Life is a Funny Business

A Very Personal Story

ALAN SHATTER

POOLBEG

Published 2017
by Poolbeg Press Ltd
123 Grange Hill, Baldoyle
Dublin 13, Ireland
www.poolbeg.com

1

A catalogue record for this book is available from the British Library.

ISBN 978-178199-810-6

Printed and bound by CPI Group (UK) Ltd, Croydon, CR0 4YY
Chapter 15 illustrations by Chiam Factor

www.poolbeg.com

ABOUT THE AUTHOR

Alan Shatter was born in Dublin on the 14th February 1951. He is a law graduate of Trinity College Dublin and has a Diploma in European Integration from the Europa Institute of the University of Amsterdam. He was a partner in the solicitors firm Gallagher Shatter for almost thirty-five years and a member of Dáil Éireann [Lower House of the Irish Parliament] during the periods 1981–2002 and 2007–2016. He is a former chairman of the Joint Oireachtas [Irish Parliament] Committee on Foreign Affairs and of the Government Task Force on Emergency Planning. He was a member of government as both Minister for Justice and Equality and Minister for Defence (2011–2014). During Ireland's Presidency of the European Union in 2013 he was President of the EU Council of Justice and Home Affairs Ministers and chaired meetings of EU Defence ministers.

He is the author of four major academic books on Irish Family Law. He is also the author of *Family Planning Irish Style*, a satire (1979) and *Laura*, a novel (1989).

He and his wife Carol live in Dublin and they have two adult children, Dylan and Kelly.

Also by Alan Shatter
from Poolbeg Press

Laura (1989)

ACKNOWLEDGEMENTS

There are two special people I want to thank for their support, encouragement and advice and for taking the time to read and constructively comment on my narrative as it developed. The first is my loving and considerate wife Carol who kept my spirits up and whose wisdom, sensitivity and insights were invaluable. The second is my great friend Jane Lehane whose enthusiasm for the project, perceptive judgement and editing skills kept me on the straight and narrow. They each helped steer me through a difficult period in my life and encouraged me to focus on the positive.

I also want to thank my partner-in-law and close friend for over four decades, Brian Gallagher, for fact-checking events in which we were both involved, and for all his incredible support, assistance and work over the last three years. Thanks are also due to Brian, Tom Cooney and Derek Freedman for their suggestions and helpful feedback.

A special thanks also to my long-lost and recently found cousin Anne Williamson who at my request doggedly identified and obtained various birth, marriage and death certificates in England to enable me to ensure the accurate portrayal of family events in this book. Thank you also to the inimitable Jacquie Branagan for undertaking the same task in Ireland, and also to Stuart Rosenblatt of the Irish Jewish Genealogical Society for his assistance in some name and place checking.

My gratitude goes to my friend Chaim Factor for his agreement to my reproducing some of his brilliant illustrations which first appeared in 1979 in *Family Planning Irish Style*.

My gratitude also goes to the great people in the Oireachtas, Trinity College, Tallaght and Ballyroan libraries and also the National Archive who helped trace vital records and material.

I also want to acknowledge the use of information and material published by Yad Vashem, The World Holocaust Remembrance Centre, Jerusalem.

My publishers, Poolbeg Press, I thank for welcoming my manuscript and enthusiastically taking on the book's publication. I am also very grateful to Gaye Shortland, for undertaking the final edit, carefully checking every sentence, making necessary corrections and for her helpful comments and insights.

Finally, I thank some others whom I pestered with individual queries and whose helpful and friendly responses restored some of my lost confidence in human nature. If my recollection of anything depicted in this book is faulty, the responsibility rests with me alone.

To Carol, Dylan, Kelly and Jane –
and in memory of Alan Benson

CONTENTS

INTRODUCTION   xi

GLOSSARY OF TERMS   xvii

CHAPTER 1   1
In the Beginning – Bereshit

CHAPTER 2   17
Moving Home

CHAPTER 3   35
Only Killing Jews

CHAPTER 4   43
Thumbs Up

CHAPTER 5   55
Adult Teenager

CHAPTER 6   65
Nightmare and Reality

CHAPTER 7   77
Lodz & Sachnin

CHAPTER 8   89
Innocents Abroad

CHAPTER 9   109
DRIPS Wet Look Coats

CHAPTER 10   127
The FLAC Years

CHAPTER 11   149
Von Tourist, Von Cup of Coffee

CHAPTER 12   167
A Wedding and Two Funerals

CHAPTER 13   177
Life Goes On

CHAPTER 14   189
*Cliffhanging, Reflections on Life
and Dead Sea Shenanigans*

CHAPTER 15   199
Family Planning Irish Style

CHAPTER 16   219
Horsehair, Two Goldfish and a Newt!

CHAPTER 17   239
Psychopaths, Ducks and a General Election

CHAPTER 18   257
Being Seen but Not Heard

Introduction

Life is a funny business that has its ups and downs. For some the ups can be very high and the downs very low. What affects how we respond to and deal with the good and the bad that life and circumstances throw up? I'm not sure there is any definitive or simplistic answer to that. I'm not going to pretend that there is or that I know of one. The most straightforward and honest answer is that it depends. On what? On many things. Temperament, intelligence, conditioning, experience, insight, emotion, education, religion, beliefs, culture, prejudice, physical and mental health, self-confidence or lack of it and much else. I expect you could easily add to this list. There may be some things you would exclude.

For many, what happens when growing up is a big part of who we are and who we become. Our experience of family and relationships is central. I have no doubt that our early years can shape who we are, how we see the world and our part in it, but I do not know the extent to which our behaviour as adults substantially derives from our positively embracing our early experiences or resiling from them. I do, however, believe that our early years impact on our values, on how we respond to adversity, and that they determine our resilience. I think they also have some impact on one of our most important characteristics: our sense of humour and what makes us laugh. In this uncertain 21st century world we inhabit, the importance of laughter and our capacity for humour are greatly undervalued.

For over thirty-five years of my life I worked insane hours and for most of those years managed to work full-time in two jobs, starting most weekdays between 5 and 6 a.m. and finishing between 10 and 11 p.m. For over twenty-five years I worked as both a solicitor and a TD [Teachta Dála i.e. Member of Parliament], and then for three years in government running two separate government departments, as the first person in the State's history to act as both Minister for Justice and Equality and also Minister for Defence. My term in government ended in some turmoil on the 7th May 2014. For me it ended unexpectedly, despite some of my political opponents and some commentators predicting my imminent demise and greeting it with enthusiasm.

Put under pressure to resign by the Taoiseach (Prime Minister), Enda Kenny, I departed under a cloud of false allegations, in which many believed, in relation to my ministerial actions. Over three years later, the conclusions of two statutory Commissions of Investigation (Fennelly & O'Higgins) and one non-statutory judicial inquiry (Cooke) have established that all of the allegations made against me which they addressed were untrue or mistaken, including those that directly resulted in my ceasing to be a member of government and which contributed to the loss of my Dáil seat in the February 2016 general election. A court case I felt compelled to bring has also resulted in our Court of Appeal concluding that I was denied a fair hearing and any opportunity to defend myself prior to the production of the Guerin Report in 2014, which resulted in my resignation from government and in which I was criticised in mistaken and damaging conclusions now entirely discredited.

I hoped in March 2017 that this issue was finally definitively resolved but, unfortunately, shortly before this book was complete, I learnt that the Supreme Court has agreed to hear an appeal challenging the Court of Appeal's decision. The objective of the appeal, funded by a government legal-costs indemnity, is to reverse the Court of Appeal's decision on a number of grounds, the primary contention being to deny my entitlement to validly challenge in the courts the procedural failures which led to the Guerin Report's mistaken conclusions. Essentially, it is about asserting that Seán Guerin SC, the author of the report, was entitled to wrongly condemn me unheard. The surreal nature of this entanglement would, in a different age, have provided a perfect script for a Franz Kafka novel.

Following the 2016 general election I found myself for the first time in my adult life with nothing to do. Shortly after becoming a member of cabinet, I decided I would not again return to legal practice and permanently ended my association with my law firm, Gallagher Shatter. So in February 2016, like all TDs who failed to be re-elected, I was unemployed. I was also embroiled in a difficult and emotionally stressful court case and awaiting the conclusion of two statutory Commissions of Investigation. My reputation had been severely damaged by the political and media frenzy in which I had been entangled. No doors opened to facilitate my positive use of the enormous domestic and international political knowledge and experience of my many years of public service. I was also essentially cut off from Fine Gael, the political party I have been a member of since 1979.

My telling the truth under oath at hearings of the Fennelly Commission of Investigation and contradicting sworn evidence given by the Taoiseach and Fine Gael leader, Enda Kenny, and also taking court action to challenge the Guerin Report, had turned me into a political pariah as far as the leadership of Fine Gael was concerned. My forthright public criticism of the catastrophic Fine Gael 2016 general election campaign, of course, did nothing to positively contribute to my popularity with those who devised it. There was also little enthusiasm for my criticism of intervention by Enda Kenny in the Fine Gael campaign in my own constituency which gave the false impression that my re-election was assured.

As I awaited the publication of outstanding reports addressing events in which I had been involved, and as the wheels of justice slowly moved forward, I was concerned that the events in which I had become ensnared were at risk of becoming an obsession. Family and close friends were enormously supportive during what was one of the most difficult periods of my life but I needed something more. In addition to their help and support, for the first time in my life I felt a need to look back to my early years to try and gain some understanding of the journey I had first embarked upon that led to my arriving in the place in which I now found myself. I realised that the frenetic multitasking, which for too long had been part of who I am, had left me little time for reflection and I doubted its value.

Revisiting the past, my early life experiences, its tragedy and comedy, for me assumed a new importance in trying to understand what helped shape my values, beliefs and character and also my actions, resilience and determination. It was the past prior to my bit part in Fine Gael's history that was primarily my personal focus, as I wished, in so far as was possible, to escape from politics, personally recalibrate and look to the future. I hoped that by reconnecting with my life prior to my time in the Dáil I might get some insight into what I should do with what remains of it, now that I have finally grown up!

I hope you will find the story of my first thirty years on this planet both interesting and entertaining. In telling it, I not only give some insight into my family background, which I have rarely publicly discussed, but also take a journey through some features of the Ireland of the 1950s, 60s and 70s. For those unfamiliar with that time, it sheds light on how far as a country we have travelled in specific areas and where we have come from. My story also provides an insight into how I have been influenced by my Jewish roots and the relevance of the past to some more recent events. For those currently experiencing one or more of life's lows, or for those who simply enjoy a laugh, I hope parts of my story make you smile at life's unpredictability, peculiarities and idiosyncrasies.

Delving into my past has, over the last year, at times made me either laugh or cry as I revisited family, old friends, people, animals and events long ago parked away in the deep recesses of my mind. It has been an extraordinary personal journey into the too-long forgotten. For those who take the time to read *Life is a Funny Business*, it is your laughter that I hope stays with you as your memory of my very personal narrative. If nothing else the "newt" (or as you may better know it, the salamander) which makes a brief appearance in Chapter 16 and which is, I expect, long since deceased, deserves to live on in memory as it is likely that it is the only newt which has ever featured in a court action heard in the Irish High Court!

Alan Shatter
24th July 2017

Glossary

Aliyah – Literally means "elevation" or "going up". It is a term that is used to describe being called up in synagogue to say a prayer on the reading of the Torah [the Old Testament] and also is a reference to moving to Israel. It is in the latter context it is used in this book. While originally it was used as a reference to visiting Jerusalem, as the place closest to God, to celebrate the Jewish Feast days, it has come to signify the return of the Jewish people to the Land of Israel. Put simply, it is a term used to refer to the immigration of Jews back to their ancestral homeland. Someone moving to Israel, and in particular Jerusalem, is perceived as moving "up" in the world to a holy and "elevated" place. He or she is referred to as "making aliyah".

Bar mitzvah – Literally means "son of the commandments". It marks the moment a Jewish boy attains the age of thirteen and automatically assumes the obligations and responsibilities of the Torah's commandments. It is also the term commonly used to refer to the coming-of-age ceremony for Jewish boys on reaching thirteen years of age. The parents celebrate raising their son into what Jewish law regards as adulthood and the boy celebrates becoming an adult. In the real world, the boy is treated no differently to other teenagers and is expected to continue his studies.

Bat mitzvah – Literally means "daughter of the commandments". It marks the moment a Jewish girl automatically assumes the obligations and responsibilities of the Torah's commandments, upon reaching twelve years of age according to Orthodox and Conservative Jewish tradition, and thirteen years of age according to Reform and Liberal/Progressive Jewish tradition. It is also the term commonly used for the coming-of-age ceremony for Jewish girls upon attaining the designated age. The parents celebrate raising their daughter into what is regarded as adulthood and the girl celebrates becoming an adult. In the real world, the girl is treated no differently to other teenagers and is expected to continue her studies.

Bereshit – Hebrew for "in the beginning". It is the first word in and Hebrew title of the first book of the Torah, also known as the Book of Genesis. It is also the title of Chapter 1 of this book.

Bimah – The elevated platform in the centre of the synagogue from where the Torah scroll is read and the service is conducted.

Kaddish – An ancient Jewish prayer in praise of God, recited by mourners and on the anniversary of a loved one's death. It is recited by the graveside, in the home in which the bereaved are sitting *shiva* and regularly recited in synagogue services.

Kichels – A round cookie made from beaten egg, caster sugar and flour.

Kiddish/Kiddush – A blessing over kosher wine said by the head of a Jewish household at the start of an evening meal ushering in the Sabbath or a Jewish festival. It may also be said after a morning Sabbath or festival synagogue service, usually followed by a celebratory snack or meal. In many synagogues, Sabbath and some festival morning services are followed by what has become known as a "kiddish" or "kiddush" which is a reception preceded by a blessing over wine. The reception may be sponsored or paid for by a member of the congregation celebrating an event, such as a bar mitzvah or bat mitzvah, an engagement or imminent marriage ceremony, the birth of a child or an anniversary or other significant occasion.

Kosher food – Food that conforms to Jewish dietary laws.

Kosher wine – Wine which conforms to Jewish dietary laws.

L'chaim – A traditional Jewish toast in Hebrew: "to life". The equivalent toast in Ireland is "Sláinte" meaning "good health".

Mazel tov – A Jewish phrase for congratulations, meaning "good luck".

Mitzvah – Literally means a commandment. The Talmud [see below] mentions that the Jewish people were given 613 mitzvot [commandments]. Colloquially, it has become common usage to refer to doing a good deed or a charitable act as a "mitzvah", as in doing something that conforms with or is in the spirit of the commandments.

Pesach [Passover] – A Jewish festival which celebrates the exodus from ancient Egypt of Jewish slaves and their families under the leadership of Moses.

Rosh Hashanah – Literally meaning "the head of the year". It is the day that marks the beginning of the Jewish New Year. In Jewish tradition, it also marks the creation of the world as described in the Torah.

Seder – A celebratory evening meal that marks the commencement of the Jewish festival of Pesach [Passover].

Shabbat – The Jewish Sabbath which commences at sunset each Friday evening and ends after sundown on Saturday night.

Shiva – Literally means "seven". It is also used to refer to the week-long period of mourning observed by Jewish people following the burial of a father, mother, spouse, son, daughter, brother or sister.

Sitting shiva – The period of mourning during which immediate family members of a deceased gather in a home together to receive visitors, say prayers and recite Kaddish.

Talmud Torah – The Talmud is a central text of Rabbinic Judaism which focuses on a way of life based on the Torah and Jewish law. Talmud Torah is the field of study of Jewish law, teaching and tradition.
Torah – In its narrowest sense and as referenced in this book, the five books of the Hebrew Bible or Old Testament.

Yom Kippur – Means "Day of Atonement". It is a strict day of rest during which Jews fast, refrain from work and attend synagogue. It is the holiest day in the Jewish calendar and is preceded by the Ten Days of Awe or Repentance, a period of introspection and repentance [teshuvah] that follows Rosh Hashanah, the Jewish New Year.

Chapter 1

In the Beginning – Bereshit

I believe most of us think we can remember more of our beginnings in this world and our early childhood than we can truly recall. I may be wrong about that. It may just be that others have powers of recall superior to mine.

My earliest memories are of feelings, emotions, people, places, incidents and events. Feelings as a young child of being loved, minded and, I admit, somewhat spoilt by two doting parents. It may be that some part of this recollection is imagined but it is as I remember it. I believe in its truth as, if I am mistaken, I doubt that I would have come through my teens and entered adulthood without some serious personal difficulties. I suspect this insight would coincide with views held by many of our current psychiatrists, psychologists, psychotherapists and social workers who believe that most, if not all, of the ills and bad behaviour of today's late teens and adults derive from their childhood experiences and that few who misbehave have real choices or bear full responsibility for their actions.

◄◎► ◄◎► ◄◎►

My first memories go back to when, together with my parents, I lived in a flat (they were called flats, not apartments, in those days) at 14 Oaklands Crescent, Rathgar, in Dublin. I remember it as Number 14, as the number seemed to follow me around a lot during my childhood. I was born on the 14th February 1951 and when I was six we moved to 14 Crannagh Park, Rathfarnham, in Dublin 14. I also have a vague memory that when we lived in Rathgar it was the Number 14 bus that we rode into town. Maybe my parents had a 14 fetish which they never revealed to me!

I was told but don't remember that I was about a year old when we took up residence in Oaklands Crescent, having moved there from a rented house adjacent to Rathgar village. The flats in Oaklands Crescent were upstairs/downstairs rentals. There were two entrance doors side by side and we lived downstairs. Desmond Kerr, an artist, lived above us in Number 13. There is still stored away in our attic a portrait he painted of me when I was about five years old.

My parents were both English and Jewish. My mum, Elaine Presburg, was born in Liverpool in 1925. Her parents, Sophie and Sidney, for many years ran a hotel in Bank Square in the seaside town of Southport and that is where she grew up. Elaine met my dad, Reuben, around 1947 when visiting distant relations who lived in Carlow and Dublin.

My dad, Reuben, was born in London in 1916. His parents, Leah and Abraham or Avraham Sachnin (more of the Sachnin later) emigrated to England in 1913 from Lodz in Russian-occupied Poland. Dad was in Dublin, visiting his older brother Jack and Jack's wife Gertrude, known to everyone as Gertie (originally Gertie Samuels). Jack was born in Lodz and had accompanied his parents to England. I never knew exactly when Jack first came to Dublin but by the time of Dad's arrival he and Gertie were married and living in Riversdale Avenue, Terenure.

The story, as I was told it, was that my parents met when Mum was visiting her Dublin relations, the Robinsons, who lived next door to Jack and Gertie. They then started dating, fell in love and married in Southport Synagogue in September 1948. Mum was twenty-three and Dad thirty-two when they married. With Jack's encouragement they returned to Ireland and settled in Dublin. Destined to be an only child, I arrived on the scene in 1951. Somewhere in the family undergrowth there was mention of Mum having a miscarriage or a stillborn child before I was born. True or not? I don't know for sure.

I remember our home in Oaklands Crescent as large but that was a child's perception. In fact, it was a relatively modest two-bedroom home. I remember a warm cosy place, smells of cooking and baking apple and rhubarb pies, cakes, sponge puddings and jam tarts. Strawberry jam tarts made of a thin flakey pastry were particular favourites of my dad's and mine, and rarely survived twenty-four hours out of the oven.

The Friday evening Shabbat [Sabbath] meal was always the highlight of the week: chopped liver, chicken soup and kneidlach [matzo-meal dumplings], roast chicken and stuffing, roast potatoes or potato kugel [pudding] and whatever was the seasonal veg. On occasion, variety was provided by home-pickled cucumbers, pickled meat or purchased kosher beef sausages.

We were members of Terenure Synagogue in Dublin and officially part of the Orthodox Jewish community. Although my parents kept kosher at home and observed some of the Jewish rituals, such as Mum on Friday night lighting the Shabbat candles, like many members of the Dublin Jewish community they were not strictly religiously observant. They attended synagogue for weddings, bar mitzvahs and other celebrations. They also did so on the Jewish High Holy days, such as Rosh Hashanah and Yom Kippur and every Pesach [Passover] we always either had our own Seder meal or participated in one in Jack and Gertie's home. This had more to do with family, tradition and being a member of the tribe than with any connection to or belief in God. My parents followed an à la carte version of Judaism. I suspect they did as much as they believed necessary to ensure that, as I grew up, I had a sufficient grounding to make my own decisions about religion.

Dad was a committed atheist. If atheism were a religion, he would have been one of its high priests! He had a straightforward view. If there was a god the Holocaust would never have happened. Religion to him was myth and superstition. Religion was amongst a number of topics regularly discussed and debated in the Shatter household when I was growing up. Looking back on it now, for a non-believer, Dad spent a lot of time discussing what is good and bad about religion!

Dad loved books. He was an avid reader and any book read was treated as a sacred text to be kept impeccably on his bookshelves. He essentially had his own mini-library. To bend a page or underline a sentence (something I do to this day) was in his atheistic world a mortal sin worthy of hell and damnation. As well as speaking English with an English accent, like his parents and brother Jack, Dad spoke fluent Yiddish and his library included a wonderful selection of Yiddish books.

He was also something of an armchair politician. The

4

great issues of the day were discussed and debated at great length in our home but he was never an activist. Both Irish and English politics were followed and in the days before Teilifís Éireann, the BBC nightly television news was part of our staple diet.

The truth is, had he been born in a different era, to parents who could afford to pay for a full second and third-level education, my dad would have been a university academic. As it was, he had left school at fifteen and worked in the Petticoat Lane market in the East End of London before coming to Ireland.

Mum was about 5'7" in height and Dad 6'1". He was extremely short-sighted in one eye and as the sight in his good eye slowly deteriorated he wore glasses with progressively thicker lenses. His short sight rendered him ineligible to join the British army to fight in the Second World War. Instead, he joined the London Home Guard. I believe the revelation of the Holocaust deeply affected him and that he felt guilty over his inability to fight against Nazi Germany. He had enormous respect and admiration for those who did. If he were still alive today, it is a perspective we would share. It is a perspective which motivated my bringing legislation before the Dáil, while Minister for Defence, which granted an amnesty and pardon to those who had deserted the Irish Defence Forces to fight on the allied side against Nazi Germany during the Second World War.

In my dad's world too many people had died because of religion and ideology. For him, a form of humanistic decency and social justice, mixed with common sense and pragmatism, was preferable to pre-ordained theological or ideological nonsense. It is to him that I attribute my aversion to extremism and fanaticism of all kinds. I also have little doubt that he sowed the seeds of my scepticism toward those often-competing and sometime-compatible compatriots – theology and ideology. At their core they are two sides of the same coin but with one distinguishing characteristic. Theological believers have the promise of an afterlife in paradise, in some heavenly retreat or in a post-messianic world to come. Ideological believers seek their version (and it varies depending on the ideology) of paradise in this life. Of course, there are some who go for a two-way bet, believing both in an ideology and a theology in the hope that if they don't create paradise in this life, they will enter it or its equivalent in the next. Personally, when it comes to betting, I believe it is more likely that you will win the Euro or Irish lotto!

I don't recall Mum expressing strong views about any of these things. What I do recall is a calmness about our home: two parents clearly in love and no shouting or upsets, though I suppose they must have had occasional disagreements. If so, I was shielded from them.

I suspect that what attracted my mum to my dad was not only his looks but also his mischievous sense of humour. There was a lot of laughter in our home during my early childhood. Both my parents had a great sense of humour and of fun. Apart from pranks and sharing jokes, Dad enjoyed making fun of some of the better-known politicians of the day.

In our home, BBC radio and black-and-white television, once we had acquired a TV set, made a major contribution. *Hancock's Half Hour* featuring Tony Hancock and Sidney James, *The Goon Show* with Peter Sellers, Harry Secombe and Spike Milligan, *The Navy Lark* starring Leslie Phillips, Hattie Jacques and Jon Pertwee, and Kenneth Horn's *Around the Horn* (it was a more innocent world!) were among the many radio programmes not to be missed. In the theatre, whenever Jimmy O'Dea, Maureen Potter or Milo

O'Shea were featuring, the Shatters would be part of the audience. Des Keogh and Rosaleen Linehan would later attract a similar Shatter following. The Christmas pantos in the Gaiety and Olympia theatres were a must and usually preceded or followed by pancakes or burgers or fish and chips in a nearby restaurant.

Dad's eclectic reading tastes included all the humorous writers of the day and his books were there for me to read as I chose as I grew older. He particularly enjoyed the works of James Joyce and Samuel Beckett, Beckett's *Waiting for Godot* being one of his favourite plays. Of Irish authors I have little doubt that one of his favourites was Brian O'Nolan, who wrote novels under the pseudonym Flann O'Brien and satirical articles published in the *Irish Times* under the pen name Myles Na gCopaleen. *At-Swim-Two-Birds* and the *Irish Times* articles were particular favourites. As a result, I became a young fan of Myles Na gCopaleen, believing that to be the real name of the author of articles which significantly contributed to my humorous view of the world.

There was no censorship in the Shatter household. There were many "risqué" (for the times) and funny books that I read and enjoyed at a time when I suspect I was too young to grasp all of their nuances but which certainly gave me interesting and unexpected insights into life!

It is good to remember the laughter as too much of it disappeared around the time my age reached double digits but it is too early to speak of that. Let's stick to the good stuff and the mysterious for now.

◄○► ◄○► ◄○►

Outside the ordinary daily family rhythm, my primary memories of Oaklands Crescent are people and incidents.

Like every child I had a bold streak. I have a memory of young trees planted on a grassy area outside the flats on the estate. I also remember that, as a three-year-old, for some reason when no one was looking I developed the habit of regularly peeing on the trunk of a small tree adjacent to our flat. I suspect that I was copying what Rebel, Jack and Gertie's dog, did whenever visiting. Rebel was an affectionate small black-and-white mongrel of uncertain lineage and we were greatly attached to each other. Rebel had an independent streak and was a regular visitor, often walking from Riversdale Avenue to Oaklands Crescent on his own and well able to find his way back home. While the other trees on the estate thrived, the one near our home died within a year of being planted. Whether I murdered it by peeing on it I genuinely do not know but I presume the acidic content of what Rebel and I regularly dumped on it did not positively contribute to its wellbeing. The dead tree was dug up and a new one planted. Some weeks later I was caught by Mum as I peed on the new tree, reprimanded and sent to my room. I never again peed on that or any other tree but nobody ever attempted to restrain Rebel from doing so. I discovered on a recent visit to Oaklands Crescent that as you exit Number 14 to the right there grows a mature tree which I suspect is the second tree that was planted when I was about four years old. But I might be mistaken – it could be the third or fourth planted in that location.

Mum always loved flowers but we had no garden in which any could grow. My recollection is that our neighbour, Desmond Kerr, was a committed gardener who had an array of flowers growing in the small garden at the back of our home, the exclusive usage of which came with the rental of his upstairs flat. I still remember beautiful tulips and daffodils growing there. They were so attractive that one spring, the entrance door left unlocked, I entered his garden with a pair of scissors and five minutes later presented Mum with a beautiful bouquet of freshly cut yellow and red flowers that Interflora would have been proud to deliver. When asked where I got them I insisted it was a secret. Retribution arrived with a knock on our door about twenty minutes later when Desmond, who had been lost in his painting, realised all of his tulips and daffodils had done an unexpected runner and concluded that I was the likely culprit. Mum warned me of a terrible punishment should I ever again steal someone's flowers but did so struggling to suppress a smile and with a familiar twinkle in her eyes. Surprisingly, I wasn't even sent to my room. When she informed Dad over dinner that evening of my criminal activity, he broke down laughing and told me that the next time I wanted to give Mum flowers I was to buy them with my pocket money.

Both downstairs and upstairs in the months that followed, the story of the great flower heist, accompanied by much laughter, was told and retold to visitors and I was rapidly forgiven by Desmond Kerr. I never again picked a flower in his garden. Perhaps the beauty of our neighbour's small garden, lovingly planted and nurtured in Oaklands Crescent, or my stealing the flowers in it to present to my mum was the catalyst in later life for my own enjoyment of gardening and growing colourful flowers and plants? Your guess is as good as mine!

◄◦► ◄◦► ◄◦►

There were, from time to time, what I regarded as unexpected visitors to Oaklands Crescent. One afternoon Mum was busy frying fish for what I was informed would be the next morning's breakfast. Farley's Rusks were my favourite breakfast food at the time and Dad was a Kellogg's Cornflakes man, so the fried fish was a bit of a mystery. I remember getting out of bed the next morning to find the breakfast table set with cold fried fish, chopped pickled herring and bagels. There were also mashed hardboiled eggs with onion, cream cheese, tomatoes and slices of cucumber. For me the highlight was the Victoria sponge cake in the centre of the table. I was allowed a glass of freshly squeezed orange juice, warned not to touch the food and told breakfast would be in half an hour after the arrival of Auntie Flossy (at least I think it was Flossy!).

I had never before seen such an extravagant table of food at breakfast time nor did I know I had an Auntie Flossy. Gertie was the only aunt I knew. I have no memory of which day this happened but it was likely a Sunday as my dad, who worked a six-day week, had not taken an early bus to work.

Face washed, teeth cleaned, hair combed and dressed by Mum, I remember I awaited with my parents the arrival of the mysterious Auntie Flossy. Eventually, later than anticipated, a taxi pulled up outside our home and a very fancily dressed, small, elderly woman exited it to be greeted by my parents at our front door as I hid a little in the background. Dad helped carry her luggage in from the taxi and she was ushered into our sitting room.

The Auntie Flossy I first met that morning had blonde and strangely curled hair, a very white face and extraordinary red lips with matching nails. It is the red on her lips that I most remember to this day. While I had often watched Mum put her lipstick on, I had never previously seen such bright red lipstick. I remember being told that she had that morning flown in to Dublin airport from somewhere in England and that she was one of Mum's relations. I do not know how long she stayed in Dublin nor where she stayed. She couldn't have stayed with us as we didn't have a spare bedroom. I also remember nothing more about Flossy, other than her arrival and that breakfast. She must have visited for more than one day but I do not remember ever meeting her again after the morning of her arrival. I think it is the breakfast that made a greater impression on me than Flossy. I can still picture us all sitting around that breakfast table and my eating Mum's delicious cold fried fish followed by sponge cake. It is the only occasion when I ate fried fish early in the morning and is the only time I can recall a cake being specially baked for breakfast. I have no idea of Auntie Flossy's age when she visited Dublin or whatever happened to her. She just appeared in my life one day and then mysteriously disappeared. I do remember asking a number of times following her visit if she would be visiting again, in the hope of Mum making another similarly spectacular breakfast.

Flossy wasn't the only visitor to appear and disappear. I understood when growing up in Oaklands Crescent that Mum had a brother called Henry Presburg who lived in Birmingham and worked for Marks and Spencer. He and Mum occasionally talked on the phone and I received birthday cards from him. I didn't know that Mum had a second brother Alfred or Alfie till one day he came visiting in Oaklands Crescent. The Alfie I remember was a jovial, somewhat overweight man with a neat beard and a big smile. I think I was told he was a taxi driver in Southport. I immediately liked my newly acquired Uncle Alfie and remember walking around Dublin's city centre with him and being bought a toy Dinky car in a shop in O'Connell Street. I do not remember how long he stayed in Dublin but he seemed to be around for a while, then went back to England never to be seen again. When inquiring about his whereabouts the story was that some years before Alfie came to Dublin he had abandoned his wife Mary and two children, Anne and Clive, and run off with another woman. I was told that after his visit to Dublin no one knew where he was living. I never got to meet any of the women in his life and I cannot recall Alfie's name ever being mentioned after we moved out of Oaklands Crescent. About two years ago one of his children, Anne, who is now seventy-three, made contact with me. I learnt that for a time after Alfie left his family they had lived with my grandparents, Sophie and Sidney, in their hotel in Southport. Alfie made no contact with them after his departure and made no effort to provide his wife or children with any financial support.

◄O► ◄O► ◄O►

Getting my first tricycle was a big event. I remember Mum and Dad walking around Oaklands Crescent as I happily cycled my new prize possession on the path. Strict instructions were issued never to cycle on the road and to be careful of pedestrians. There were a lot of young families residing in Oaklands Crescent and few cars drove into the estate. Many happy hours were spent cycling on the path with friends and showing off my first bike. It was all going really well till one summer afternoon I got it into my head that I wanted to see how fast I could go. Deciding the path was holding me back, I cycled onto the road and blasted off, pedalling as fast as possible. I can still recall the terror of realising I had lost all control as I crashed straight into a wall at the entrance to the estate and tore the skin off all my knuckles and both knees. Mum must have heard my screams as she came running out to pick up the sobbing bloodied casualty lying on the road with his tricycle's bent front wheel resting on his chest. The sight of blood ensured remonstrations were postponed as child and bike were picked up and carried home. I was fortunate that day that a car had not driven into the estate as I careered into the wall as there was no way a driver would have seen me coming at speed and I could have been killed. It was a lesson spelled out in no uncertain terms after my wounds had been washed and bandaged. The lesson was unnecessary. I had never been so scared in my short life and there was no way I was going to repeat the performance. The front wheel of the tricycle was fixed and, from then on, I was strictly a pavement man!

◄o► ◄o► ◄o►

Dad had a shop called Junior Wear located in Dublin's Nassau Street in which he sold children's clothes. In those days traffic travelled both ways on Nassau Street and there was a bus stop directly outside the shop. There were never more than two assistants employed by him and the shop, which he rented, was our family's only source of income. I remember often visiting the shop as a young child. It closed when I was about eleven years old. There was much discussion between my parents at home before its closure which Dad attributed to a reduction in customers because CIE had removed the bus stop. Looking back that explanation makes little sense. To this day successful shops trade from the same location. The reality is, of course, that an intellectual who loves books does not usually make for a good businessman. One of the tragedies of my dad's life is that he ran a business located directly opposite the walls of one of Dublin's major universities, Trinity College, but never had any opportunity to study there nor to obtain the degrees required to teach inside its walls.

In his London days Dad had primarily sold women's

clothes in Petticoat Lane and had also learned how to cut cloth and manufacture clothes. After Junior Wear closed he rented two floors in a premises located in Dublin's Dame Street and, in partnership with another, ran a CMT business, that is "Cut, Make and Trim".

Women's coats, suits, dresses and skirts were manufactured and in the early days the business went well. Dad was the principal cutter and his partner the principal machinist. Clothes were supplied to a number of shops around Dublin and the business benefited from some small manufacturing contracts from Dunne's Stores. At its height there were about twelve people employed.

When I was about thirteen, Dad discovered his partner was fiddling the books and embezzling some of the profits and he ended the partnership. It took a couple of weeks to persuade the partner to simply leave. He finally did so under threat that if he didn't go the gardaí [police] would be called. I still remember Dad, partly irritated and partly amused, talking at home of his partner ludicrously and repetitively singing "Stand by Me" for the two weeks prior to his forced departure. I think that is why I have always hated that song. Whenever it is played on radio I always change to an alternative radio station or turn the radio off.

Dad's CMT business carried on till I was about seventeen. It closed the year prior to my doing my Leaving Certificate examination. The sight in his good eye had deteriorated and he was no longer able to properly see or follow designs, cut cloth or deal with the business accounts. The business had never greatly grown and Dunne's Stores had long ceased giving him work. He was unemployed in his early fifties and, because of his deteriorating eyesight, unemployable. He was still able to see sufficiently to get around and a few more years would pass before he suffered a detached retina, rendering him almost completely blind. It is a condition that for some can be rectified today by an operation but in the Ireland of the 1960s no such operation was available.

I am fortunate in that it seems I inherited my mum's not my dad's eyesight – and also her height. Had I a choice I would have opted to be 6'1" in height but not at the cost of going blind.

Chapter 2

Moving Home

When I was about six years old we moved to a three-bedroom semi-detached house in Crannagh Park. It was in a new estate under construction in Rathfarnham on land formerly owned by Lambe Brothers who supplied fruit used to make Fruitfield jams. 14 Crannagh Park would be the only home purchased by my dad and the final home in which he and my mum lived.

I still remember the excitement of moving in. The house had what appeared to me to be a huge garden at the back. Even the front garden was bigger than the small patch of land cultivated by Desmond Kerr in Oaklands Crescent. Dad's business must have been doing well at the time as the house was beautifully decorated compared to Oaklands Crescent and within a couple of weeks of our move it was fully furnished, carpeted and curtained. Every delivery was met with great excitement and Mum fussed over the furniture deliveries to ensure no damage was done to wallpaper as beds, couches, chairs and tables were carried

17

in by the delivery men.

My bedroom had a wardrobe, a chest of drawers and a bedside table with a side light. In Oaklands Crescent my bedroom had only a chest of drawers. My Crannagh bedroom also had grey curtains with bright toadstools in a variety of colours and sizes. Unfortunately, the curtains turned out to be a bad choice as during the course of various childhood illnesses – such as flu, chickenpox and mumps – when I had a high temperature, I imagined or had nightmares of the toadstools jumping out of the curtains and coming to get me. It was terrifying and probably explains why in my young days I could never eat mushrooms! Today, they number among my favourite vegetables.

Shortly after we moved into Crannagh, a carpenter arrived and constructed bookshelves in our sitting room in alcoves on either side of the fireplace into which Dad meticulously placed his books, organised by author and category. The categories originally included classics, philosophy, politics, history, religion, Yiddish, comedy, sport and a mix of novels, but as the years passed they got jumbled and he didn't seem to mind. He was a dedicated reader of *Punch*, the English satirical magazine. Each magazine was saved and at the end of each year that year's magazines were beautifully bound in a red cover and had pride of place on the top bookshelf.

Amongst the cardboard boxes filled with books that arrived from Oaklands Crescent were two boxes containing my Christmas comic annuals, such as the *Beezer*, the *Dandy* and the *Hotspur* accompanied by all of the then published Enid Blyton *Noddy* books. I also had lots of books about animals and some about prehistoric times with illustrations of dinosaurs. Bookshelves were constructed and mounted on the wall in my own bedroom and I proudly placed all my books onto the shelves with lots of space left for new acquisitions.

I don't remember exactly when I learnt to read on my own but I think I became a reader at a very young age. Reading and sport, all types of sport, were two of my favourite things in the world. In the years following our arrival in Crannagh, the bookshelves in my bedroom rapidly filled up with *The Famous Five*, *Billy Bunter*, *Just William*, and many of my dad's classics, such as *The Wind in the Willows*, *Treasure Island*, *The Three Musketeers*, *Oliver Twist* and *Gulliver's Travels*.

Soon after our arrival in Crannagh grass seed was sown front and back, flower beds and a vegetable patch created, and fruit trees and bushes planted, with the help of Michael Flood who became our gardener. Michael lived in Woodview Cottages beside Rathfarnham village and had knocked on our door shortly after we moved in, offering his services as a gardener. He ended up gardening for a number of families in Crannagh.

Victoria plums, damsons, apples, pears, gooseberries, strawberries and raspberries provided a wonderful selection of homegrown summer fruits for desserts, jams, pies and puddings. At a young age I was not only involved in picking the fruit we grew but also in helping to take care of the vegetable patch and plants under my mum's watchful eyes. Summer in our home was synonymous with the smells of apples or gooseberries stewing or pies baking in the oven.

Every summer until I was about sixteen Michael cut our grass and helped keep the garden tidy. I remember a kindly, tall, occasionally red-faced man who prior to my teens I used to follow around the garden chatting away and who on dry days always spent time, when his work was finished, kicking a soccer ball with me. We would make a goal with cricket stumps or a couple of garden stakes and he would play goalie as I tried to kick balls past him and score. In the early days I also remember him always stopping work to enjoy a cup of tea and a piece of whatever was the latest pie or cake Mum had baked.

Following the arrival in Crannagh of a man who called himself Paddy the Vegetable Man I took to naming people by the job they did. As a result, Michael became known forever more as Michael the Gardener.

Paddy arrived on the scene shortly after we moved in. Although it took almost three years for the construction of our estate to be entirely completed, there were already families living on the adjacent Ballytore Road, Rathfarnham Park and Crannagh Road. Once a week, summer and winter, Paddy the Vegetable Man arrived in his blue open van selling fresh vegetables, fruit and eggs. Mum was one of his regular customers and when I was on school holidays, if he was in a good humour, he occasionally permitted me to ride a short distance along our road in his van with him. I recall that for over twelve years he sold produce in our estate. Then one day he stopped coming. I do not know whether he fell ill, died or whether by then the viability of his business had been fatally undermined by the arrival of supermarkets. By then I was in my late teens, the circumstances of our family had dramatically changed and we only occasionally purchased something from him.

Crannagh Park and its neighbouring streets must have been a major attraction for door-to-door salesmen. For about two years we also had a weekly visit from the Lemonade Man who drove a van full of Taylor-Keith lemonade and, by the time I reached ten, we had regular summer visits from Mr Whippy, the Ice Cream Man. We also, of course, had daily milk deliveries, postal deliveries and the Newspaper Man delivered the *Irish Times* and other morning papers. Apart from salesmen the estate was also visited by the Pig Man who collected weekly food-waste to feed to his pigs. Mum declined a waste-collection bin when one day he knocked on our door and offered one to her. As we didn't eat pork because it wasn't kosher she concluded we shouldn't contribute to feeding his pigs! But now I am getting a bit ahead of myself, so we will return to the early days in Crannagh Park.

Shortly after we moved in, construction stopped in Crannagh and did not restart for at least a year. During our first summer there strawberries grew wild on some of the land adjacent to our home on which eventually more houses were destined to be built. As a child I didn't understand why so many strawberries were growing there but I enjoyed picking and eating them. Looking back, I presume they were plants which survived Lambe's departure.

We had the same postman for many years. I can still recall his face but I can no longer remember his name. I have a great memory for facts, events, laws and court judgements but, unusually for someone involved in politics for over thirty years, I am dreadful at remembering people's names. I am embarrassed that I no longer remember our postman's name as he was a great friend during my childhood. On school breaks and school holidays, until I reached my teens, I frequently cycled around Crannagh Park and its adjacent roads with him jabbering away about all sorts of things as he delivered the post. I think TV programmes and sport were our main topics of conversation.

◄o► ◄o► ◄o►

I loved soccer and cricket and I was a dedicated Shamrock Rovers and Tottenham Hotspur fan. Our postman was into soccer and Gaelic football and followed Dublin. I knew nothing about the GAA and what I originally learnt about it largely came from him.

Dublin Maccabi, located in Kimmage Road West, was the Jewish Community's Sports club. During the winter, soccer and rugby were the main sports played and, in the summer, cricket and tennis. As I grew up, Dad and I often together watched the Maccabi teams' soccer and rugby matches and in the summer Mum joined us to watch some of the cricket. The Maccabi cricket team, Carlisle Cricket Club, was very successful and over the years a number of members of the team played for Ireland. No Gaelic football or hurling was played in Maccabi. The GAA was perceived within the Jewish community as a very Catholic organisation and there was no tradition of Jewish involvement in it.

I went with Mum and Dad for regular walks in Bushy Park in Terenure which had numerous GAA and soccer pitches. Dad and I frequently kicked around a soccer ball in the Park, in Maccabi and in our back garden. I watched and enjoyed my first Gaelic football match in Bushy Park and overheard a conversation between a spectator whose son was playing and my dad about something called "the ban". I later said to Dad that when I got older I wanted to play both soccer and Gaelic football and he explained to me that, because of this thing called "the ban" imposed by the GAA, I could only play one of them. Because he was born in England, until our visits to Bushy Park Dad took little interest in the GAA. I think he only first learnt of the ban during the conversation there that I recall.

I was probably around eight at the time and in the weeks that followed I must have driven our postman demented. As he was into GAA, I wanted to get as much information from him as I could about the ban. To this day I remember saying that I could not understand why, if you played a game in which you could only kick the ball, you were forbidden by the GAA from playing a game in which you could not only kick but also pick up the ball and throw it. Didn't goalkeepers do both? And playing soccer didn't ban you from playing rugby. I just couldn't understand it and I jibber-jabbered on and on along this theme. Of course, today, I understand the historical background though I still believe the rule, long since rescinded, was daft.

The postman's simple explanation to me was that soccer and rugby were regarded as foreign English games and that was why! But didn't we have our own international soccer and rugby teams and match commentaries of their games that I loved listening to on Radio Éireann? If Radio Éireann could broadcast commentaries on not only games played by our international soccer and rugby teams but also GAA games played by Dublin's football team, why couldn't I play both? And didn't a lot of countries in addition to England play soccer and rugby? And so on and on and on! I can't recall for how many weeks I continued along this line but he must have been a kind man of enormous patience and good humour because he put up with me. He never really defended the ban, just explained its background. To an Irish boy with two English parents it just made no sense.

Soccer was my game of choice. Following a substantial part of the estate being built and occupied, on the majority of afternoons after school, once school homework was done, a lot of my time was spent playing soccer on the road near my home or, when there was only a few boys to play with, in our back garden. In the years that followed I played schoolboy league soccer which I loved but I have for many years regretted that when growing up I never played Gaelic football. I think I could have been a reasonable player. I would eventually get onto the pitch in Croke Park but that was in my teenage years as an athlete, running in what were called the Tailteann Games.

Dad supported Arsenal and had started attending Arsenal's matches in the English First Division (the forerunner of the Premiership) as a young boy living in London. The rivalry between Arsenal and their North London neighbours Tottenham Hotspur (Spurs) was both intense and legendary, as it still is today. For devilment and because, at the time, they were more successful than Arsenal I became a Spurs supporter. It was a fun recipe for the daily exchange of inventive and humorous banter between myself and Dad.

It was the early 1960s and the era of the great Spurs team that did the double by winning both the League and FA Cup. I can still to this day remember the names of most of the players. Spurs' success coincided with Shamrock Rover's dominance of the domestic soccer scene. Sunday afternoon meant heading off to Glenmalure Park in Milltown to watch Shamrock Rovers with Dad or to away matches when played in Dublin in Dalymount, Tolka or Richmond Park. Mum occasionally, on a dry and sunny Sunday, would join us in Milltown where we had membership tickets that gave access to tea, cakes and great sandwiches at half time. I meticulously kept scrapbooks, one of which I still retain, with newspaper cutouts of match reports and league tables which included reports of all the international team's matches in the early 60s. As with Spurs, I can still reel off the names of some of the great Rovers players of those days.

My dream of playing for Rovers never materialised but before Glenmalure's sacred pitch was turned into a housing estate, as a young TD I did get to play on it. In 1986, at my request, the Kilcoyne brothers, who owned the Milltown ground, freely made it available for a celebrity soccer tournament that I organised to raise funds for research into cystic fibrosis. We raised about £5,000 that day. The late, great, much lamented Dermot Morgan of *Father Ted* fame, who died far too young, was one of those who togged out to play. So also did former Miss Ireland, Olivia Tracey, who had no inhibitions sharing a changing room with the other players. (Before anyone jumps to conclusions, the teams were mixed and most people arrived in their track suits, so "changing" primarily involved co-ordinating team jerseys and lending football boots to those who had none).

The summer months meant cricket competed with soccer. Dad loved cricket. As well as Carlisle Cricket Club, we both followed the Surrey County cricket team and we played cricket together regularly in our back garden, taking turns at bowling and batting. We were frequently joined by some of my friends from school or the neighbourhood. During the summer school holidays there were daily cricket matches in the Shatter back garden which caused consternation to our next-door neighbour, Vera Delaney, who lived in Number 12.

Vera and her husband Charlie moved into Crannagh around the same time as us. They had no children and Vera's love and all-consuming hobby was her garden. Her back garden was spectacularly planted with a pond in the centre containing a wonderful variety of water lilies that flowered in the summer. Cricket in our back garden meant lots of balls being hit over the wall into Vera's garden and the risk of damage to rare flowers lovingly cultivated during the year both outdoors and in her heated greenhouse. Balls over the wall were also an ever-present danger to the glass in her greenhouse, which miraculously only once got broken. They also regularly landed on lilies in her pond. Vera understandably was not enthusiastic about our cricketing exploits nor did she appreciate me or one of my friends climbing over the wall to retrieve an errant ball. As I grew up, we had various battles over balls. We then reached an agreement. I was given permission to climb over her wall once a day to retrieve balls but all my pals were banned. This was subject to the condition that I climb the wall at the bottom of the garden where she had a compost heap enclosed in a low bricked area, as she had flower beds and shrubs all along the wall up to that point. I had no difficulty with this as first standing on the low bricked area made the climb both easier and quicker. Sometimes Vera would throw balls back over the wall and visiting her garden was unnecessary. Other times balls were confiscated when she became annoyed by their frequency. As I child, I viewed Vera as difficult and a bit of a grump but she was a kindly woman who simply invested a lot of her time in her garden and was stuck with a sport-obsessed child living next door whose balls, like missiles in a war zone, were an ever-present danger.

Every Christmas we were invited into Number 12 for home-baked Christmas cake, a cup of tea and an exchange of presents. Vera knew I loved books and invariably she had purchased a book for me and a box of chocolates for my parents. Mum bought Vera various Christmas presents over the years which she always thoughtfully wrapped in colourful Christmas paper. I no longer remember any particular present given to her – I suspect because, perversely, what Vera made most fuss over each Christmas was the beauty or novelty of the wrapping paper. Over the cup of tea, as exchanged presents were unwrapped, there was much oohing and aahing by Vera over the "exotic" or "special" paper which she focused on. She always opened her presents carefully and then neatly folded the paper and stored it in her dining-room chest of drawers. For her it seemed the Christmas paper was the highlight. I have no recollection of there being anything unique about Mum's Christmas paper and could never figure out why Vera took the wrapping paper so seriously.

One of my missions on some occasions when Mum was baking was to knock on Vera's front door and deliver a cake or a pie to her. I think it was one of Mum's ways of thanking her for putting up with the noise of screaming kids in our back garden and the regular arrival in hers of balls of all shapes and sizes.

The O'Driscolls, our neighbours on the other side in Number 16, had a large back garden, mainly covered in grass. They had their own children and were never upset by flying balls or my hopping over the wall to retrieve them.

◄0► ◄0► ◄0►

Up until the age of ten, life growing up seemed uncomplicated. If there were complications at home, I was oblivious to them. The most complex issue seemed to centre around my schooling. I started off in Rathgar National School, a primary school on Rathgar Avenue, which I attended from January 1956 until June 1957.

I have only four memories of Rathgar National. The classroom seemed very large with a lot of pupils in it. I think the teacher in charge was teaching more than one year in the same room. The playground was concrete and if you fell when playing soccer, you grazed your knees. There was a great chipper just a short distance from the school which those who dared could visit during a school break to buy chips. And my final memory is of the day I was sent to the principal, John Corsgadden, for continuously dropping my pencil on the floor in class. At least that is how I remember it but maybe I did something more serious because being sent to the principal was a big deal. Stories abounded of the principal having a cane which he used on bold boys. I have no idea of whether the stories were myth or true. Looking back, I have no recollection of any distressed pupil in the school complaining of being caned. Nevertheless, the cane was a substantial fear factor and there was no way I was submitting myself to it. I remember sitting for a while on a chair or a bench outside the principal's room and then returning to class. When asked by the teacher, I simply told her I had been warned to behave. I didn't mention I had not spoken to the principal. I arrived the next day at school in trepidation that I would be called out for not doing so and for telling untruths but to my enormous relief nothing was said.

In those days Rathgar National was a Methodist-managed school divided into a boys-only and girls-only section. Even the playgrounds were separated by gender. In September 1957, my parents moved me to Stratford Junior School in Rathgar. Stratford was a mixed-gender Jewish private primary school. I have no memories of my time there other than the fact that I was a Stratford pupil for only one academic year. I then moved on to The High School Junior School, a boys-only predominantly Church of Ireland school. Like its Senior School, it was located at that time at 40 Harcourt Street on a site currently occupied by An Garda Síochána [Guardians of the Peace], our police force.

I'm fairly certain that as I started my first term as a pupil in High School, one of the pupils commencing first year in the girls' section of Rathgar National school was someone destined to play a big role in my life: Carol Danker, who today is better known as my wife Carol Shatter! Upon completing her primary education in Rathgar, Carol became a pupil in the Diocesan Girls' Secondary School located on Adelaide Road in Dublin's city centre, just a five-minute walk from High School's Harcourt Street premises. Despite the proximity of the two schools we didn't first meet each other until I was eighteen and in the middle of my Leaving Certificate exams and she was just fifteen and in the middle of her Intermediate Certificate exams. Ironically, three years after Carol completed her secondary schooling in Diocesan, it amalgamated with High School, creating a mixed-gender school located in what originally had been High School's sports ground in Danum, Rathgar. We obviously set the precedent for the schools coming together!

I loved High School and quickly settled down there. I liked all of the Junior School teachers but my particular favourite was Dorothy Blakeney who I stayed in touch with until her death some years ago. As a teacher, I remember Dorothy as always being good-humoured and bringing a real sense of joy and anticipation to her teaching. There was nothing unpredictable about her and she smiled a lot. When being taught in her Junior School class I looked forward to being in school and saw her homework exercises as a challenge to enjoy.

I was competitive and always wanted to get top marks. I did well in the Junior School and recall annually featuring in the school Prize Day presentations. In High School's Junior School I was definitely a goody two-shoes and regarded by my classmates as something of a swot. However, I got away with being labelled a swot as I was a useful playground soccer player and was a sure thing to score goals for whatever team I played on at the school break.

In my final Junior School year, I finished top of the class in the summer exams but after my first year in the Senior School my academic standards substantially declined – but more of that later.

◄○► ◄○► ◄○►

Most but not all of our summer vacations were spent in Ireland. I have a vague memory of once, as a small boy, visiting my grandparents Sophie and Sidney (my mum's parents) in Southport. They also visited Dublin a few times.

Jersey and Birmingham are the only two destinations I remember definitely flying to before I reached my teens. My only memory of Jersey is being out at sea with my parents in a speed boat steered by my dad. I think I was only about seven at the time and I assume Dad's eyesight did not then detrimentally affect his capacity to steer the boat. I remember more of our visit to Birmingham where we stayed with Mum's brother Henry and his wife Delphine. I don't know exactly how long we stayed in their home but I can recall rows between Henry and Delphine over the length of our stay.

We must have been in Birmingham for at least two weeks as I still remember the newsagent's at the top of their road and the spectacular selection of comics on the shelves, some of which I had never seen in Dublin. The colour of the roads and the paths were different to those I was familiar with in Dublin and I know that I walked to the newsagent's to buy more than one edition of the comics I regularly purchased each week and read in Dublin.

While there I decided I didn't like Henry very much. I was destined to be in his company on only two further occasions: when he and Delphine came to Dublin, staying two days for my bar mitzvah, and when twenty-two months later in the early morning he flew in to Dublin for less than a day.

The highlight of the Birmingham trip was a visit with my dad to Edgbaston, the home ground of Warwickshire County

Cricket club, to watch the last day of a test match between England and the West Indies. The English team scored over 500 runs in their second innings and the West Indies got into terrible trouble, losing seven wickets in the afternoon, but they managed to hold out for a draw. Freddie Trueman, who played for Yorkshire, was one of my cricket heroes and I saw him bowl out two of the Windies batsmen.

On most summer holidays we spent a few days in hotels or guest houses in Bray or Portmarnock and on about three occasions we spent a week in Butlin's Holiday Camp in Mosney, County Meath. Butlins is where I first learnt to play table tennis and after we first stayed there a net, bats and balls were purchased, the net mounted on our dining-room table and table tennis was added to the Shatters' sporting activities.

◄०► ◄०► ◄०►

A couple of years after moving into Crannagh, a TV was purchased, an aerial installed and the world of BBC and then UTV opened up. Sport, comedy, politics and soaps were avidly watched as was *The Late Late Show* once Teilifís Éireann commenced broadcasting. Dad and I regularly watched *Dixon of Dock Green* on BBC, a series about daily life in a London police station, and Mum and I became addicted to ITV's *Coronation Street*. Dad couldn't stand *Coronation Street* which of course runs to this day. *Doctor Who*, *The Twilight Zone* and *Match of the Day*, covering the English Leagues First Division were my favourite programmes. During the summer holidays my idea of heaven was watching England playing test cricket on our small black-and-white screen while licking an ice cream delivered by Mr Whippy. If I wasn't playing or watching soccer or cricket, just sitting in the garden on a

31

sunny day reading was the next best thing.

Being born on the 14th February meant my birthday coincided with Valentine's Day. Birthday cards always arrived in the post and our postman used to joke that I had a surprising number of girlfriends for a young man. Birthdays meant a party and my mum was a great party-organiser. If she didn't bake the birthday cake, an ice-cream cake would be the centrepiece, decorated with birthday candles.

◄o► ◄o► ◄o►

Buses were the main family mode of transport but when I was about eight we got our first car, a red Vauxhall that my mum proudly drove. It was great having a car. On wet mornings, instead of us getting a bus, Mum drove me to school and dropped Dad off at work. Dad didn't drive because of his deteriorating eyesight. I no longer walked to Terenure with Mum to do the shopping. She now drove us there. On weekends we also ceased to be dependent on my Uncle Jack to go to Dún Laoghaire for a walk on the pier and a visit to Teddy's, famous for its whipped ice cream. During the summer we could drive to the beaches in Portmarnock, Donabate and Brittas Bay whenever we chose. Picnicking in the sand dunes in Brittas Bay and playing on Brittas Beach was a particular favourite.

Soon after our arrival in Crannagh, I had learnt to ride a two-wheel bike. By the age of nine I was cycling all over and, on occasion, got into trouble for cycling too far from home without my mum's permission. I remember a gang of us cycled up the Dublin Mountains one sunny summer's day when Mum thought I was playing in a friend's house. We walked up a sloping field to investigate the ruins of the Hell Fire Club, a notorious place in 18th century Dublin.

We had been told that two hundred years earlier wild parties used to take place in the club and that it was haunted by the ghosts of some of the party-goers. We just saw a broken-down building and nothing unusual. It was very disappointing and we believed a waste of time. Another time I got into trouble when my Uncle Jack, driving his car, spotted me cycling in Ranelagh. A school friend lived there and one sunny summer's day during the school holidays I had decided on a whim, without telling anyone, to go visit.

◄○► ◄○► ◄○►

In addition to my parents, prior to my teens, the other adult relative who featured to a major degree in my life was my Uncle Jack. At weekends I frequently accompanied him to Edmonstown Golf Club where he was a member and walked the golf course with him when he was playing. He always paid me for caddying and wheeling around his golf clubs and we regularly played together on the putting green when golf was over. During school holidays, from a relatively early age, I used to spend some of my time assisting unpacking or packing parcels and stacking shelves in his business, the Continental Jewellers, located on Ormond Quay. He imported Irish souvenirs, watches and jewellery as a wholesale business and sold them on to shops all over the country. The colourful leprechauns that he sold were made in and imported from Hong Kong, as were many of the other souvenirs he stocked.

Jack's business also supplied jewellery and watches to the Grafton Jewellers, trading in a retail shop located in the middle of Dublin's Grafton Street. My Aunt Gertie and her brother Willie Samuels, who played cricket for Ireland, were partners in the Grafton Jewellers which they successfully ran together. Following Willie's death during my teens, the business continued with Willie's wife Elsie taking his place. Whenever as a youngster I was wandering around town, the jewellery shop was one of my regular ports of call and where I most frequently met Gertie.

Jack and Gertie had a beautiful piano in their home but I have no recollection of anyone ever playing it. It was many years later that I learnt Jack had been a brilliant musician who played violin as a member of the London Symphony Concert Orchestra in the 1930s. The only existing record of his doing so is his fleeting appearance, together with other members of the orchestra, at the very end of Alfred Hitchcock's British thriller film *The 39 Steps* which was first screened in 1935.

Jack was a regular visitor to our home, much more than Gertie, and would join in playing football or table tennis. The other regular family visitor was Jack and Gertie's dog, Rebel, who fairly rapidly after our move to Crannagh, having been walked over to us by Jack a couple of times, learnt the route and visited on his own. He continued to visit, even for a period after going almost totally blind, until he died during my teens at the old age, for a dog, of fourteen years. Unfortunately, this is not the last time the number 14 features in my story associated with death nor was Rebel's the only death I had to come to terms with growing up.

Chapter 3

Only Killing Jews

My dad had a group of friends, all of whom worked in the city centre and ran their own businesses. Where today Brown Thomas is located in Grafton Street, Switzers was located during my childhood and into my early adult years.

Switzers was a major department store which had in its basement a large restaurant. At the back of the restaurant, adjacent to the Gents' toilets, there was a large oblong table that could comfortably accommodate about eight people and more at a squeeze. From Monday through to Friday for about twenty years this table was reserved by Dad and his friends for lunch. Out of a group of about twelve, between six and ten would turn up. They ran a variety of different retail shops in Dublin, some big, some small, employed a significant number of people and were all members of Dublin's Jewish community. From time to time family members, wives, girlfriends, sons and daughters squeezed into the seating along the back wall and joined in the lunch.

Wednesday was a half day at school and from the time I

started at High School I regularly turned up for the Wednesday lunch. On school holidays I did so once or twice a week and was always fussed over. I really enjoyed the Switzers lunches. The food was great, there was always a lot of joking and laughter at the table and some of my dad's friends were extrovert characters.

Mum and Dad met up with some of the same people and their wives at weekends and everyone from time to time visited each other's homes. They also, on occasion, went out as a group to horse races in Phoenix Park, Punchestown, Leopardstown or the Curragh racecourse and I was usually taken along.

◄o► ◄o► ◄o►

Sometime after my tenth birthday Mum developed health problems. I didn't really understand what was wrong. Both of her parents, Sophie and Sidney, died in the period immediately preceding her becoming unwell and their deaths may have deeply affected her. Of course, her illness could have been triggered by something else. Like most ten-year-olds I did not know the full story of my parents' day-to-day lives nor did I know of every event that impacted on them. Did something happen between Mum and Dad that escaped my notice? It is possible but I don't think so. Did someone say or do something that upended her equilibrium or which utterly undermined her self-confidence? I simply do not know. What I do know and remember is that her personality changed. She lost her infectious exuberance and started to spend a lot of time during the day in bed. There were days she didn't leave the bedroom other than to visit the bathroom. There were also some days when she seemed perfectly okay. Dad employed a part-time housekeeper to tidy the house and she cooked some of our meals. Over a period of three to four years Mum spent time in a variety of hospitals and nursing homes and Dad and I, both in the evenings and at weekends, regularly travelled by either bus or taxi to visit her. I remember many such visits to the psychiatric wing in St James's Hospital. She was prescribed various medications and sometimes just seemed out of it or behaved oddly. She stopped driving her car and rarely went out. I regularly cycled to H. Williams supermarket in Terenure (which is today a Centra shop) to do the household shopping. I remember her on one occasion, having returned from hospital very distressed and crying after electric-shock therapy, saying she would never go back to hospital again.

Her behaviour became increasingly erratic and unpredictable. From being a loving, happy, soft-spoken, tactile parent she became distracted, irritable and distant. Without warning her mood and demeanour could change. One minute she could be the Mum I had grown up knowing and loving, the next a semi-detached stranger lost in her own thoughts. As time passed, the mood swings became more frequent and her negative moods grew in duration. I know there were occasions when I was very upset by her behaviour but I recollect that over time I learnt to adapt to and cope with what was happening.

When having a bad time she was never unkind to me, just became withdrawn and locked into her own world with little interest in what was happening around her. I understood that I could no longer rely on her to help me with my homework, to do the shopping or to prepare supper. I started to cook basic food, such as cheese on toast, scrambled eggs, mushroom omelettes and slowly graduated to other dishes. I also from time to time cooked suppers for her, bringing them up to her bedroom and trying to encourage her to eat. Sometimes she ate what I brought upstairs and cheered up but mostly she picked at it and it languished cold and uneatable on her plate until I disposed of it in our kitchen bin.

At the start of Mum's deterioration there were moments when I got very upset and nights when I quietly cried myself to sleep. However, at an early stage I understood she was unwell as Dad regularly explained. I believe that, in the midst of all the upset, I learnt to be both resilient and self-reliant.

There were moments during those years when Mum seemed to get well and would resume driving and go out again. She would then suddenly, without warning, relapse. Dad became increasingly distressed and arguments between my parents became a regular occurrence. Mum grew very thin and there was great concern that she was not eating enough. Over those years the family doctor, Manny Berber, who was a kindly man, made regular house calls to our home and when he did there were always lengthy conversations between him and my dad. Looking back to that time now, I believe it likely that, amongst other things, she was suffering from anorexia. She had a poor self-image and I remember her standing in front of her bedroom mirror pronouncing herself fat when she was as thin as a rake and her clothes were literally falling off her. By then she was no longer the vivacious, attractive young woman of early family photos but a preoccupied, slight and fragile victim of her destructive demons. Unfortunately, there was no real understanding of anorexia in the early 1960s.

◄o► ◄o► ◄o►

It is strange how odd things stand out from your childhood and are remembered and other stuff is totally forgotten. Dublin city centre was less crowded in those days than it is today and perceived to be safe. During the school holidays it wasn't unusual for me, on my own, to get the 16 or 16A bus to meet up with some of my school friends in O'Connell Street to go to a movie in the Savoy or Adelphi cinemas or to go to the Grafton Cinema located close to the Grafton Jewellers to watch cartoons. After school, when I had reached the age of about ten, some of us occasionally wandered into town to mess around before getting the bus home. I got into trouble on a few occasions for arriving home late and the dinner getting overcooked!

Sometime in April or May 1961, outside Clery's Department store in O'Connell Street, I took a double-decker bus home. As usual, I sat downstairs on the bus. I always sat downstairs, if possible, as in those days smokers sat upstairs and I hated the smell of smoke. The bus was fairly full. I sat beside a man who I now reckon must have been in his early fifties. He was reading the *Evening Herald* which had an enormous headline on its front page about the trial of Adolf Eichmann.

I knew something about Eichmann who was one of Hitler's Nazi henchmen and had played a central role in the extermination of six million Jews in the Holocaust. His kidnapping by Israeli Mossad [Secret Service] agents in Argentina the previous year had been the subject of much animated conversation at home and amongst my dad's friends at the Switzers dinner table. By then I regularly read stories reported in the *Irish Times* and had read whatever it had published about Eichmann. Either my dad or mum also each week bought the *Jewish Chronicle*, a weekly paper published in England. I occasionally looked through it and had read articles and stories about Eichmann there.

I was a nosey child and stared at the *Herald* story, trying to read it. The man must have noticed as after a few moments he turned to me and said: "I don't know why they don't leave that fella alone. He only killed Jews and it all happened a long time ago."

I won't pretend that at the age of ten I knew all about the Holocaust but I reckon I knew a good deal more than most Irish ten-year-olds. I came from a home where these things were discussed with a father who had a growing library, with books about World War Two and the foundation of Israel. Eichmann's role in the Holocaust was something I knew about. I was stunned by the casual dismissal of Eichmann's inhumanity and cruelty and, unusually for me, rendered totally speechless.

I didn't respond and sat silent for the rest of that journey until I stepped off the bus at my Rathfarnham Road stop. As I walked home I felt guilty about my silence and that night discussed the man's comment with both Mum and Dad. Mum assured me that I was wise to say nothing as he was probably an anti-Semite and Dad advised me that had I attempted to argue with him no good would have come from it. The incident must have had a profound impact because it has always stayed with me.

A few days later I was back in town and purchased William Shirer's *The Rise and Fall of the Third Reich*, the thickest book I had ever bought. I was determined to learn as much as I could about Germany's role in World War Two and how the Holocaust occurred. I read the book during that year's summer school holidays and on many nights, after Mum and Dad thought I had fallen asleep, read it under my bed covers by the light of a torch.

Growing up in Dublin I had experienced very little anti-Semitism. The children growing up in Crannagh Park regularly played together on the road and we were all in and out of each other's homes. There was one family though, living at the top of the road, a reasonable distance from our house, of which I was wary. There was one son, older than me, with whom I got on well, and a second younger one who, on a number of occasions, called me a dirty Jew. I may have been wrong but I believed he could only be repeating something he had heard his parents say. I ended up giving all members of that family a wide berth. When in my forties, during an election campaign, out canvassing one evening in Dublin South constituency, I instantly recognised the guy who answered a door I knocked on as the child who had called me a dirty Jew when I was around eleven or twelve years old. He announced himself to me as a former neighbour in Crannagh Park and greeted me as a long-lost friend. I feigned friendship, apologised for disturbing him and simply explained it was a canvass call. I said no more and he assured me of his number one vote! Not believing his word, I rapidly ended the conversation. As I walked out of his gate, the slightly annoyed Fine Gael canvasser accompanying me emphasised to me the importance of my being more proactive in "tying down the number ones". The truth is, I didn't want his number one vote. Standing that evening at his door I was still a young boy being called a dirty Jew.

Chapter 4

Thumbs Up

Although Dad worked Saturday mornings, most Saturdays I attended synagogue. Abraham (Abe) and Sarah (Sadie) Josephson lived in 20 Crannagh Park and were among a number of Jewish families living nearby. On a Saturday morning I often called into their home around half past nine and walked with Abe to Terenure Synagogue. At that time there were approximately 3,300 members of the Irish Jewish community, most of whom lived in Dublin. There were three large synagogues, two medium-size ones (one of which was in Cork) and three small ones and on a Saturday Terenure Synagogue was reasonably full. I enjoyed the service and meeting up with a lot of my age group there. Until I was fourteen I was a regular attendee and I reckon by then, if I had possessed a decent singing voice, I could have conducted most of the service myself. Unfortunately, I am tone deaf and can't sing to save my life! Often, after the Shabbat service, the Josephsons had a kiddish in their home. I always enjoyed their kiddish at which I drank a small amount of sweet kosher wine and ate Sadie Josephson's delicious homemade kichel cookies and sponge cake.

Despite my dad's atheism he was anxious that I receive a Jewish education and understood my Jewish roots. On Sunday mornings I attended religious (Talmud Torah) classes in Stratford College for about an hour and a half. While I enjoyed synagogue, I hated the classes. I believed that some of the teachers held their positions due more to personal religious observance than their teaching skills. One of the teachers, a Mr Lev, regularly threatened pupils with a black strap he kept in his desk, had a short fuse and was not slow to hit any pupil he regarded as disruptive. I learnt practically nothing of value in his classes and regularly complained about them at home. Apart from my dislike of Lev, my main memory is of the day one of the older pupils arrived before class with a garden shears, cut the black strap into small pieces and then laid the pieces together on top of Lev's desk. With the pieces pushed together the strap looked intact and undamaged. Lev arrived about five minutes later and looked puzzled to find the strap on the desk instead of in his desk drawer. He just looked at it, left it where it was and commenced class. After a few minutes had passed the culprit roared Lev's name together with an expletive from the back of the class, Lev grabbed his strap to hit him, it disintegrated and parts of it fell to the floor as the offending pupil sprinted out of the classroom. Lev turned red and started screaming at the class but he no longer had his strap and we all fell about laughing. I hadn't mentioned Lev's strap to my parents but when I returned home I couldn't resist telling Dad the story of what had happened. I was almost twelve and due to commence bar mitzvah classes. Dad told me that he believed no teacher was entitled to hit a pupil. He said that type of teacher should not be tolerated and he determined to arrange for my bar mitzvah and religious classes elsewhere.

Like all Jewish boys I was scheduled to have my bar mitzvah when I reached thirteen years old. This required my reading an extract from the Torah in synagogue and reciting other religious readings in Hebrew. Shortly after the strap incident, I started attending bar mitzvah classes twice a week after school with the Gavron sisters (Becky and Lillie) who taught in their home located just off the South Circular Road, near to Clanbrassil Street. Clanbrassil Street, when I was growing up, had various kosher butcher shops, a kosher delicatessen and a bakery and I had regularly shopped there with both Mum and Dad and Uncle Jack. The general area, because of its Jewish connections and many Jewish residents during the first half of the 1900s, had become known as Little Jerusalem and was familiar territory. On Sunday mornings in the 1950s and 60s it was a focal point for members of the Jewish community to congregate, shop, meet up and gossip. Today, Clanbrassil Street is utterly changed and retains none of its Jewish heritage.

Several of my Jewish pals attending High School were also being taught by the Gavrons as we were all scheduled to have bar mitzvahs within a few weeks of each other. The Gavrons were very special. They were kind, wonderful people and brilliant teachers. I hugely enjoyed their classes and, amazingly, they taught me to sing my bar mitzvah readings in a way I hadn't believed possible. Their home was about a five-minute walk from Dublin's Leonard's Corner. The Number 16 bus stop was located about thirty yards down from the corner, right outside a small bakery that baked great bread and delicious cakes. I loved the smells of baking as I stood waiting for my bus and often purchased some bread or cakes to take home with me.

◄O► ◄O► ◄O►

During the year before my bar mitzvah Mum's health

continued to deteriorate. She had some good spells but was frequently in and out of hospitals and psychiatric nursing homes. On one occasion she was rushed to hospital by ambulance after taking an overdose of prescribed tablets. It was not known whether she had deliberately overdosed or had accidentally taken too many tablets. I was in a friend's house and Dad, on his return from work, had found her lying unconscious on their bed and was unable to revive her. She remained in hospital for about six weeks and then returned home and was in good spirits for about three weeks until her health again deteriorated.

◄◦► ◄◦► ◄◦►

Despite Mum's health problems, arrangements for celebrating my bar mitzvah were made. A pre-bar mitzvah Friday-night dinner for visitors was organised at Jack and Gertie's home and on the Saturday, after the morning bar mitzvah synagogue service, a lunch was organised for relations and friends in the hall attached to Terenure synagogue. Bar mitzvah invitations were printed and posted and in the weeks preceding the event the excitement built up. At least two months beforehand I knew my portion of the service so well I think I could have sung it blindfold. I wasn't nervous about my role but increasingly anxious about my mum's ability to cope with it all and worried that by the time it came around she might be back in hospital. I knew she was taking medication at the time and in the weeks leading into the bar mitzvah everything seemed to settle down. She seemed more cheerful and together than she had been for a long time and my dad started to loosen up and look less tense. I wondered whether as a result of the approaching bar mitzvah she had turned a corner and was on the road to a permanent recovery. Although she recommended baking and a jam tart made an appearance for the first time in over a year, I remained nervous about how it would all turn out.

On Friday, the day before my bar mitzvah, Henry Presburg and Delphine flew in from Birmingham. Gertie had two brothers who were doctors in London, Leslie and Eddie Samuels, who also flew into Dublin for the event. Eddie was accompanied by his wife Molly and Leslie by his son Basil. Friday night's pre-bar mitzvah Shabbat evening meal went well and was uneventful. It was essentially a family event. Even Dad and Uncle Jack's mother, my grandmother Leah, who could be very difficult, behaved well. She lived permanently with Jack and Gertie and did what she could to make Gertie's life miserable – but more about Leah later.

My Saturday bar mitzvah day arrived and it was cloudy and cold, not unusual for February. My parents and I left home just before nine to walk to Terenure Synagogue and arrived on time for the quarter-past-nine start to the service. By a quarter to ten the synagogue was practically full, accommodating the Saturday morning regulars, all my parents' guests and my Jewish school friends. I sat downstairs in the synagogue between Dad and Uncle Jack. I still remember Mum, wearing a glamorous yellow wide-brimmed new hat, specially purchased for the occasion, sitting proudly in the centre of the front row of the balcony upstairs in the women-only section of the synagogue, happily smiling down at me throughout the service.

I have two other memories of that service. Upon my completing singing my portion of the service on the bimah (the raised platform or podium in the synagogue from which the service is conducted), with a huge sense of relief I turned to look at Dad who was standing beside me and was surprised to discover him wiping tears from his eyes. Crying at bar mitzvahs must be a family trait as I was destined to repeat Dad's performance many years later when my son Dylan sang his bar mitzvah portion on the bimah in Dublin's Adelaide Road Synagogue and then again in our Dublin home where we held my daughter Kelly's bat mitzvah. (My scepticism toward religion I have learnt doesn't inhibit my emotional reaction to some aspects of Jewish ritual.)

My second vivid memory of the service, apart from all the shouts of mazel tov as I stepped off the bimah, comes from the speech delivered by the then Chief Rabbi of Ireland, Dr Isaac Cohen. As the rest of the congregation quietly listened to what he said, my role was to stand facing him looking respectful, interested and earnest. Unfortunately, disaster struck within a couple of minutes of the start of his speech. I have no recollection of anything Dr Cohen said but to this day recall that upon his emphasising something or other he believed important he inadvertently spat straight into my right eye. Until the speech ended I was engaged in a personal struggle to avoid being consumed by a fit of the giggles. In my head, to divert an insane desire to burst out laughing, I repetitively counted from one to a hundred and then started over again, a technique I have deployed many times since to avoid catastrophe on serious occasions.

◄O► ◄O► ◄O►

Counting to a hundred proved particularly helpful in May 2011 during the historic visit of Queen Elizabeth to Ireland. The visit took place just nine weeks after I had become Minister for Justice and Equality and Minister for Defence in the newly formed government after the February 2011 general election. In my role as Minister for Defence I had to formally greet the Queen and Prince Philip upon their arrival for a commemoration ceremony at Dublin's Garden of Remembrance. The garden is a memorial dedicated "to all of those who gave their lives in the cause of Irish freedom". A column was formed with the Queen and our fantastic then President, Mary McAleese, at its head and others, including me, walking slowly and solemnly, two by two, behind them. We walked down some steps and then by the side of the cruciform pool of the garden where various former Taoisigh [prime ministers] sat. We then walked up the steps to where the large cross stands, in front of which both the Queen and the President were to lay wreaths. My difficulty arose before we reached the steps as I approached where Albert Reynolds was seated.

Albert was a former Fianna Fáil Taoiseach, now deceased, who took political risks in making an enormous and greatly undervalued contribution to the Irish peace process. The Provisional IRA's "complete cessation of military operations" (or complete ceasefire) after over twenty-five years of murder and mayhem in Northern Ireland occurred on 31st August 2004 when Albert was Taoiseach.*

At the time I was on the Fine Gael back benches, having been sacked as spokesperson on Justice by John Bruton for being involved in an unsuccessful attempt earlier in 2004 to remove John as Fine Gael's leader (conduct of mine I came to regard as dishonourable and have for many years regretted). Both Albert and I were members of the Riverview Club (now David Lloyd's) in Clonskeagh in South Dublin and on a number of occasions from mid-June into July 2004 we bumped into each other at the club, usually sometime between nine and ten in the evening, after Albert had finished swimming in the indoor pool and I had

---

*The ceasefire occurred eight and a half months after the Downing Street Declaration. The Provos announced the end of the ceasefire at 7pm on the 9th February 1996 and a minute later two people were killed in a massive bomb explosion in London's Canary Wharf. On the 20th July 1997 the ceasefire was restored and became permanent. In the intervening period six further victims of Provo violence died, including Detective Garda Jerry McCabe who was killed on the 7th June 1996 during the attempted robbery of a post office in Adare, County Limerick.

finished playing tennis. We talked politics and, in particular, he confided in me about some of what was happening behind the scenes in the effort to end violence in Northern Ireland. At the time Albert was coming under terrible political pressure as a consequence of atrocities committed by the Provisional IRA, being criticised by political opponents, including some of my Fine Gael colleagues and some commentators, for not issuing more strident condemnations of the Provos' conduct. He frequently publicly criticised the Provos but was being particularly careful in the language he used in order to ensure the peace discussions were not fatally damaged by anything said. Sinn Féin, the Provos' political wing, were scheduled to have a day-long conference towards the end of July. There were rumours and some media speculation that a ceasefire would be announced at the conference.

We bumped into each other one evening on a day when it seemed the political and media hounds of hell were in pursuit of Albert. He confided in me that the rumours were wrong. He believed a ceasefire likely but not until the end of August or early September. He was worried that once the conference was over he would be in enormous political difficulty, particularly if there was another Provo-perpetrated atrocity. I encouraged him to continue on the path he was travelling as the political risks were worth the enormous prize of peace.

I was surprised at the extent to which Albert confided in me over those weeks. He never asked that I keep our conversations confidential. I assume he presumed that I would and I did. I never mentioned anything he shared with me to anyone in Fine Gael or in the media. I presume for his own reasons at that time Albert wanted to explore what was happening with someone outside the process. Our conversations occurred as an accident of circumstances.

Well, that is the background to Albert inadvertently

getting me into trouble at the Garden of Remembrance. The world's television cameras and media were fixating on all of us as we walked in the direction of the cross. Cameras were, of course, primarily following the Queen and the President but I assumed they occasionally scanned down our line. Looking ahead, maintaining a serious expression, I saw Albert out of the corner of my right eye greet me with a big smile and give me an enthusiastic thumbs-up. It was the first time our paths had crossed since my ministerial appointment. I have always had a difficulty taking myself seriously at ceremonials and, a bit like the occasion when the Chief Rabbi spat in my eye, I had to struggle not to smile in response to Albert. Had I presented, on camera or in photos later published, smiling at that moment in the Garden of Remembrance it would have looked weird and could have been personally politically ruinous. My difficulties increased during the wreath-laying ceremony. I was positioned standing immediately behind the Queen and at risk of being constantly on camera. My only function was to stand still and look sombre. As I did, I quietly fought with myself to contain my continuing amusement at Albert's thumbs-up and wondered what the reaction would have been had I returned it. Although the event was both serious and historic, I was struggling to take my role in it seriously in so far as it required that I stand still and stare at the Queen's back. Fortunately, I managed to maintain a serious ministerial appearance in the face of adversity!

Filmed footage of me standing behind the Queen, before and during the wreath-laying ceremony and while the Last Post was movingly played by an Irish army soldier, went around the world and is still occasionally broadcast in documentaries and other TV programmes. On Christmas Day 2011, I was inundated with texts from friends telling me that an extract of the footage had been screened during the Queen's annual televised Christmas Message. Whenever I see it, I remember Albert and just recall that as I stood behind the Queen I was frantically and repetitively counting up to one hundred in my head to avoid disaster.

As I write this book, I realise that had my mum been alive in 2011 she would have been intrigued by my role that day in the Garden of Remembrance. During my childhood, from the time we had a television, she always enjoyed watching the Queen's Message broadcast Christmas Day on the BBC. It was a link to her English heritage.

◄◦► ◄◦► ◄◦►

Now back to where I started: my bar mitzvah. When the Chief Rabbi's speech ended he gave me a big smile. With enormous relief I relaxed and smiled back.

After his speech the service fairly rapidly concluded. All our guests made their way to the synagogue hall for lunch which was preceded by some drinks, sponge cake, chopped herring, smoked salmon and bagels. Everything seemed to be going well till we sat down for lunch. Then Mum started acting strangely and began to slur her words. She didn't want to eat anything but just incoherently and incessantly talked. Both Dad and I simultaneously concluded that she was drunk as a result of a mixture of medication and alcohol, despite her having had only a couple of drinks. I had yet to deliver my bar mitzvah speech and I knew there were a couple of presentations to be made to me. I could see the alarm register on Dad's face that before it was all over Mum might do or say something awful or possibly just collapse.

Fortunately, our fears were not realised. She talked throughout the meal and I recall feeling embarrassed and uncomfortable because of her behaviour. But, apart from Mum, Dad and me there were only five others at our table

– Gertie, Jack, the two Presburgs and Grandmother Leah –
and they just seemed to get on with their meals.

Shortly prior to the start of the speeches at the end of the
meal, Mum quietened down. I delivered a short speech (my
first ever) which I had composed and written with Dad's help
the previous weekend. Someone (I do not remember who)
then made a short speech praising my bar mitzvah
performance and presented me with a certificate recording
that ten trees had or would be planted in Israel to celebrate
my becoming an adult. (The theory being that your bar
mitzvah day marks your entry into adulthood.) A brief speech
by my Uncle Jack was next, about what a grand lad I was,
and he presented me with a watch which had my name and
the date of my bar mitzvah in the Jewish calendar engraved
on its back. The lunch ended with a brief thank-you from
Dad to everyone present for joining us on my "special day".

With that it was all over.

As the guests departed some came over for repeat mazel
tovs, to thank my parents for the meal and to hand me
envelopes, each of which contained a congratulatory card
accompanied by a bar mitzvah present of a cheque. I can't
recall how much I received in bar mitzvah gifts but it must
have been a serious sum as a few days later Mum took me
into a local branch of Bank of Ireland to open a deposit
account and to lodge it all.

When everyone had departed we walked home in the
rain, accompanied by the Gavron sisters. As they both were
strictly Orthodox and religiously observant they would not
travel in a car or a bus on the Sabbath. They had walked
from South Circular Road to Terenure Synagogue early
that morning and the weather was too bad for them to
walk all the way back. The walk home was difficult
because Mum was unwell as a result of her cocktail of
medication and alcohol and she continuously muttered

apologies for walking slowly and talked incoherently about the lunch. The Gavron sisters pretended not to notice.

When we arrived home Dad helped Mum go straight to bed. The rest of the afternoon was then spent with the Gavrons in our sitting room, reprising my bar mitzvah performance and talking about other bar mitzvahs scheduled for the coming weeks. I may be wrong in my recollection or it just may have been my perception but I can recall no exuberance in our post-bar-mitzvah conversation that Saturday afternoon. I think Dad and I were upset over Mum's condition and just filling in time with the Gavrons until it became dark outside, Shabbat ended and Dad could phone for a taxi to drive them home.

I don't recall much more about that weekend, other than later that evening watching a rerun on television of an international rugby match played by Ireland that afternoon and Mum on the Sunday confessing to very little memory of the luncheon or my delivering my speech and having to be filled in on how it had all gone. She repeated her apology for her condition, saying she should have realised she should not have drunk alcohol.

The truth is, I don't think her getting drunk was anticipated as a possibility by either of my parents as little alcohol was ever consumed in our home, save for Dad on the odd occasion on an evening or a weekend putting a small amount of rum in his coffee. To this day, I am not a great drinker but enjoy an occasional Jamaican rum and Coke or a Mai Tai, which is a rum-based cocktail with orange and pineapple juice. I also make a killer sherry and rum trifle. I don't know whether my liking for rum is inherited and is part of my DNA or whether when drinking rum I am subconsciously maintaining some connection with my dad. I am sure that could be a subject for analysis if anyone was curious enough to pursue it!

Chapter 5

Adult Teenager

After attaining adulthood according to the Jewish religion, I transferred from High School's Junior to its Senior School the following September. Having been a stellar pupil in the Junior School, in my first three years as a Senior School pupil I was a good deal less than stellar. I attribute this to my growing obsession with sport, my increasing boredom with some of the school subjects taught and my spending far more time reading books of my own choosing than studying or spending time on my homework. I suspect some would also attribute to family events my scholastic decline over those years, from the top to somewhere close to the bottom of my class in exam results (save for history which I thoroughly enjoyed and which was taught by a fantastic teacher, Ronnie Wallace). If I was on the outside looking in, I might also do so but, having been on the inside looking out, I am not convinced it would be an accurate perspective.

◄◊► ◄◊► ◄◊►

In the summer of 1964, having played in a trial match, I became a member of Port Vale schoolboys' soccer club which played in the Dublin Schoolboy League. (The club had no connection to the English League club of the same name). Home games were played in Bushy Park, Terenure, and in the 1964/65 season I was a regular, playing on the under-14s team. I played in the attack and my positions varied. I played on the right or left wing or inside right or inside left. I was equally proficient with either foot and often switched positions during a match. The team's manager, whose face I remember but whose name I can no longer recall, determined my position for each match. Dad watched all our home matches but I have no memory of Mum ever accompanying him. Away matches were played all over Dublin and mostly as a team we would meet up at the relevant bus stop and then bus to them.

At weekends in August we trained together. We also trained early in the evening on Tuesdays and Thursdays until the autumn arrived, it got dark early and the park was closed by 5 p.m. Then, to be as fit as possible, I regularly got out of bed in the early morning before school and did a twenty- to thirty-minute jog around the block near our house. Some evenings I repeated the performance. Crannagh Park circled around into an extension built on to Crannagh Road, continued back around into Ballytore Road and then I could turn back into Crannagh Park and end up outside Number 14. Most mornings, unless the weather was really awful, I did a series of circuits, then showered, breakfasted and caught the bus to school.

◄o► ◄o► ◄o►

After I had played the first three or four away Schoolboy League matches for Port Vale I learnt never to sit beside the team manager on the bus. I discovered that when sitting beside him he placed his hand on one of my legs and on two or three occasions attempted to fiddle around inside my trousers. As a thirteen-year-old it didn't seem right and made me feel uncomfortable. I played soccer with Port Vale for four years and whenever we travelled after that to away games I always kept my distance from him. He was a thin man I remember as being in his late thirties or early forties and I assume he treated other boys similarly as after a short time most of the team carefully avoided sitting beside him but I do not recall any of us discussing his conduct nor did I mention it to my parents. His behaviour, so many years ago, was something long forgotten by me until shortly before I started writing this book. It was, of course, child abuse but I don't believe his behaviour had any negative impact on me. My experience was mild compared to the horrific levels of abuse experienced over past years in Ireland by far too many children.

However, perhaps not only what I later learnt about widespread child physical and sexual abuse, but also my experience as a thirteen-year-old boy, subconsciously incentivised my determination both as a lawyer and a TD to confront the perpetrators of such abuse, to improve our child protection services and to tighten up our laws to ensure those who commit or cover up child abuse are criminally prosecuted. Criminal legislation I originated and had enacted in 2012, within sixteen months of becoming Minister for Justice, today plays a very important role in criminalising individuals who learn of a child being sexually abused and fail to report the abuse to the gardaí. The removal of child protection services from the dysfunctional Health Service Executive, the creation of Tusla (the Child and Family Agency) and a separate government Department of Children with a senior cabinet minister, plus the successful incorporation into the Irish Constitution of a Children's Rights Amendment, all originated from reforms I first advocated a long time prior to my being in government. They were all over the preceding years taken up and advocated by various groups and organisations as well as by some other political parties. Ultimately they formed part of Fine Gael's election platform in 2011 and were both incorporated into and implemented by the 2011 Programme for Government which I helped negotiate and which was agreed between Fine Gael and the Labour Party.

◄०► ◄०► ◄०►

One afternoon each week there was school rugby training in Danum, High School's sports ground in Rathgar. While I enjoyed watching rugby, soccer was my first love and I had to be careful to ensure I did not find myself selected to play on a school rugby team. The school rugby matches played on a Saturday coincided with Port Vale's soccer matches which I did not want to miss. To prevent being selected, I avoided tackling as much as I could get away with. My doing so also ensured I suffered no rugby injury that would prevent me playing soccer. However, when fifteen years old this strategy failed. I was very fit and the fastest runner of all my contemporaries. One fine afternoon in Danum I made the mistake at training of scoring about eight or nine tries when playing on the team of also-rans (the possibles) against our Junior Cup Team (the probables). I was on the right wing and each time the ball came out to me I sprinted for the line, successfully swerved past opposing players and scored a try, leaving floundering Cup Team players in my wake. For three of the tries I ran almost the entire length of the pitch. Much to my shock the next morning my name was included on the team sheet posted on the school notice board to play in that Saturday's Junior Cup match against Blackrock College. As a result, I missed our Schoolboy League soccer match that Saturday. As it turned out, it was my only appearance on one of the school's rugby cup teams. We were clobbered by Blackrock and the few times during the match the ball came my way I was buried by Blackrock tackles. They were a team playing at a much higher level than High School and we were not at the races!

On many an occasion during my first three years in the Senior School, homework played second fiddle to soccer. After school, if not playing soccer on our road, I often lined up cricket stumps in our back garden, put on my soccer boots and practiced for ages sprinting around the stumps, guiding the ball around using only my left or right foot or passing from one foot to the other. As an alternative, I would go on a three-mile run through Rathfarnham, Rathgar and Terenure. Being fit had a far greater priority than academic success.

In the Junior School I had been very studious and did not need parental supervision for homework to be properly completed. In the Senior School I did as little homework as possible. In my world homework had ceased to be important and my grades rapidly deteriorated. I had a simple ambition: when seventeen or eighteen to play for Shamrock Rovers and then for Spurs!

◄○► ◄○► ◄○►

Then, soccer got me into trouble. Well, perhaps to be more accurate, I got myself into trouble! Dublin Maccabi, the Jewish community's sports club, had two teams playing in the adult Amateur League. I started training on Thursday evenings with members of the Maccabi teams. The Club had lights, which meant you could have a kick around in the dark during the winter. The Amateur League matches were played on a Sunday and I got onto the second team. So I was now playing two matches every weekend, one on a Saturday and the second on a Sunday.

Near the end of the rugby match against Blackrock College I had pulled a muscle in my back. Our family doctor disliked rugby, believing it to be a dangerous sport. In addition to recommending physiotherapy, he gave me a note for High School asking I be indefinitely excused rugby training because of my back injury. When recovered from the injury, instead of resuming Tuesday rugby training, I opted for Maccabi's Tuesday evening soccer training which until then I had only occasionally joined because of rugby training earlier on Tuesday afternoons.

At that time Port Vale were doing very well, had won a series of games and were serious contenders to win our division of the Schoolboy League. There were two evening papers in those days, the *Evening Herald* and the *Evening Press*. Over two Saturdays each took turns in sending a photographer to take pictures of the team. On each occasion I was hunkered down in the front row for the photo and easily identifiable. Week one we appeared in the *Herald*. Week two in the *Press*. Each time the pictures appeared on a Tuesday evening when the papers reported the weekend's Schoolboy and Amateur League match results.

The Wednesday morning after our picture appeared in the *Evening Press*, a couple of minutes after the start of Latin class our Latin teacher, who was my school group's rugby coach, let out a roar at me, shouting how come my picture was in the paper when I couldn't play rugby because of a back injury? I immediately realised he was an *Evening*

Press reader! He was known in the school to be both a rugby fanatic and to have a bad temper. He also specialised, on occasion, in giving pupils a thump on the back of the head. He seemed to break into a gallop in my direction. Before you could say "Virgil" I was out the door like the clappers. His classroom was on the second floor of the school and as I sprinted down the corridor he insanely chased after me, ordering me to stop. I suppose I have never been good at obeying orders! I kept going, clattered down the stairs and, arriving on the ground floor, sprinted into the office of the principal, Dr Ralph Reynolds, a scholarly and kindly man who I greatly liked. My general grades at that time may not have been good but I had never been in trouble in the school. I also had a good reputation as the school's best athlete for my age, having the previous summer been one of a small number of boys who represented the school in athletic competitions.

As Dr Reynolds looked up startled from his desk at the uninvited visitor who had rushed into his office, behind him, panting and dishevelled, came the Latin teacher. Before he could catch his breath, I asked him very loudly to "Please explain to Dr Reynolds why you want to hit me". Muttering something about a misunderstanding, he retreated and went back up the stairs. Dr Reynolds, with a broad smile, then asked me if everything was alright. I assured him it was and returned to Latin class. Nothing more was ever said about the incident and the Latin teacher never again attempted to hit me, although within a couple of weeks he resumed giving an occasional clatter to other pupils in my class.

I enjoyed Latin and Roman history and the crazy teacher who chased me was in fact a really good teacher of both. In the year leading into my Intermediate (now called Junior) Certificate exams I again started to study seriously. Thanks to his teaching, I achieved a very good mark in my Latin exam and two years later went on to easily pass Latin in Trinity College's matriculation exam. But what I best remember is the chase down the corridor with the teacher in hot pursuit!

There was one other occasion during my six years in the Senior School when a teacher threatened me with violence. During Fifth Year the school initiated a weekly Civics class. A part-time teacher in his mid-forties, with an odd and bullying personality, was recruited to teach Civics. His classroom was a prefab located in the school grounds adjacent to the school's permanent buildings. It was a classroom also used by other teachers and, on occasions when it rained during our lunch break, was occupied by pupils eating their sandwiches and chatting. One day, it started lashing rain a few minutes into the break and, together with other boys, I walked into the classroom to discover him sitting behind his desk reading the morning paper. He had arrived early for our class which was scheduled for one-thirty. He roared at us to get out. He was relatively new in the school and I started to explain that the teachers always allowed use of the room during school break when it was raining. He was having none of it and ordered us out into the rain. I thought his conduct irrational and refused to be bullied by him. I refused to leave by simply replying "No" when he again ordered me out after most of the others had retreated out of the room. With that he bounded out from behind his desk, grabbed me by the lapels of my school blazer, hoisted me off the ground and pinned me against the wall. Red-faced and angry, he lifted his right arm. Before anything further happened, I enquired whether we should visit Dr Reynolds before or after he hit me. He hesitated, slowly lowered me to the ground and said something about visiting him after class. With that he returned to his desk and I sat at the back of the class to eat my sandwiches. A few minutes later, some of those who had exited trickled back into the classroom, soaking wet from the rain.

Civics class lasted forty minutes and at its end I immediately went up to the teacher to enquire whether we should now go and visit the principal. He muttered something about prior commitments, saying leave it till next week. Of course, we never made that visit. He was another teacher who occasionally during that year hit pupils but he never again came near me. Not only was he a bully, he was a dreadful teacher and his classes were useless and boring.

I have no doubt that I would have dealt differently and less confidently with each of those incidents if not for my dad impressing on me that no teacher had any right to hit a pupil. Both my parents were totally opposed to corporal punishment. I had witnessed each of those teachers striking my friends in class and at home discussed some of the incidents that had occurred and I was angry over what I had seen. I believe I was angered by the gratuitous violence as well as my powerlessness to intervene to protect a pal. I was determined never to become one of their victims. I had also noticed that once either of them hit one boy, inevitably within a few weeks he would find a reason to hit the same boy again without fear of consequences. As far as I was concerned I was never going to be that boy.

Now I don't want anyone to get the wrong impression. I loved my years in High School, most of the teachers were brilliant (there are always exceptions), some both brilliant and seriously eccentric, and the majority never lifted their hands to pupils. Other than confronting a school bully when sixteen, I was involved in no other similar incidents nor did I ever get into any other trouble.

As a teenager I was definitely precocious and at the age of fifteen believed I was in love with a girl in another school who was also doing her Intermediate Certificate exams. My problem was she was very studious and inevitably on course for between six to eight Honours. At the start of our fourth year I think my teachers expected I might fail the exam. As far as I was concerned no way was that going to happen. I worked my socks off during that year and took grinds in Irish and maths, my two worst subjects, and ended up miraculously with four Honours and two decent Passes. I missed my final exam which I hoped would result in another Honour and I will come to the reason for that shortly. I know the Irish teacher was astonished that I achieved a decent mark in Irish as my mock exam earlier that year had been a disaster. He attributed the result to some last-minute material he had given us to rote-learn. I attributed it to the grinds I attended of which he was unaware and to my working hard to ensure I did not fail a subject in which I correctly anticipated my girlfriend would excel and get Honours!

But I have got ahead of myself. In the years leading up to my Intermediate Certificate exams there was a lot more going on than my schooling, playing soccer, attending Shamrock Rovers matches, training, reading books and chasing girls. It is one of the more difficult periods in my life to discuss but I believe the time has come to open up that door and walk through it.

Chapter 6

Nightmare and Reality

Much of the laughter that had been part of our home as I was growing up gradually evaporated in the years immediately preceding my bar mitzvah. By the time my bar mitzvah was over the laughter had stopped. I remember my home as a sad, sombre place throughout 1964 and 1965 when I was thirteen and fourteen years old.

My mum was continually unwell and in and out of hospital. There was a second occasion when she was rushed to hospital in an ambulance after taking an overdose. Dad appeared very stressed and was under pressure because of emerging business difficulties. When at home Mum rarely went out and continued to spend a lot of time in bed. She also had become incredibly thin and on some hospital stays was intravenously fed.

Mum was prescribed a cocktail of pills and vitamins and Dad had to ensure they were properly taken as she could not be relied on to take them herself or to take the correct quantity. We employed a housekeeper weekdays to cook and to ensure Mum did not overdose when taking her tablets at lunchtime when I was at school and Dad was in town. At weekends I took over the cooking as Dad was too shortsighted for preparing food and cooking anything beyond a boiled egg or a toasted cheese sandwich. Roast beef with Yorkshire pudding and roast potatoes became my speciality Sunday dinner. I cheated by buying the horseradish sauce instead of making it myself.

Mum had some days when she was quiet and distracted and others when she was delusional and angry. Whether the delusion and anger were part of her illness or the unintended side effects of her medication I do not know. Looking back on it now, I suspect the latter. There were also days of normality when for no identifiable reason she seemed to just snap out of it.

We started to regularly have Friday-night Shabbat meals in Jack and Gertie's home. Occasionally, Mum accompanied us but more often, when not in hospital, took to bed. When driven home by Jack we always returned with a plate of food which she would pick at but largely leave.

When Christmas 1964 arrived, for the first time she was unable to visit Vera Delaney to deliver our Christmas present. I dropped in to Vera, accompanied by Dad, with a box of chocolate liqueurs and went to some trouble to wrap them in nice paper. For our return home Vera gave us some Christmas cake for Mum which she never ate. What none of us knew at the time was that 1964 would be her last Christmas.

Christmas school holidays in 1965 commenced when school ended on Friday the 17th December. In the days before, Mum had been going through a bad spell and Dr Berber visited her at home on the Saturday. There was talk of depression and her returning to hospital after Christmas. After the doctor had left I overheard her telling Dad she never wanted to go back to another hospital. She had said this before. On the Sunday she seemed to buck up and for a couple of days everything was normal.

On Tuesday the 21st December, having spent my morning messing around with friends on the street, I briefly returned home, then shortly after one o'clock I headed off to get a bus into town to meet Dad in Switzers for lunch. Mum was in a cheerful humour and I suggested she drive us both into town for lunch but as usual she chose to stay at home. I caught the Number 16 bus and got to Switzers at about a quarter to two.

I loved town that time of year. The Grafton Street Christmas decorations looked great and Switzers windows fronting onto the street were full of cartoon characters. After lunch I dropped into the Grafton Jewellers to say hello to Gertie and then spent some time in a bookshop checking out the Christmas comic annuals and other books. Although Jewish, we always exchanged Christmas Day presents and every Christmas my mum and dad bought me three or four books, including a couple of my favourite annuals. Dad had asked me whether I was not a bit too old for the annuals. Acknowledging I was for some, I had promised to identify those that I would enjoy. I remember one was a soccer annual with lots of pictures and stories about teams playing in England, including a feature on Spurs and the World Cup scheduled to take place in England in 1966.

Sometime after three o'clock I headed for home.

It was a dry, cold, sunny December afternoon and instead of getting the bus I decided to jog home. On dry days I often jogged home from school and it seemed a good idea. Mum had been in good humour when I left the house, so I decided to give her a surprise. A bread strike had been taking place in Dublin for a number of weeks and bread could not be purchased in our local shop or supermarket. It was still being baked in local bakeries, so I decided to jog first to the bakery shop beside the bus stop near Leonard's Corner which I used to frequent after my bar mitzvah lessons with the Gavron sisters. Having bought some bread, I continued jogging home. It was only as I reached Terenure village that I was passed by a Number 16 bus. Had I caught the bus I would have got home about five minutes earlier.

As I walked up our driveway before I reached the front door there was a strong smell of gas. The smell was even stronger when I opened the door. Running into our breakfast room, I found the kitchen door locked. Bizarrely, what was happening resembled a nightmare I had awoken from just a few nights earlier. I instantly knew Mum was in the kitchen. I climbed out the breakfast-room window, grabbed a big rock in the garden and broke one of the kitchen windows high up on the side wall of our house to let the gas escape. After that I climbed back into the breakfast room, dialled 999 and called for an ambulance. I then ran and knocked on Vera Delaney's front door, told her what I had found and that I needed her help. Going through her house, I ran to the end of her garden to where I could more easily climb over her wall near the compost heap enclosure and get back into our garden. Opening our side door, which I had mistakenly believed to be locked, I let Vera in. Vera held our dustbin steady as I stood on it to reach the ledge of the kitchen window. I then put my arm through the broken pane of glass, flicked up the window catch and climbed through the window into the kitchen.

I found my mum lying still, curled up in a ball on the floor, her head on a pillow beside the oven door with a coat over her. All the taps on the gas cooker and oven were open and the smell of gas was overwhelming. Holding my breath, I instantly turned off the gas, opened the doors leading into the garden and quickly opened all the kitchen windows. Vera rushed into the kitchen together with Michael who had just arrived to do some gardening. We moved Mum away from the oven door and stretched her out on the floor. She didn't react and there was no sign of life.

At that very moment the ambulance arrived and she was rushed to the Meath Hospital in Heytesbury Street. After the ambulance's departure, I phoned Dad and told him Mum had tried to gas herself. Within fifteen minutes he arrived home, driven by a friend, Louis Verby, whose business was close to Dad's premises in Dame Street. Before Dad arrived Vera, Michael and I opened every window in the house to get rid of the gas. Dad stayed for a few minutes to check I was okay and then, leaving me with Vera, was driven to the Meath Hospital.

Just before Dad's arrival I had phoned Dr Berber to tell him what had happened. He told me that by phoning the ambulance so quickly I might have saved her life. He was wrong. She had no pulse on the ambulance journey and after arriving in the hospital Dad was told she had been dead for some time. Uncle Jack joined my dad in the hospital and, as Dad was totally distraught, Jack, in response to a doctor's request, formally identified Mum's body in the hospital mortuary.

I remember very little of the rest of that day. I'm sure I was traumatised. I do remember that when Dad returned from the hospital I described to him everything that had happened upon my arriving home and what I had done. I know we hugged and cried but I have no idea what else was said. There were many visitors to our home that evening but, other than Jack and Gertie, I have no memory of who they were or of when we finally went to bed. I do remember sleeping with Dad in his bed that night. Neither of us wanted to sleep alone. We talked about Mum and her illness for hours. At some stage I fell into an exhausted sleep.

When I woke up in the morning Dad was already in the breakfast room drinking a cup of tea. I'm not sure he had slept at all as his eyes were red and he looked dreadful. We again slept together the next night and during the nights that followed. A few weeks would pass before I again slept alone in my own bedroom.

Around midday that Wednesday, two very nice and sympathetic gardaí from Rathfarnham Garda station called to our home and explained that because of the circumstances of my mum's death they had to take a statement from each of us. Yet again, I explained what had happened, a guard wrote it all out and I signed the statement. Dad did the same. I would later learn that statements were completed also on that Wednesday by Vera and Michael.

◄○► ◄○► ◄○►

The funeral took place in the Jewish cemetery in Dolphin's Barn in Dublin, on the Thursday. My memories of the funeral are scanty. I remember being brought into a room where I saw my mum's body lying in a coffin, standing beside my dad in the small synagogue while prayers were said after we had walked in behind her coffin, walking behind the coffin with Dad to the burial plot, more prayers after the coffin had been placed in a hole dug in the ground and then saying Kaddish, which is a prayer in praise of God recited by mourners. Then back in the synagogue and, after more prayers, sitting down on a hard wooden bench as a stream of people shook our hands, muttering meaningless words of sympathy. It all seemed unreal.

Mum's brother Henry flew in that morning for the funeral and as soon as it was over took a taxi back to the airport and was gone. I have always regarded Henry's swift departure as surprising but I do not know the reason for it. The funeral was followed by a week of sitting shiva in our home and unless it was essential that Henry return to Birmingham he would have been expected to remain with us in Dublin throughout that week.

Shiva for members of the Orthodox Jewish community is the week-long mourning period following the death of a spouse, parent, child or sibling, during which prayer services take place in your home where you remain to be visited, fed and comforted by friends and relations. In each prayer service the Kaddish is recited by the male mourners. Gertie, Jack and my grandmother Leah spent the entire week of shiva in the house with us, Jack and Gertie going home at night while my grandmother decided to overnight throughout the week in our spare bedroom.

Each day, except over the Sabbath, we had prayers at eight in the morning and at eight in the evening and there was a constant stream of well-meaning people visiting throughout the day. Every day, both for prayers and during the afternoon, some of my dad's Switzers lunchtime friends came to our home and they were a welcome presence among the many strangers, both Jewish and non-Jewish, who turned up. I had never realised that my mum and dad knew so many people. There were also visits from all my friends and some of our Crannagh Park neighbours.

The primary purpose of shiva is to provide an environment of comfort and support for the bereaved. But, while the Switzers group and my closest friends' visits were welcome, the truth is both Dad and I found the whole week horrendous. Throughout the week we were both distraught and our grief wasn't helped by being entangled in a religious ritual of repetitive prayers that lacked logic and meaning. Because of my regular synagogue attendance, I was familiar with and understood all the prayers recited in Hebrew in our home. Praising every morning and evening an almighty God who, if he existed and was truly powerful, could stand by and watch my mum kill herself by lying down in front of an open gas oven was for me repugnant nonsense. It was during that week that I became a secular Irish Jew. To some this description may be contradictory. To me, it is an honest description of who I am.

Over the years, I have learnt that being not only Irish but also Jewish is part of who I am and how I view the world. I believe that it is one of the reasons why I constantly ask questions to establish the truth of things and I have so frequently challenged perceived wisdom, false narratives, prejudice and injustice. I am not sure whether it is a matter of culture, tribal identity, conditioning or just something that is part of my DNA. Perhaps it is a mixture of all of those things. I do know that argument and questioning is at the very heart of Jewish tradition. Throughout Jewish history debate and discussion on issues of religious importance has always been vigorous, valued and played a central and crucial role for those in search of wisdom and truth. I have also learnt that my non-observance of Jewish religious ritual is of no relevance to how I am perceived, treated or depicted by others and, in particular, by those who are consciously or subconsciously anti-Semitic or whose insights have been influenced by anti-Semitic tropes. There is nothing new in this. It is consistent with the global Jewish experience over thousands of years.

Shiva over, Dad sat me down and said he never wanted me to go through that experience again. When he died I was not to sit shiva. The day shiva ended was also the moment for Grandmother Leah to make an announcement.

She was moving permanently into our home to cook meals and be of help. Within a few days Gertie and Jack, in a number of car journeys, moved all my grandmother's clothes and belongings from Riversdale Avenue to Crannagh Park. Her moving in would ultimately prove to be disastrous but Dad and I were too upset at the time to give it much thought.

◄o► ◄o► ◄o►

About three weeks later, on the 21st January 1966, I found myself in the Dublin Coroner's court with Dad for an inquest held into my mum's death. I have a memory of taking an oath holding the Old Testament. I then confirmed on oath that the statement I had signed the day after Mum's death was indeed mine and that its contents were true. Dad and each of the others who had signed statements went through the same ritual and medical reports were handed to the coroner. The coroner then pronounced that Mum's death was due to "carbon monoxide poisoning inhaled" at her home on the 21st December 1965 "at a time when she was of unsound mind". The word "suicide" was not mentioned by him. As a fourteen-year-old, I simply understood that Mum was unwell when she died and that she had committed suicide.

Recently, when visiting the National Archive and examining the coroner's file, I discovered the autopsy and medical reports read by the coroner. Mum was forty at the time of her death and Dad was forty-nine. The reports revealed that not only had she been diagnosed before her death as suffering from depression but was, according to the pathologist at the time of her death, "an emaciated adult female who appeared to be older than her stated age". I have no doubt that she was suffering from anorexia but in those days the complexity of this serious eating disorder was neither acknowledged nor understood.

Before the coroner concluded the proceedings, he commended me for my swift action upon arriving home. I didn't believe I deserved any commendation. If I had not gone into town for lunch that day my mum might still have been alive. She might also have still been alive had I gone straight home after lunch. And did I really need to jog home instead of travelling by bus? Would the bus not have got me home quicker? And if there was no bread strike I would have run through Rathmines and Rathgar to Rathfarnham which was quicker than the Leonard's Corner, Harold's Cross, Terenure route that I had taken. Why had I decided to go buy bread when bread wasn't much of a surprise anyway? And why had the bread strike happened and been allowed to go on for so long? Why should anyone die because of a bread strike? Bread strikes aren't supposed to kill. I had a myriad of uncomfortable reflections and unanswerable questions.

And there was one other question but I answered it myself. Why had I climbed over Vera Delaney's back garden wall when returning to my house and not just simply run back with Vera and gone through the side garden door? I knew the answer to that question. In my nightmare I had found Mum lying dead in our kitchen, her head inside the gas oven. Due to the side garden door being locked, Vera and I could not get into the back garden together and I had lost time before I climbed through the kitchen window. I had to run back through Vera's house, climb over her back-garden wall and then unlock the side door to let her in. Later I realised that my nightmare had impacted on how I reacted that dreadful afternoon. The main differences between my nightmare and reality were that I found my mum lying down, her head on a pillow, in front of, not inside, the gas oven and discovered our side garden door unlocked when opening it for Vera. Whether it had been left unlocked or had been unlocked by my mum to enable Michael the gardener to get in to cut the grass, I do not know. I do know that Michael had not featured in my nightmare. It was only when Dad told me that she had died a long time before I found her that I understood any extra time I had taken unnecessarily climbing over Vera's wall didn't matter. What I will never know is whether Mum's suicide could have been prevented had I told my dad about my nightmare the morning after it had occurred. I think during our lives we all experience nightmarish moments which are part of our reality but few of us expect a real nightmare we experience while sleeping to turn into reality. What I do know is that my mum's suicide was a terrible waste of a good life blighted by an illness that nobody fully understood.

Chapter 7

Lodz & Sachnin

I returned to school after the Christmas holidays and on the first day back to school I was accompanied by my dad who informed Dr Reynolds of Mum's death. Later that day Dr Reynolds sent for me, expressed his sorrow at the news and said that he was always available if any day in school I wanted to call into his room for a chat.

Dad had delayed returning to work until the new school term started and we then settled down into a routine. Each morning we took the bus together as I travelled to school and Dad to work. Either the housekeeper or my grandmother cooked meals. Unless I went to soccer training in Maccabi, most evenings were spent doing school homework, reading or watching television. Mid-week some of Dad's friends met up for a card game upstairs in Maccabi and he joined the game, holding the cards right up to his nose so he could see them. After soccer training, I frequently played table tennis in Maccabi until sometime between ten and ten-thirty.

In the weeks following my mum's death Uncle Jack had visited our home more frequently than usual and on Sunday mornings from early spring I caddied for him in Edmonstown. Lunch there was usually followed by his collecting Dad and my grandmother for a drive to Dún Laoghaire and, on dry afternoons, a walk down the pier. I continued to play a soccer match every Saturday and once Easter arrived athletics training started. But things hadn't settled down at home and my grandmother's presence had become a problem.

I never knew the full story of Grandmother Leah's life before she lived with Jack and Gertie and then moved in with us. I assume it must have been difficult as her husband, Abraham (my grandfather), died in England in 1934 in the middle of the great economic depression and she never remarried.

Jack was almost one year old in 1913 when he arrived in England from Lodz with Leah and Abraham. I do not know how many relations remained living in Lodz after their departure, their names or the extent to which my grandparents maintained any contact with them after arriving in London. They exist in old family photographs, looking solemn and formally dressed in their best clothes, beckoning across the decades for a recognition I cannot give them. I do know that I am fortunate that Leah and Abraham did not remain in Lodz. Had they done so, I would never have been born!

Lodz, Poland's second largest city, was under Tsarist Russian control when Leah and Abraham left and travelled to England with Jack. The family surname was Sachnin not Shatter, and my uncle's original name was Jankel not Jack. When arriving in England neither Leah nor Abraham spoke any English and English officialdom attributed Shatter as a surname to them and Jankel over time evolved into Jack.

(My father's name on his birth certificate of 1916 is Reuben Shatter not Reuben Sachnin.) A year or so after Abraham's arrival in England he was followed there by his brother and officialdom conferred on him the surname Stamp. The family story is that, when something was said to him that he didn't understand about stamping his papers, he questioningly repeated the word "stamp" and ended up with Stamp as his anglicised surname! As a result there were two Sachnin brothers living in England, one known as Shatter, the other as Stamp. Whether the "Stamp" family exists today I do not know as during my life I have not known of any family contacts between the Shatters and the Stamps.

In 1934, the same year his father died, Jack became a naturalised British citizen. His naturalisation certificate records the grant of naturalisation to "Jankel Sachnin, known as Jack Shatter" born in Lodz on the 16th December 1912 and then resident in 2 Sheba Street, Spitalfields, London E1. Today, this certificate hangs as a memory of Jack on my study wall. To preserve the original family name, our home in Ballinteer has a plaque naming it *Sachnin*. I do not know whether any other Sachnins originating from Lodz emigrated during the early 20th century to any other part of the world or whether they continued to live in Lodz until the outbreak of the Second World War.

Lodz at the turn of the nineteenth into the twentieth century had a thriving Jewish community of approximately 100,000 people which continued to grow and by 1939 was in the region of 230,000. It was roughly one third of the city's population and one of the largest Jewish communities in Europe. Lodz was at that time a major centre of Jewish learning and culture. Prior to the outbreak of the Second World War a small number left Lodz and moved further east to Warsaw and other cities in fear of a German invasion and Nazi persecution.

The German army invaded Poland on the 1st September 1939 and entered Lodz on the 8th September. From the moment of the Germans' arrival in Lodz, Jews were terrorised and attacked in the streets, their shops and homes plundered and businesses taken over. In the early weeks of Nazi occupation a number were tortured and murdered. By the end of December 1939 over 70,000 Jewish inhabitants had been expelled or fled to the Soviet Union and some had been deported as slave labour to work in Nazi labour camps. Jewish institutions were closed and by the 17th November 1939 all synagogues were destroyed. From that date all Jews were required to wear a yellow star. The Lodz Ghetto was established in February 1940 and 164,000 Jews were compelled to live within the ghetto which was sealed off from the outside world in May 1940. Jews living outside Lodz and from other parts of Europe were also deported into the Ghetto. During its existence an estimated 19,700 deportees arrived from Germany, Austria, Czechoslovakia and Luxembourg. Sanitary conditions were horrendous with no fully functioning sewerage system, food was scarce, there was very limited running water, no coal or wood for heating and virtually no clothes or shoes beyond people's possessions. The ghetto area of just under four square kilometres became the most densely populated part of Lodz. Outside the entrance to the ghetto, signs were erected: "Wohngebiet Der JUDEN: Betreten VERBOTEN" [Jewish Residential Area: Entry Forbidden]. Any Jew caught outside the Ghetto could be shot on sight.

A series of mass deportations from the ghetto to the Nazi death camp at Chelmno, 55 kilometres north-west of Lodz, commenced in January 1942. By the end of May 1942, over

57,000 had been sent to Chelmo to be gassed. In September 1942 the "Gehsperre Aktion" (roughly translates as "Lock-up Action") was initiated and the ghetto's hospital closed. In the period from the 3rd to the 12th of September 1942, 15,681 children (aged 10 and under) and the sick and the elderly (those over 65) were sent to Chelmo for extermination. Those sent to Chelmo were transported in five-ton trucks to the train station outside the ghetto from where they were taken to the death camp. In the 1940 to 1944 period, approximately 43,000 Jews imprisoned within the ghetto died of starvation and disease, including epidemics of typhoid, dysentery, typhus and tuberculosis. Some were simply shot. Between October 1942 and May 1944 there were no major deportations from the ghetto, then in June 1944 over 7,000 more of the Ghetto's inhabitants were transported to Chelmo. The concluding act of the Nazi genocide of the Lodz Jewish community was the transportation in August 1944 of 72,000 people to the Auschwitz-Birkenau death camp. It is estimated that only 5,000 to 7,000 Jews from the Lodz Ghetto survived the war.

To this day, I do not know how many relations, if any, of my grandparents lived in Lodz or other parts of Eastern Europe and perished during the Holocaust. It is something that was never discussed as I was growing up. There must have been some as Uncle Jack and Grandmother Leah were the only relations on my dad's side of our family that I knew. In fact, I grew up in what could accurately be described as a largely relation-free zone. Reflecting on it now, it is surprising that my dad never discussed our family history as so many other things were discussed and debated during my childhood.

The months following Mum's funeral were very difficult. Dad tried unsuccessfully to hide his distress and blamed himself for not ensuring Mum was immediately hospitalised after Dr Berber's visit to our home just three days before her death. My grandmother, who believed her residing with us to be helpful, constantly criticised Dad either for not doing more to prevent Mum's suicide or for not being as successful as Jack was in his business. She was a difficult, damaged and embittered woman, who during her years living with Jack and Gertie constantly complained that Gertie wasn't good enough for Jack and criticised Gertie for what she regarded as her inability to become pregnant. (I do not know the true reason for the difficulties experienced by Jack and Gertie in conceiving). When I returned home from school my grandmother always had something unpleasant to say about someone and even complained about the expense involved in feeding the two pet guinea pigs I kept in a hutch in our back garden!

One afternoon in April or May I explained to Jack what was happening at home, expressed concern about the effect of her behaviour on Dad and asked if he could try and arrange for her return to his house in Riversdale Avenue. He promised to talk to Gertie. It was only after he had done so that I learnt of her persecution of Gertie. There were no circumstances in which Gertie would ever again allow her to reside in Riversdale Avenue. When I learnt why, I could not argue.

◄o► ◄o► ◄o►

I was used to Jack leaving Dublin for a couple of weeks to go to international trade fairs and visit Hong Kong and Japan to purchase supplies for his business. His leaving Dublin together with Gertie for a couple of weeks in June

1966 wasn't anything unusual as far as I was concerned. Dad continued to be upset and distracted but that didn't ring any new alarm bells for me as a fifteen-year-old. About two weeks after the start of the school summer holidays Dad told me we were both flying to London the next day and that we were booked into a hotel for a few days. Gertie was there, staying with Leslie Samuels, her brother. I learnt that Jack had been diagnosed with cancer and had travelled to London for an operation. He had been in hospital for almost two weeks and could now have visitors. Dad hadn't told me earlier because he didn't want to upset me any sooner than necessary.

The next day we flew to London. Our visit to London was traumatic. Jack had been diagnosed as suffering from throat and mouth cancer. He was a regular but not a chain cigarette-smoker. I was warned by Dad before we visited him in hospital that the visit would be upsetting, that we could not stay long and that Jack would be unable to speak. His tongue had been removed as part of the operation.

Jack was only fifty-four but when we saw him in hospital he looked seventy-four. The Jack I knew was tall, fit, suntanned, self-confident, talkative and very likeable. The Jack I saw lying on the hospital bed looked old, pale, thin, distressed and could only grunt in response to conversation or nod a "yes" or " no". He was unable to eat and was being drip-fed.

Gertie was with Jack when we first visited. His head was propped up on three pillows and when he saw me he attempted a smile but could not sustain it. Before we set foot in the hospital Dad had warned me that Jack was very sick but I did not expect what I saw and had difficulty speaking to him. I think I must have been in shock.

We stayed in London for five days and visited Jack twice a day. He was being taught by a nurse to eat and swallow small portions of soft food, such as mashed potato, stewed apple, stewed apple, custard and jelly, and finding it very difficult not to choke on it. We were assured he would eventually be able to eat on his own but I understood he would never again be able to taste his food. He was, by the time of our visit, drinking small amounts of water and slightly warm tea through a straw. Jack was also being taught how to form words and speak without a tongue. In Jack's presence Gertie was being positive and encouraging but, away from his hospital bed, she and Dad talked gravely in whispers about Jack's condition and prospects for recovery.

The doctors were hopeful. The cancerous cells they believed had been fully removed. He was to have further treatment on his return to Dublin and provided the cancer did not reappear Jack could live for many years. Both Gertie and Dad were sceptical of this prognosis and, opening up to me, my dad expressed his doubts.

◄○► ◄○► ◄○►

I have two other memories of that visit to London. It was the era of the Beatles, Flower Power and Carnaby Street's moment of fame. One afternoon we visited Carnaby Street and Dad bought me a black shirt covered all over with tiny red and yellow roses. We also went for a walk around London's East End and the places of his childhood. I think the highlight was visiting Petticoat Lane market. He explained to me the area had changed. In his day, it had been largely the home of Jewish immigrants. When we visited, many of those there originated from the West Indies, India and Pakistan. It had substantially but not totally lost its Jewish identity.

◄○► ◄○► ◄○►

July 1966 was dominated by the FIFA World Cup Finals which were held in England from 11th July to 30th July. The Republic of Ireland had failed to qualify, having been eliminated from the tournament by Spain. With my dad, I cheered on the English team as we watched matches the team played on our small black-and-white television at home in Crannagh Park. For me, the biggest disappointment was the absence from the English team of Spurs star forward Jimmy Greaves as a result of an injury. The highlight was England's 4-2 defeat of West Germany in Wembley Stadium. What was particularly special was the hat trick scored by West Ham's Geoff Hurst, who I had watched just over a year earlier score two great goals for West Ham in a friendly match against Shamrock Rovers played in Dalymount Park. There was, of course, no possibility of Dad and me supporting Germany. I can still remember both of us cheering with excitement and hugging when the final whistle blew.

◄O► ◄O► ◄O►

It wasn't until early September that Jack returned to Dublin. When he did, he was thin but looked surprisingly well. It was only when he tried to talk that you knew something was wrong. With difficulty I could understand what he said and as the months passed his speech slowly improved as did his ability to swallow food. I think swallowing is a more accurate description than "eating food".

By mid-October he was going to work daily for a few hours. In his absence the Continental Jewellers had continued in business under a very able employee who had worked with him for many years.

By March 1967 Jack was back on the golf course in

Edmonstown and, although he had regained only some of his lost weight, he appeared fully recovered. He was also able to speak more clearly with a voice sounding entirely different to his pre-operation voice. Then suddenly in early May he again became ill. The cancer had returned and within a short time Jack was a patient in the Royal Victoria Eye and Ear Hospital in Dublin. He was destined to remain in hospital until his death.

Jack's final weeks were horrific. The cancer had spread throughout his body and entered his pancreas. He was in continuous and terrible pain. His only treatment was increasing levels of painkillers. I was told he would not recover and visited him in hospital every day after school and at weekends. The hospital, located on Adelaide Road, was only a seven-minute walk from High School.

When his condition further deteriorated I was discouraged from visiting but continued to do so. My Intermediate Certificate exams took place when Jack was in hospital and at the end of each day's exam I visited the hospital before going home. By that time Jack could barely speak and I remember one afternoon, as I walked down the hospital corridor to his room, hearing Gertie pleading with a doctor to give him extra painkillers because of the terrible pain he was suffering. He died, aged fifty-five, two days before my last exam.

For the second time in eighteen months Dad sat shiva, this time with Gertie and my grandmother in Riversdale Avenue. If I had any remaining doubts about the existence of a god, the horror and pain suffered by Jack in the last twelve months of his life extinguished them.

I have, of course, attended many funeral services throughout my life and visited many of those bereaved in their homes after the death of a spouse, partner, parent or child. I do so out of respect and affection for those deceased or to be supportive to the bereaved. I find it very difficult to stomach sermons at funerals giving thanks for God's goodness and talk of the deceased again meeting in the afterlife loved ones previously deceased. I recognise and understand the comfort such comment can give to religiously devout family members and friends and its value and importance to many millions of people. I respect those who have strong faith in a God and the afterlife but cannot pretend I fully understand it. To me, it is only understandable as a fictitious comfort blanket at a time of unbearable stress, ensuring that when confronted by death or tragedy you retain your sanity. There is a part of me which hopes that I am wrong.

Perhaps, had Dad been a believer, the final years of his life would have been happier and less stressful. Perhaps he might have lived longer. For the truth is Jack's death following on so rapidly from my mum's suicide left an indelible mark and he never fully came to terms with their loss. I believe after Jack's death his only real remaining interest was my welfare and education and, beyond that, he simply gave up on life.

My grandmother Leah continuing to live with us ensured he was given no space to grieve and to recover from Mum's or Jack's death. During the final year of Jack's life, when not blaming Dad for my mum's death, she was complaining that it was Dad not Jack who should have got cancer. In the years after Jack's death she loudly and regularly complained that it was Dad not Jack who should have died. I can still hear her cruel taunt "It's you who should be dead". It is ingrained in my memory. Despite my pleading with him to insist she move out and live elsewhere, he maintained he could not do so because she was too elderly to live alone. At that time, finance was not an issue in getting her alternative accommodation as Jack had left some property to Dad to secure him financially. The fact is that, despite all of the verbal abuse she showered down on him, he felt an obligation towards her as his mother. I suspect that he also tolerated her abuse after Mum's death because he wrongly believed that he deserved it.

Chapter 8

Innocents Abroad

Jack was an astute businessman. While his main business was Continental Jewellers, he had also during his life acquired a number of investment properties. Two properties were in the joint names of Jack and my dad and upon Jack's death Dad became their sole owner. In addition, Jack left in his will a third property to my dad and a small rental shop to be managed by Dad for my benefit. Jack was clearly concerned about Dad's finances and capacity to continue in business and anxious that he be financially secure. Three of the four were commercial properties with a variety of business tenants and one was residential.

The residential property was on Kenilworth Road in Dublin, a three-storey redbrick house which was divided into two separate residences. An elderly woman lived alone and rent free in the basement and continued to do so until she died four years after Jack's death. I believe she had lived there for decades and was supposed to pay about four pounds a month that neither my uncle nor my dad ever collected. The ground floor and upstairs of the house was rented as a single residence. I do not remember whether it was vacant or occupied when Jack died but I do recall that during my late teens it was rented at some stage by the musician and singer Luke Kelly who, together with Ronnie Drew, Ciaran Bourke and Barney McKenna was one of the founding members of The Dubliners. The Dubliners were a legendary Irish Folk band on the local and international stage. Luke Kelly had a brilliant voice and they had already achieved substantial success. To this day one of my favourite songs is Luke Kelly's rendition of "On Raglan Road", from a poem written by the great Patrick Kavanagh.

I remember visiting Kenilworth Road a number of times with Dad and various conversations between him and Luke Kelly. Dad liked Luke Kelly and their conversations were never confined to discussing issues relating to the house. However, the main reason for the visits was his intermittent failure to pay his monthly rent on time. Luke Kelly was always pleasant, mild-mannered and apologetic when we visited but did not always appear sober. On some occasions the rent arrears were paid when we called, on other occasions promises were made that arrears would shortly be paid but the promises were not always kept.

By that time Dad, because of his short sight, had closed his clothes-manufacturing business, had growing bank borrowings and his only source of income derived from rents received from the various properties. Rents received from two of the other properties had also dried up because of the tenants alleging commercial difficulties. I wasn't convinced that one of his commercial tenants was telling him the truth. I was concerned that Dad was being given the runaround and that advantage was being taken of his kind nature and lack of business acumen. However, I think the manner in which Luke Kelly dealt with Dad had more to do with him having a somewhat disorganised lifestyle than any badness. Eventually, he moved out of Kenilworth Road. Subsequent to his departure, Dad sold the house and discharged his bank debt.

Following the closure of his business, I suspect lengthy conversations with non-paying tenants gave Dad something to do and contributed to his reluctance to take any legal action to recover accumulating rent arrears. I also believe he was anxious to avoid the confrontation and upset involved in court proceedings. An added complication was that the offender who owed Dad the most money had in the past regularly played golf with Jack in Edmonstown. Dad was reluctant to sue someone he believed to have been one of Jack's friends and with whom he himself was on friendly terms. It was only after the guy purchased a new house and it became clear my dad was being misled about his commercial difficulties that any meaningful legal action was taken. Even after that I remember a conversation in which he asked Dad to call off the scheduled court case and give him an extra few weeks to pay the rental arrears. The explanation – he didn't expect furnishing the new house he had purchased to turn out to be so costly!

◄○► ◄○► ◄○►

The summer after Mum's death I had joined Crusaders Athletics Club. There were a number of athletic clubs across Dublin and the various athletic meetings organised by the Irish Amateur Athletics Union held what were called Youth Events and also open adult graded races. I participated in both and enjoyed competing. In inter-club competition I ran the half and quarter mile races and in High School everything from the 100 yards to the mile. In my last two years in High School I was the schools athletics captain. The races were most times in miles not metres or kilometres in those days. The best athlete in Crusaders was Derek McClean whose specialty was the half mile and his main Irish competitor was the great Noel Carroll of Clonliffe Harriers. Both ran for Ireland in international competition and in the Olympics. Two members of the Jewish community, brothers David and Bernard White, who were older than me, also competed for Crusaders, so there were a couple of familiar faces when I first joined. On occasion I trained with Derek McClean and, while I won and featured in the top three in many of the races I competed in as a fifteen to nineteen-year-old, I never achieved the standard and times of McClean or Carroll. Whether I could have done so if I had continued to run competitively after my first year in Trinity College I do not know. I know I gave up athletics at too young an age (and I will get to that) but I also think I was simply not good enough.

I loved competitive running and I believe my daily training routine through my last three years in school and participating in athletic meetings kept me on an even keel and ensured I did not go off the rails. I ran in many meetings in Santry Stadium, subsequently named Morton Stadium after Billy Morton who I knew and who encouraged many great international athletes to come to Dublin to compete in the stadium. There were always some youth and graded races to bolster the race programme in between the main events which attracted the crowds and I got to compete in some of those.

At that time the National Athletics and Cultural Association (NACA), formed in 1922 under the patronage of the GAA , ran its own athletic meetings. It was an all-Ireland body and was in competition with the Irish Amateur Athletics Union whose remit was confined to the

26 counties of the Irish Republic. It was the IAAU which represented Ireland at Olympic Games and there was bad blood between the two organisations. I have no recollection of how it came about but together with John Hanratty, who joined Crusaders around the same time I did, I competed in what were called the Tailteann Games in Croke Park, organised by the NACA. (The original Tailteann Games are said to have first occurred as "funeral games" originating in Pre-Christian Ireland in honour of a deceased ancient Irish queen named Tailte.) It was my first time in Croke Park and it was a big adventure. We didn't tell anyone we were members of Crusaders and competing in athletic competitions organised by the enemy. We felt like two adventurers entering an alien and forbidden land. I have no clear memory of the outcome of the races in which we competed. I recently found a medal in an old box of memorabilia at home which I think I may have won in Croke Park for finishing in the top three in one of the races but I am not certain that is the origin of the medal.

John Hanratty was a real Dub and I was a product of South Dublin with a posh, slightly English accent. We were total opposites and became friends almost instantly when we met in Crusaders. John's races were the mile and half mile. For about two years we regularly trained together, competed in the same athletic meetings and often against each other. We also did not confine competing to our best distances. I was faster than John but he had greater endurance. Any occasion I ran against him in the mile, John won. Any occasion he tried the quarter mile (440 yards), I won. In the half mile, if I could stay with him until the final 200 yards he had no chance. If he managed to outpace me in the early stages of the race there was always a danger that I would be unable to catch him before the finishing line.

On my 17th birthday, almost eight months after Jack's

death, Gertie bought a new car and gave me her three-year-old Mini-Minor which was maroon with a grey roof. Jack, prior to his death, had said that he wanted me to have his car but, as I was too young to drive, it had been sold. Having learnt to drive, I drove with John Hanratty to Belfast to compete in an athletics meeting being held in Paisley Park. It was 1968 and Ian Paisley was becoming a notorious figure for his anti-Catholic extreme Unionist rhetoric. Paisley Park had no connection to Ian Paisley. It was simply at that time being used as a venue for Northern Ireland athletics meetings. I had never driven to Northern Ireland before and neither of us knew our way around Belfast. We had directions to the venue but got lost. I parked the car outside a pub and John accompanied me in to ask the barman the way. It was around lunchtime and there were a few men in the bar. Upon my seeking directions to Paisley Park all conversation stopped and everybody just stared at us. The only words from the barman in a deep Belfast accent were "You better leave NOW!". It dawned on me that I had been misunderstood and that it was assumed I had asked something about Ian Paisley. Nothing more was said. John and I exited rapidly, jumped into the car and drove off.

I do not know where we stopped but presume we were two innocents abroad in the heart of nationalist Catholic Belfast. We struggled with the written note of directions given to us before leaving Dublin and eventually found the athletics ground without again stopping to ask for help.

◄O► ◄O► ◄O►

I could not then have anticipated that over forty-four years later I would visit Belfast and the Stormont Parliament as Minister for Justice and Defence representing the Irish government, accompanied by Garda Commissioner, Martin Callinan, to meet with David Ford, the Northern Ireland Minister for Justice and the North's Chief Constable, Matt Baggott.

I also could not have foreseen that I would attend a historic and groundbreaking State dinner to mark the first visit of a British monarch to the Republic since Irish independence – in fact, the first visit of a British monarch since George V's visit 100 years before. The dinner was held in Dublin Castle on the evening of the 18th May 2011, just over two months after my appointment as a cabinet minister.

The security for the State visit was intense and both the Departments of Justice and Defence were involved in the advance planning. As I was both Minister for Justice and Minister for Defence it was all relatively straightforward to coordinate at ministerial level. Although I had to consult with myself at regular intervals, meetings I had with myself did not have to be specifically scheduled in the Departmental ministerial diaries!

The security arrangements required the fullest co-operation and engagement between the Garda Síochána and the Defence Forces. It was essential to not only ensure the safety of Queen Elizabeth and Prince Philip but to also ensure that the various events and engagements ran smoothly, were not disrupted by the small minority of protesters opposed to the visit or by hoax bomb or other security threats. No threat could be ignored or discounted because of the minority of extremists still engaged in violence on the island of Ireland. The task was complicated by the attitude of the then Minister for Public Expenditure and Reform, Brendan Howlin, who in the lead up to the visit was opposed to the allocation of the additional finance required to fund the anticipated Garda overtime bill relating to the provision of essential and comprehensive security.

The importance of strict security was starkly illustrated

during the State dinner held in Dublin Castle. In advance of the dinner a full security sweep had been undertaken and the Castle put in lockdown pending the guests' arrival. Upon their arrival all the guests lined up for a meet and greet with the Queen and Prince Philip and then everyone sat at their assigned tables. I was sitting at a table with my daughter Kelly who was substituting for my wife Carol who was competing in a golf tournament in England. Amongst those sitting at the same table were Garda Commissioner Martin Callinan and the very able Chief of Staff of the Defence Forces, Seán McCann, and their wives.

After everyone had sat down and just before President McAleese and the Queen were about to speak the Commissioner received a message, leaned over to me and quietly informed me that they had received a phone call containing a bomb threat. We both believed it was a hoax as a thorough job had been done to ensure the building was safe and the Castle had been fully secured. The Queen's speech was going to receive global media attention and we knew it would be a considerable coup for the caller if the event was disrupted by our clearing the building. We were both totally aware of the horrendous consequences should we make the wrong decision.

We decided to keep the threat to ourselves. Nóirín O'Sullivan, who succeeded Martin Callinan as Garda Commissioner, was the Deputy Commissioner in charge of Garda operations around the Castle that night. She was instructed that the building be again discreetly and thoroughly checked.

Before dinner was served President McAleese and the Queen delivered eloquent and historic addresses without incident. During the course of the speeches the Deputy Commissioner gave the all-clear but I don't believe either Martin Callinan and I truly relaxed until the meal was eaten and the event successfully concluded.

It is a coincidence that on the very week I am writing this chapter, sixty-six-year-old Donal Billings from County Longford, having four weeks ago been convicted by the Special Criminal Court, has been sentenced to eight-and-a-half years imprisonment for possessing explosives in May 2011 and, amongst other charges, for making a phone call falsely claiming that two mortars were set for Dublin Castle on the night of the State dinner.

◄o► ◄o► ◄o►

Of course, all of this was light years away on that afternoon in 1968 when I competed in both the quarter and half mile races in Belfast's Paisley Park.

In the twelve months following Jack's death I lost myself in sport. I continued to play soccer during the 1967/68 season and on weekday evenings, when not training under lights in Maccabi or playing table tennis there, usually between eight and ten, went on five-mile runs through parts of South Dublin and picked up along the route a few school pals who joined in. There could be between five to ten of us out running on any evening.

On one occasion, after ten, running through a poorly lit residential street in Rathgar we spotted our Latin teacher's car parked with the windows steamed up. Within our group were two pals from High School who had been at the receiving end of his backhanders. Having run past the car, one of them silently crept back, looked through a steamed-up window and returned to report that the teacher was in some disarray in the back of the car with a woman. A plan was hatched. We all silently surrounded the car and started shaking it as we loudly and repetitively called out his surname, and then sprinted off into the darkness. As we did so, he jumped up inside the car, startled and shirtless, trying to figure out what had just happened. Teenagers can be very cruel! We all laughed our way home that night.

What wasn't a laughing matter was the kick I received in the testicles during that soccer season. I was selected to participate in a trial match involving twenty-two players from the Schoolboy League for some representative game that was to take place. It was a bitterly cold winter's day with light snow falling on and off throughout the match. About ten to fifteen minutes into the game I was standing on the halfway line in the centre of the field when our goalkeeper kicked the ball into the other side's half. I outpaced the defenders and reached the ball about ten yards outside the opposing team's penalty area. At that stage the only person between me and the goal was the goalkeeper, desperately sprinting out of the penalty area in my direction. The ball bounced awkwardly on the hard-frozen surface. We both went for it. The goalkeeper missed the ball and kicked me full belt in the crotch. It was a total accident. I have a memory of screaming, falling, then blacking out and sometime later lying face down on the ground surrounded by players with an indescribable pain between my legs. It was as if my testicles had imploded. Having turned me over, somebody got the bright idea of extending the elastic from my shorts and pouring cold water inside over my aching parts. The cold didn't increase my sense of happiness but did temporarily have a numbing effect. After about five or six minutes the game resumed as I hobbled to the sideline. There were no substitutes in those days, not even in trial matches, so about ten minutes later I tentatively jogged back onto the pitch. I played out the rest of the match but could barely run and just passed on a few balls that came my way. Of course, I didn't get selected for the post-trial team. Fortunately, other than severe bruising (literally black and blue), I suffered no lasting physical

injury but I do think for my remaining years playing soccer
I was a somewhat windy tackler!

◄o► ◄o► ◄o►

The Six Day War between Israel and its surrounding Arab
nations took place from the 5th to the 10th June 1967.
Although it occurred while I was doing my Intermediate
Certificate exams, like my dad I followed media reports of
the war. Egypt had closed the important sea route through
the Straits of Tiran to Israel's major port of Eilat to both
Israeli ships and other ships carrying strategic materials to
Israel. By doing so, it also blockaded access by ships located
in Eilat to the Red Sea. Just days beforehand, the Egyptian
President, Gamel Abdul Nasser, had informed the United
Nations that its Emergency Force (UNEF) was no longer
wanted in the Sinai Peninsula as he ordered a concentration
of his army there. Nasser's objective, detailed in his fiery
rhetoric, was the total destruction of the Israeli State. Israel,
anticipating a massive attack by Egypt, Syria and Jordan,
launched a pre-emptive strike and obliterated the planes of
the Egyptian, Syrian and Jordanian Air Force. Within six
days the war was over, Israel having captured East
Jerusalem and the West Bank from Jordan, the Gaza Strip
and the Sinai Peninsula up to the Suez Canal from Egypt
and the Golan Heights from Syria.*

---

*The Sinai was returned by Israel to Egypt under the terms of a peace treaty
concluded in 1979. Under a peace treaty concluded in 1994, 380 square
kilometres of land were returned by Israel to Jordan. A year after Israel
successfully defended itself in the Yom Kippur War of 1973, at an Arab League
Summit held in Rabat the Palestinian Liberation Organisation (the PLO) was
recognised as the sole representative of the Palestinian people. As a result, Egypt
did not seek the return of Gaza nor did Jordan seek the return of the West Bank,
territories over which each had ruled since 1948. Jordan retains a "special role"
in relation to Muslim Holy shrines in Jerusalem.

At the start of the Six Day War my dad had been hugely concerned about its outcome. Discussion in the Shatter household was focused on the fact that the Israeli state was not yet twenty years old. Dad firmly believed that Israel's continued existence was crucial to the safety of world Jewry and the only insurance against a second Holocaust. The world had largely looked the other way as Jews were targeted and persecuted in Nazi Germany during the 1930s and borders had been closed to tens of thousands desperate to leave Germany and escape anti-Semitic persecution. Those who sought them were denied visas to reside in the Irish state. Even after the end of World War Two, when it became known that six million Jews had perished as a result of Nazi barbarity, Jewish survivors of the concentration camps had been blocked by the British from entering Palestine despite there already being a sizeable existing Jewish population. The Irish State after World War Two had also kept its doors firmly closed to concentration-camp survivors, ensuring those given visas for permanent residence never reached double figures.*

Israel's extraordinary victory in June 1967 was an enormous relief but there was no family celebration as when it occurred Jack was gravely ill in the Eye and Ear Hospital with no possibility of recovery.

Jack and Gertie had visited Israel but Dad had never travelled there. Following the Six Day War and Jack's death, I was determined to do so.

---

*In a speech delivered by me as Minister for Justice and Defence on Holocaust Memorial Day, 27th January 2012, referencing the Second World War, I stated that "we should no longer be in denial that in the context of the Holocaust Irish neutrality was a principle of moral bankruptcy". John Bruton, as Taoiseach in 1995, also speaking on Holocaust Memorial Day, acknowledged and apologised for the Irish State's failures, including its failure to admit Jewish refugees, asserting that the Holocaust "was not the product of an alien culture. It happened in Europe in living memory. It was a product of intolerance, bigotry and a distorted concept of nationalism".

◄○► ◄○► ◄○►

In early 1968 I arranged to spend July and August of that year working in a kibbutz called Ma'anit in Northern Israel, near the city of Hadera. During those two months I worked a six-day week, starting at 5 a.m. and finishing at 1p.m. with a half-hour breakfast break at 8 a.m. At the start I was picking apples in the kibbutz's enormous orchard. I then graduated to moving irrigation pipes in the cotton and watermelon fields. Together with others, I lifted pipes dripping with mud above my head, carrying them onto the back of a trailer. They were then driven to a new location to be relaid and reconnected to irrigate another area overnight. It was hard work but there was great camaraderie between the kibbutzniks who were permanent residents of Ma'anit and those, like me, who were temporarily living and working there over the summer months.

In return for our work we received food and lodgings, eating our meals every day in the large communal dining room. Although it was a socialist secular kibbutz, the Friday night Shabbat evening meal was always special.

As we finished work by lunchtime each day, afternoons were spent indoors relaxing, reading, playing chess or table tennis, or outdoors swimming or playing soccer in the hot Israeli summer sun. I remember playing many hours of afternoon soccer in intense heat and enjoying it immensely.

The kibbutz also arranged trips to enable its volunteer workers visit different parts of Israel and some of the areas captured during the Six Day War. Visits were made to Haifa, Tel Aviv, Jerusalem, the Golan Heights, Gaza, Ramallah and Bethlehem, places I was destined to visit again either as a TD or as a government minister. I could not have guessed in 1968 that I would in the future meet many leading Israeli and Palestinian politicians. On the Israeli side they include former President Chaim Hertzog, who was born in Belfast in 1918, had lived and been brought up in Dublin between 1919 and 1935, and whose father Isaac Herzog had been Chief Rabbi of the Irish Free State and subsequently British Mandated Palestine and then Israel; former President and Prime Minister, Shimon Peres; and the current Prime Minister, Benjamin Netanyahu. On the Palestinian side they include former President, Yasser Arafat, and current President, Mahmoud Abbas. I have also met with many of those on both sides who have engaged over many years in attempts, through discussions, to resolve the long-enduring conflict between Israelis and Palestinians and secure a permanent peaceful resolution of disputed issues.

What was to be my first of many visits over the years to the Old City of Jerusalem was truly extraordinary. Jerusalem had been in the front line in 1948 in the Israeli War of Independence when the surrounding Arab States attacked Israel, having rejected the resolution adopted by the United Nations to create two states – an independent Jewish Israeli State and an independent Arab Palestinian State – and to make Jerusalem an international city under United Nations administration. The Arab nations of Egypt, Jordan, Syria, Lebanon and Iraq had failed in their objective of bringing about the stillbirth of the nascent Israeli state and to achieve their stated mission of massacring its Jewish population. When the 1948 war ended Jerusalem had been divided – West Jerusalem falling under Israeli jurisdiction and East Jerusalem, including the Old City, falling under Jordanian jurisdiction. Israel's victory in 1967 in the Six Day War had resulted in Jerusalem again becoming a united city and for the first time in nineteen years Israelis and Jews from every corner of the globe had access to the Western Wall, the surviving part of the sacred Jewish Temple destroyed by the Romans in 70 AD.

Walking through the narrow, cobbled streets of the Old City of Jerusalem with the wondrous aroma of spices emanating from the warren of shops of the Arab souk felt like being transported back to a different mystical historical era. Arriving at the ancient stones of the Temple's revered Western Wall, I saw a large number of people milling around and many standing by the Wall in prayer, the ultra-Orthodox amongst them swaying backwards and forwards, muttering their words to God as if in a trance. It is the most sacred place in the world to the Jewish people and has been a focal point of Jewish prayer across the centuries. For someone who regards himself as a secular Jew, I was surprised by the depth of the emotion I felt just being there, a feeling that has been replicated on every occasion I have returned. My emotional reaction is always a surprise as still to this day it is being in the precinct of the historical Wall that elicits my response. For me, prayer still has no meaningful role. I think the emotion is in part generated by a sadness I feel for the millions of Jews who have in past centuries lost their lives or whose lives have been blighted by anti-Semitism and for no reason other than being Jewish. It is accompanied by a deep respect for tradition and a sense of awe at the vibrancy of the joy displayed by those of religious faith at their closeness to what is a remnant of one of the four great Temple walls constructed by Herod, the King of Judaea, over 2,000 years ago.

The reverence in which King Herod is today held by some partly contributes to his still being referenced as Herod the Great. It is not generally known that Herod, having first gained and then lost his kingdom, ultimately recovered and secured it by obtaining the support of the Senate of Ancient Rome. At that time Mark Antony and Octavian jointly ruled the Roman Empire and Herod was regarded by them as an important ally. His forty-year reign over large tracts of modern Israel, including Jerusalem, and which extended into parts of today's Jordan, Syria and Lebanon was marked by political intrigue, bloody family quarrels, extraordinary battles, terror and cruelty as well as complex alliances, substantial economic development, stunning architecture and massive construction. Today's political commentators would give Herod very mixed reviews!

In 1968 Israel was a proud country filled with hope. Proud of (and also relieved by) its victory and hopeful that it would be involved in no more wars. This was the perspective of the permanent residents of Ma'anit, one of whose members, Eliahu Goshen, I learnt had been killed during the Six Day War.

Amongst the kibbutz members were a significant number who had survived the concentration camps, the cruel tattoos of their concentration-camp identification numbers clearly visible above their wrists. The hope they and others felt was accompanied by both doubt and cynicism, based on their worldly experience, that Israelis would ever be left to lead their lives in total peace freed from threats of terror, war and annihilation. The concentration-camp survivors had years earlier been confronted by their own mortality and, having once felt abandoned by the outside world, believed it crucial that Israel remained strong and able to defend itself. It is a perspective which reflected my dad's insights and which I believe to be as valid today as it was in 1968, almost fifty years ago.

I made good friends amongst the kibbutzniks and was encouraged to either stay and settle in Israel or to come back and settle after I had finished school in Dublin. It was even suggested that I should trial with an Israeli soccer team playing in the Israeli League but I did not take the suggestion seriously. I was worried about my dad, living alone with my grandmother persecuting him back in Dublin, and his deteriorating eyesight. I had to return to Dublin to do my Leaving Certificate and knew I could not simply abandon him and make my home in Israel either before or after my exams.

Today, I wonder how different my life would have been had I in my late teens or had Carol and I after our marriage trod a different path and chosen to emigrate to Israel. It is a country with which I feel a close bond and in which I have a deep interest but Ireland has always felt like home. I think I could have temporarily enjoyed a communal kibbutz life but I believe I would eventually have grown weary of collective living. Some of the young people I met during my two months in Ma'anit felt suffocated by it, whilst their parents understandably viewed kibbutz life as providing security, a safe haven from a difficult world and peace of mind. I am something of an individualist and like determining my own path rather than being required to travel a road map determined by others. Having a kibbutz committee or manager designate the work I should do would not have sat well with me. I could, however, envisage living in an Israeli city or town and becoming engrossed in day-to-day Israeli life and possibly Israeli politics. Knowing my personality, I doubt I could have stood back and not attempted to assist addressing concerns and issues that have since the State's foundation dominated Israeli discourse, such as the security of the Israeli State, disputes between secular and religiously observant Jews, human rights, social and economic issues, the Israeli/Palestinian conflict and Israel's difficult relationship with its mostly hostile neighbouring states and the rest of the world.

◄◐► ◄◐► ◄◐►

As my flight took off from Tel Aviv airport at the end of August 1968 I had no doubt that I would one day return. However, I did not anticipate that I would do so on a number of occasions both as a member of Dáil Éireann and later as a cabinet minister to discuss complex issues of enormous difficulty with both Israelis and Palestinians. Over the years they have included discussing with both sides Israel's security concerns, the hardships of daily life experienced by Palestinians, realistically progressing a peace process, ending terrorism and violence and the need to understand and address the fears of the other; with Palestinians their adulation and acclaim of terrorists as martyrs, their educational system and dysfunctional civil institutions; with residents of the Israeli town of Sderot the fear and disruption experienced as a result of being repetitively targeted by rockets fired from Gaza; and with residents of Gaza their limited freedom, fears and sense of despair, infrastructural and resource deficiencies, commercial difficulties, extensive unemployment and the death and destruction resulting from Israel defending itself from attacks by Hamas and other extremist groups intent on Israel's destruction.

While Israel has gone from strength to strength and its population has almost trebled since I first visited almost 50 years ago, the long-yearned-for hope of Israelis for an end to wars and permanent peace and security still remains tragically elusive, as does the desire of Palestinians for the establishment of an independent, sovereign, viable and united Palestinian state. Indeed, the divisions within Israeli society and between Palestinians today seem greater than

106

Relatives in Lodz beckoning across the decades for recognition

Sydney and Sophie Presburg
(Maternal grandparents at a birthday party)

Reuben and Jack Shatter with their father Abraham

Wedding photograph: Reuben and Elaine Shatter

Back: Jack and Reuben
Front: Gertie, Leah and Elaine

Reuben and Elaine with Alan
(Back garden Riversdale Avenue)

Jack playing the violin, London 1930s

Alan

Elaine and Alan

Leah, Reuben, Alan and Jack, with Rebel, Jack's dog

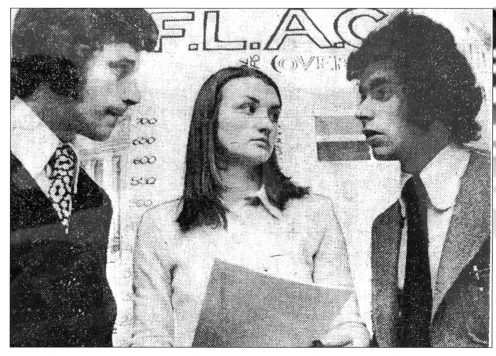

At the Free Legal Advice Centres conference in Jury's Hotel were, from left: David Molony, chairman; Anne Colley, secretary; and Alan Shatter, director. December 1972.

Friam, Alan, Carol, Betty, Reuben (Wedding day 23rd September 1973)

Reuben and Alan, on Alan's on wedding day

Carol on her Graduation
Day 1975

Alan, 1978 Jerusalem, the Western Wall in the background

Picture of young Kelly and Dylan

Photo of Alan taken at publication and launch in 1977 of first edition of *Family Law in the Republic of Ireland* in the headquarters of the Law Society, Blackhall Place, Dublin

Carol and Alan at launch of second edition of *Family Law in the Republic of Ireland*, July 1981
(Photograph: Paddy Whelan, the *Irish Times*)

Carol congratulating Alan on his first being elected to Dáil Éireann to represent Dublin South constituency at the count in Ballinteer Community Centre, June 1981 (Photograph: Paddy Whelan, the *Irish Times*)

Ben Briscoe TD, Chaim Hertzog (President of Israel), Mervyn Taylor TD and Alan Shatter
(Israel President Official visit to Ireland, June 1985)

they were when I first visited in 1968 in the aftermath of the Six Day War. The latter divisions are starkly illustrated by the reality that one Palestinian faction, Hamas, after Israel's withdrawal from Gaza in 2006, through a bloody coup took control of Gaza and has for over a decade ruled the territory with an iron fist, while another faction, Fatah, controls the Palestinian Authority which governs part of the West Bank. Continuing hostility and rivalry between Hamas and Fatah, which has prevented Palestinian President Mahmoud Abbas from visiting Gaza since 2006, has resulted in Gaza and the West Bank evolving into two separate Palestinian political entities, a fact that until very recently has been largely ignored by many states, international organisations, diplomats, politicians and commentators. Internal Palestinian differences and the total absence of trust between Israelis and Palestinians in positions of political leadership and their mutual incapacity to engage in any constructive and credible dialogue gives little cause for optimism that any substantive progress in achieving a permanent end to conflict and a mutually beneficial, constructive, peaceful and harmonious co-existence will be achieved any time soon.

Chapter 9

DRIPS Wet Look Coats

September 1968 marked the start of my final year in High School. I was determined to do well in my Leaving Certificate exams and to become a Trinity College undergraduate. Attaining the grades required was just one of the obstacles to overcome. The other was working out what I would do should I get there! Fitting in with the caricatured aspirations of Jewish parents for their children, I believe I had been conditioned to assume that I would either become a doctor or a lawyer. Having spent so much of my young life in and out of hospitals and observed the deaths of both my mum and my uncle, I determined medicine was not for me. I wanted a life free of the smell of hospital disinfectant in so far as possible.

Following my Intermediate Certificate exams, I opted for the Fifth and Sixth Year school subjects consistent with becoming a Trinity law (legal science) student rather than a medical student. As a consequence, I did not study either chemistry or physics for the Trinity matriculation or the

Leaving Certificate exam, two subjects crucial to entering medical school. By the start of Sixth Year I was concerned that I had made a fundamental mistake.

Out of interest I had taken an optional school subject, biology, for Fifth and Sixth year. We had an incredibly talented biology teacher, Mary White, and I loved the subject. I became fascinated by genetics, as I have continued to be throughout my life, and started reading additional material that went well beyond the course specified for Trinity's matriculation exam in biology or the Leaving Certificates equivalent exams. By the start of my final school year I was thinking seriously about becoming a geneticist and was advised that if I wished to do so I should first qualify as a doctor. (I do not believe that advice would be given today.) As a result, like many a Sixth Year secondary-school student, I became confused about what I wished to do with the rest of my life. (I still am!) I determined to get the best grades possible to ensure that I qualified to enter Trinity College with study options and could take some time to make my final decision.

I applied to do a General Studies course, taking English, history and philosophy in first year, and discovered I could simultaneously take a one-year night-time Leaving Certificate course in chemistry and physics, and at the end of the academic year do Leaving Certificate examinations in both subjects. My objective was to have the opportunity of switching into either medicine or law in the following academic year and not make a decision solely based on my lacking Leaving Certificate Honours in the two science subjects. Having made that decision, I stopped obsessing on the problem and took my final year in High School more seriously than any preceding senior school year.

There were two school friends who played an enormously important role in my life during my Fifth and Sixth school years, to whom I will always be grateful and with whom, unfortunately, for many years I lost touch. They are Fred Jackson, who for many years was a consultant haematologist in Waterford Regional Hospital and is a Professor of Medicine of the Royal College of Surgeons Ireland (RCSI), and John Silverstone who became an accountant, emigrated to England and currently lectures in accountantcy.

During my last two years in school my grandmother had become increasingly difficult to live with, giving both my dad and me continuing grief. It had reached the stage where being at home was both distressing and unpleasant and not conducive to study. Dad partly solved the problem she created for him by spending four nights every week in Maccabi either watching television or playing cards. When no longer working, he spent the daytime meeting up with friends in town. I solved the problem by spending a large part of my after-school time in John Silverstone's home where I studied with John, and lesser time in Fred Jackson's home where Fred, who was brilliant at mathematics, assisted me with maths. We were both scheduled to do Honours Maths in the Trinity Matriculation and in the Leaving Certificate, and I was struggling with the subject and badly needed the help Fred willingly gave me.

Though I always returned home to sleep at night, for a time I was a virtual lodger in the Silverstone home, not just studying there but also eating regularly with John's family. His parents, Leslie and Sybil, were genuinely good and kind people and made me feel welcome and part of the family. Looking back on it now, I believe their kindness provided me with crucial support during a personally painful and difficult time in my life. Unfortunately, some months before the Leaving Certificate exams relationships sundered as a result of a row between me and John's dad over something to do with the Maccabi soccer team on which John and I were playing. I have no idea today what the row was about nor who said what but I recollect I said something inappropriate in the heat of the moment which offended John's dad and which ended my relationship with John. I have no doubt I was in the wrong and do not know why I did not immediately apologise. I do recollect some weeks later apologising and attempting to mend fences but to no avail. John and I did not re-establish our close friendship but recently we reconnected with each other.

Outside of studying, continuing to play soccer and running in various athletic meetings, little else of note happened during my last year in school until I was in the middle of my Leaving Certificate exams. Fortunately, I did well in the Trinity matriculation exam which took place about five weeks before the Leaving. Just before the start of the Leaving I learnt I had secured sufficient Honours in the matric to get into Trinity. As a result, the Leaving was less pressurised than I'd originally expected.

◄O► ◄O► ◄O►

The weather during the Leaving Cert exams was glorious, each day being dry, sunny and warm, and during our lunchtime breaks I left the school and went for a walk around St Stephen's Green to get some fresh air, eat a sandwich and quietly focus on the afternoon exam. During one lunchtime visit to the Green, as I strolled past the duck pond closest to the Grafton Street entrance, I spotted a very pretty girl dressed in the green Diocesan School uniform with a snow-white blouse, sitting on a park bench engrossed in a study book and oblivious to the pedestrians passing by. She had longish black hair, deep-brown sparkling eyes and an attractive suntan that contrasted with her white blouse. Totally beguiled and jettisoning all thoughts of my afternoon Leaving Certificate paper, I stopped, said "Hi" and asked if she was also doing the Leaving Certificate. The answer was "No, the Intermediate Certificate". Feeling awkward and slightly embarrassed, I cracked some totally forgettable joke, wished her well and resumed my walk. Ten steps too late I realised that I had not introduced myself nor had I found out her name. The truth is, I was a shy youth and just stopping and engaging with a girl I did not know and had never previously met was, for me, a big deal.

I continued to stroll through St Stephen's Green during the remaining lunch breaks till the exams ended. Despite my keeping an obsessive lookout, I did not meet the girl again. Exams over, I had no idea where she lived, how to find her or discover her name.

Athletics training and competing for Crusaders at athletic meetings became my main post-exam focus. Just over two weeks later, the Maccabi club had its summer sports day which involved various children's races for different ages over a series of distances. Although eighteen years old I could still run in the under-eighteen races, one's age at the beginning of January determining eligibility. Halfway through the afternoon I recognised the Stephen's Green girl as she sprinted past spectators and won the under-sixteen girls 220 yards race. She repeated the performance in the 100 yards. I was surprised to discover she was part of the Jewish community and realised this was a golden opportunity to get to know her. The competitions and prize-giving over, I drove Dad, who had come along to spectate, home and speedily returned to the Maccabi grounds – but I was too late. She had departed before my return. But I now knew her name as it had been announced over a loudspeaker both times she won a race and again announced during the prize-giving. I learnt that she was the first cousin of one of my teammates on the Maccabi soccer team and by the afternoon's end I had successfully secured her phone number from him.

It took about three days for me to work up the courage to phone and when I finally made the call her mum answered and told me she was out. I left a message, she called back and by the end of our first date I knew I was in love. That date marked the start of a relationship that has lasted for over forty-eight years. Little did we know at the time that the girl, Carol Danker, was destined to become my wife in September 1973 just before her twentieth birthday. I was only twenty-two when we married and we were both at the time Trinity College students.

◄o► ◄o► ◄o►

I really enjoyed my first year in Trinity. I was studying three subjects I found intellectually stimulating and reading for each subject books and articles that were engrossing. In our first year as boyfriend and girlfriend, Carol was subjected to my reading extracts to her from Geoffrey Chaucer's *Canterbury Tales* (not all of them at the time probably regarded as entirely suitable for a sixteen-year-old girl) and prattling on about philosophy. Amongst the philosophical works studied were those of René Descartes, including his widely known proposition "Cogito ergo sum", commonly translated into "I think, therefore I am". The proposition originated in French in his *Discourse on Method* and then reappeared in its better-known Latin form in his *Meditations on First Philosophy*. The phrase, which is concerned with establishing the reality of personal existence, has throughout my life had an existential relevance.

For me, thinking rationally prior to addressing or responding to events is at the very core of human engagement. This does not mean that emotion should play no role or that the impact of emotion on others should be ignored. What it requires is an understanding that simply surrendering to and acting in response to emotion alone without rational thought and analysis increases the risk of unanticipated and sometimes damaging consequences. (Of course, rational analysis provides no absolute protection against such consequences where conclusions reached are mistaken or others are consumed by emotion or are malign and simply intent on doing you damage.) Too many wars and tragedies have occurred as a result of individuals reacting to events like automatons, with anger and without rational thought, and too much false news or information has been manufactured by individuals with malign motives and reported by media outlets without necessary verification and careful analysis. The capacity to analyse and think things through and actually doing so should, I believe, play a central role in human discourse and engagement. Doing what is right and telling the truth is, of course, also of central importance. Unfortunately, as I would later discover, in politics, as in other walks of life, not only do some people act without rational analysis and aforethought but it is also the self-serving modus operandi of some to simply shoot their mouths off and maliciously denigrate those who value rational thought and knowledge of relevant facts. On occasion, I have learnt that for some neither doing what is right nor telling the truth is a priority. But enough of this rambling, to which I will return in a different context in another book, and back to Trinity Year One.

◄◦► ◄◦► ◄◦►

Sports-wise my focus during my first year in Trinity was athletics. Apart from competing in inter-college races and getting my university athletic colours, the highlight of the year was a tour of the Netherlands by the College athletics team shortly before Easter. We competed against three different university teams in various parts of the country and I fell in love with Amsterdam. I wasn't to know at the time that the Trinity team's visit to the Netherlands would later on substantially influence where I would choose to undertake my post-graduate education.

By Easter 1970, I finally opted for law instead of medicine and abandoned the possibility of becoming a geneticist. I did so because of the fact I would have had to first work as a doctor in a hospital for a number of years. I knew I would not be able to overcome my aversion to hospitals which for me had become synonymous with death. There was no difficulty in my transferring to First Year Legal Science at the start of the next academic year (1970/71) and suddenly I was as free as a bird for the next five months. I did not need to take General Studies exams nor exams in Leaving Certificate chemistry and physics.

◄०► ◄०► ◄०►

By then, due to most of his rental tenants being in substantial rent arrears, Dad was in increasing financial difficulty. The modest rent paid by the tenant of the small shop Jack had willed to me only made a minimal contribution to necessary expenditure. There was not only the issue of food on the table and general household expenses but also payment of university fees for my four-year Legal Science course, the purchase of required text books and my general day-to-day expenses. I determined to work and generate some real income. The question was what to do and how to earn something beyond a basic income as someone's employee?

Due to Dad's involvement in the fashion trade and conversation at home over the years about fashion trends, as a teenager I had developed an awareness and interest in evolving clothes fashions. I was then fascinated by the latest thing, the arrival of the "wet look" coat. It was the latest craze and it seemed that every teenage girl and women of all ages regarded the wet-look coat as the most fashionable and desired thing in town. You were not an "in" person unless you wore the wet look! It was literally the hottest fashion item.

I got the bright idea of designing, manufacturing and selling wet-look coats. Although he was out of the business, Dad had the expertise to advise me how to go about it. He introduced me to a guy based in Dublin's Francis Street, who had his own CMT business and who had the capacity to manufacture coats provided he was supplied with designs to follow. Dad also pointed me in the direction of a company based in Trim, County Meath, that manufactured industrial PVC. This shiny plastic material, otherwise known as polyvinyl chloride, was at the time widely used as wet-look clothing fabric but the industrial version was thicker – and cheaper. Large rolls of PVC could be purchased relatively inexpensively. I drove to Trim and discovered they had every colour in the rainbow and some more. Enormous rolls of PVC in yellow, blue, green, red, white and black were available for immediate purchase. Upon examining the product, I believed it presented a great opportunity to create low-cost nicely styled wet-look coats. All I needed was the money to purchase the rolls of PVC required to get started. My bar mitzvah money, which had lain dormant and untouched in the Bank of Ireland account opened with my mum six years earlier, provided the required resources.

Every Saturday and Sunday there was an outdoor market, called the Dandelion Market, located in a car park off Dublin's Leeson Street. A stall could be hired for a relatively small sum (I think it was £20 for the two days) and crowds of people visited the market every weekend. It was for me the ideal location.

Having toured around many of the city-centre women's fashion stores to view the coats on sale, I sat down at our breakfast-room table to design my own style. With Dad's help I prepared the cut-out patterns the manufacturer required and within a week I was in business.

The rolls of PVC were too large to be put either inside my Mini-Minor or in the boot. A roof rack was purchased and, if properly tied down, two rolls of PVC could be transported on the car roof on each trip. My first two rolls delivered to Francis Street were red and blue. The styles designed were for maxis, midis and minis to be made in various sizes.

Before investing any more time or money I wanted to test the market. At half past seven on a Saturday morning in late April 1970, within twelve days of delivering the two rolls to the manufacturer, I drove expectantly to the Leeson Street Market, my car packed with coats, a long mirror and a portable clothes rail. Coat-rail assembled and filled with red and blue coats on hangers, I waited for the market to open. I had clipped a sign onto the front of the stall which I had painted and illustrated. It read: "DRIPS Wet Look Coats."

The coats were priced substantially below wet-look coat regular retail shop prices: minis £5, midis £6 and maxis £7.50. They walked off the coat-rail. By four o'clock on that first Saturday, not only had I sold all my coats but I also held deposits from a number of enthusiastic customers who, because of my limited stock, were unable to purchase a coat in their required size or chosen colour.

In the days and weeks that followed I made multiple trips to Trim to collect PVC rolls in every colour available. My main difficulty was in securing from my CMT man in Francis Street the quantity of coats I required to operate the stall on two full days every weekend.

Another difficulty was transporting the number of coats I could sell in one early-morning car trip to Leeson Street and in serving the quantity of customers, particularly between eleven and four each day. Dad came down to lend a hand but, because of his restricted sight, was unable to read the different size numbers on the coats or to record sales in my sales book. Within a short time I employed someone to work with me and that enabled me to bring additional coats to the market by driving back home early each Saturday and Sunday morning and returning before the market opened while the first batch were minded. In the weeks that followed, sales generated between £500 to £1,000 per week. Bad weather was bad for business as fewer people visited the market but, even on weekends it rained, a reasonable number of coats sold. About 50% of the money received from sales was pure profit.

The entirety of that summer was dominated by my wet-look-coat venture. When I wasn't driving backwards and forwards to Trim I was transporting coats from Francis Street to our garage in Crannagh Park which had become a storeroom. The capacity to manufacture the coats was increased and I started selling them to a small number of boutique shops around town and in the suburbs.

I then expanded into selling shirts in the market and multicoloured waistcoats both in the market and to the boutiques. It had bothered me that the coats hung on my portable clothes rail but I had no product sitting on the long table that came with the stall. I was determined to make use of it. Driving around the city centre I spotted two men's shops having unseasonal sales of shirts and deduced they might be having some business difficulties. Upon enquiring, I discovered they had overstocked in particular colours and sizes and were anxious to sell them. In one shop in Middle Abbey Street I purchased one hundred shirts at £1 each. They sold with ease in the market at £1.50 to £2. The second shop in Capel Street allowed me to take a variety of shirts on a sale-or-return basis as the shop-owner knew and liked my dad. The following Saturday the shirts were put on display on my market stall. I had agreed with the shop-owner from whom I had purchased the 100 shirts that he would pack the shirt boxes with a proportional number of shirts between Sizes 14 and 17 and a variety of different colours. Upon opening the boxes, I discovered that about forty were a mix of Size 17 and 17 ½ and about thirty-five shirts were an awful red colour. For the first hour I was angry that I had been conned. I regarded the Size 17s as very large and the peculiar shade of red as weird, and couldn't figure how I would sell them. I was entirely wrong. The 17s and the red shirts totally sold out during that Saturday. I discovered that large men had a difficulty getting shirts that fitted comfortably. Few purchased just one Size 17 – most took two or three shirts at the one time. A number of happy customers promised to return if I continued to stock the bigger sizes. I had accidentally discovered a gap in the market. I returned to the same shop the following week and purchased as many large shirts as the owner was willing to sell at £1 each.

In the months that followed I developed a relationship with a variety of shops in the city centre who sold me shirts they regarded as dead stock for less than I would have had to pay the original shirt companies if I had bought shirts directly from them.

Encouraged by the success of my shirt sales, I kept a look-out for new opportunities. Driving a car piled full of coats just two months into my venture, I spotted multi-coloured Spanish bedspreads with tassels advertised in the window of Frawley's department store at the junction of Francis and Thomas Street, selling for £3 each. Parking the car I went in, had a look, purchased two and took them home. I had an idea and wanted to check it out. Opening them both up on our sitting-room floor, checking the fabric and pattern, taking some measurements and drawing some designs confirmed my suspicions. If cut and sewn carefully, three trendy waistcoats could be created from two bedspreads with the tassels hanging down and there was even enough cloth left over to include an attractive breast pocket. Two days later, a design cut-out together with written instructions prepared, I returned to Thomas Street and purchased thirty bedspreads, delivering them one hundred yards down the road to my Francis Street manufacturer. We agreed a price for his work and two weeks later my first waistcoats went on sale for £5.50 each, hanging from a smaller rail I acquired. In the weeks and months that followed, hundreds of waistcoats were sold. I continued to buy the bedspreads from various shop assistants working in Frawleys and I have no recollection of ever being asked what I was doing with so many of them.

Working in the Dandelion Market was both great fun and tough. By each Sunday evening I was fairly wrecked and during cold and wet winter days it could be miserable. Great care was required to ensure stock was fully covered and protected from rain and, when it was busy, to keep an eye out for shoplifters. I had one incident where a number of women were trying on coats and, as I talked to one customer, another just strolled off and disappeared into the crowded market wearing a coat. But there was also a lot of laughter and banter. Most of the customers were very nice and happy to purchase a bargain. I had many return visits from satisfied customers, bringing relations and friends with them. It also wasn't unusual for three or four customers who had arrived together to each leave with a wet-look coat after much lively negotiation between them to first decide who would purchase which style in what colour. The style and size chosen was usually determined by the wearer's height and weight and I always tried to gently encourage a customer to buy the length and cut that looked best on them. Unfortunately, I wasn't always successful in doing so. I still recall the very large and excitable mother who arrived with two very large teenage daughters. Despite my best diplomatic endeavours, all three insisted on buying and immediately wearing three seriously undersized mini wet-look yellow coats. Happily departing, they presented as three overripe, extraordinarily life-size, mobile bananas bursting out of their skins!

When the market was quiet I did stuff to attract custom that I would today regard as mortifying. There was another stall opposite mine selling kettles, pots and pans and a good-humoured banter developed between me and the stallholder to attract attention. I would loudly warn people that his kettles leaked, which he would then theatrically disprove and in retaliation he loudly alleged that customers would get wet if they wore "DRIPS" coats in the rain. "DRIPS is the name and drips is the game!" he would shout. I thought it was great advertising. Crowds would gather around both stalls and generate sales to our mutual benefit. I suppose that it was all good training for speaking through a megaphone outside churches in Dublin South constituency during the general election campaigns of the early 1980s in which I successfully competed as a Fine Gael candidate and secured and later retained a Dáil seat.

‹o› ‹o› ‹o›

Christmas 1970 arrived and I had completed my first term in Legal Science. I was enjoying my legal studies while at the same time running my business and spending my weekends in the Dandelion Market. Prior to Christmas an opportunity arose to trade directly Mondays through to Saturdays out of a large shop in Capel Street. The original company leasing the shop had gone out of business and small sections of space were being rented out on a weekly basis to different sole traders to sell a variety of goods. Recruiting another CMT women's clothes manufacturer created the possibility of more than doubling my weekly stock and I secured some additional more sophisticated coats from other suppliers. I realised it was impossible for me to run both the Dandelion Market and the Capel Street operation and also carry on with my studies and sought out a former school pal to partner me on the Capel Street venture. It opened the first week in December 1970 and closed by the end of January 1971. My pal was averse to getting out of bed early in the mornings and unable to get to Capel Street much before 12 noon, could not be relied upon to collect PVC from Trim nor to collect manufactured coats when ready. (Later on he became a successful businessman!) I hadn't the time to supervise the Capel Street business and rapidly decided the best thing to do was to close it down. A month later I ended my Dandelion Market activities and my business involvements.

I had given up athletics training to create time to run my business and was concerned that if I did not bail out and take my studies more seriously I could have trouble passing my first-year examinations in Legal Science. I was also determined to do better than simply pass. The competitive instinct which had motivated me when a Junior School pupil in High School kicked in. I wanted to finish first year Legal Science as one of the top three in my year and I knew, if I continued to be distracted, achieving that was impossible. Moreover, my business venture had been very successful and I had accumulated substantial savings in a short period of time, so money had temporarily ceased to be a problem. I sold off my last remaining stock to a couple of boutiques and ended my brief career in the fashion trade.

I look back at that time with fond memories. As a nineteen-year-old I had no realistic perception of how well the Dandelion Market venture had gone. I recollect Dad one wet Sunday afternoon coming down to the market to check that I was okay and listening to me complaining about only taking in about £500 so far that weekend. He pointed to a guy beside me selling trinkets for a few shillings each and asked did I not realise that he was lucky on any weekend to earn more than £50 to £60? It was a thought that had never occurred to me.

◄○► ◄○► ◄○►

For the remainder of the academic year I focused on my studies, working most weekday evenings in Trinity's library until it closed at ten. I revisited topics covered in the early months of the first-year Legal Science course and made up for lost ground. When not studying, attending lectures or sleeping, I spent time with Carol, frequently collecting her from school in the afternoons and giving her a lift home. She was the only girl in her class whose boyfriend drove a car and this added to her street cred with some of her school pals. On some evenings she sneaked into Trinity's library and studied beside me for her Leaving Certificate exams while I was engrossed in reading legal textbooks and court judgements.

The exams came and went and I achieved my objective of making the top three as I did in all subsequent end-of-academic-year exams in Legal Science.

I continued to play soccer with Maccabi for another couple of years but never again competed in an athletics meeting or represented Crusaders or Trinity College running the quarter or half mile. I had continued some regular late-night jogging but, because of my Dandelion Market involvement and my objective to get top marks in my law exams, once first-year law lectures started I had no time for the intensive training of previous years. I think part of the reason was I did not believe my times would improve enough to attain Olympic standard. Put simply, I did not think my athletic results justified the time commitment devoted to training.

Looking back on it now, I realise that for a 19/20-year-old I was far too serious and driven. I do not believe my life would have worked out any differently had I simply graduated as a Trinity law student with middling grades rather than coming first in my final year but I know that at the time achieving that first for me was of enormous importance. By the time I did so my dad had died, so I could have had no subconscious agenda to impress him nor did I believe he was following my progress from some heavenly retreat. By the commencement of second-year Legal Science I had two all-consuming passions: Carol Danker and the law.

If I could tread the same path and start again, I would be somewhat less passionate about the law, resume my athletics training, compete as a runner and play soccer for at least another fifteen years and participate to a greater extent than I did in college social life. In relation to Carol nothing would change. I remain amazed that she put up with the totally driven, far too serious, obsessive boyfriend and husband she had accidentally acquired as a result of a casual exam-day lunchtime visit to St Stephen's Green.

Chapter 10

The FLAC Years

During the spring of 1970 circumstances at home had changed. My grandmother's behaviour in the preceding twelve months had became increasingly erratic as a result of what was diagnosed as the onset of Alzheimer's. On a couple of occasions she went wandering from home, could not find her way back and was returned by strangers. She was clearly unwell and could not be left alone. In her lucid moments she continued to verbally abuse my dad. There were moments of minor amusement. Carol had become a regular visitor to Crannagh Park. On occasion she wore her hair tied back and on other occasions she wore it loose, hanging down over her shoulders. My grandmother was convinced I had two girlfriends. She wasn't slow to tell me that the one with the long hair was alright but that she really didn't like the one with the tied-back hair and instructed me that I should get rid of her. To eliminate one topic of contention, I agreed that my relationship with the girl who tied her hair back would end!

As a result of my grandmother's condition and her need for 24/7 care, my dad arranged for her to move into the Jewish Home located in Denmark Hill, Leinster Road West, in Dublin. Her departure dramatically changed the atmosphere in our house and both Dad and I started spending more time at home than either of us had done since Mum's death. This didn't mean Dad escaped entirely from my grandmother's verbal assaults. He insisted we visit her at least three times per week and when she was lucid, immediately upon arrival, he was subjected to a verbal onslaught. The new refrain was to accuse him of locking her away in the Jewish Home, saying had Jack still been alive he would not have treated her that way. And it was he, not Jack, who should be dead. Of course, she was not locked away but under the care of a full-time nursing and care staff. When not lucid her speech was rambling and incoherent but at least then she did not give Dad a hard time. No matter her condition, I always found visiting her stressful but Dad, at least outwardly, presented as stoic and concealed any stress he felt. My dad persisted with visiting three times a week until the Alzheimer's entirely took over and she was incapable of recognising anybody. The visits still continued but less frequently for the remaining part of his life.

◄o► ◄o► ◄o►

Second year Legal Science commenced in early October 1971. Two years earlier a group of law students had founded the Free Legal Advice Centres, now better known as FLAC. Their purpose was to provide free legal advice and assistance to those who required legal help but could not afford to pay for it. FLAC's work was confined to civil law and excluded criminal law. A state-funded statutory criminal legal-aid scheme provided legal advice and court representation for those charged with criminal offences but no such scheme applied to any other area of law. Law centres were opened in various parts of Dublin, operating one evening a week, staffed by law student volunteers from Trinity and UCD (University College Dublin). Each centre was managed by a volunteer student director and had a panel of solicitors attached to it who took turns helping the students with back-up advice and assistance. Solicitors and barristers on a panel also voluntarily represented FLAC clients in court proceedings for free.

At the start of second-year Law I started helping out every Friday night in the FLAC Centre operating out of St Agnes's Social Service Centre on the grounds of St Agnes's Church in Crumlin. I never anticipated my doing so would substantially shape a large portion of my life. The centre officially opened from seven-thirty till nine but most Friday evenings we didn't finish till between ten-thirty and eleven because of the number of people seeking legal help. The overwhelming majority were women with marital and family problems: battered wives, wives of husbands beating children, unsupported dependent wives and children, deserted wives, wives of husbands with alcohol and gambling addiction problems, wives of husbands engaged in affairs, unmarried mothers with dependent children receiving little or no financial help from their child's father. There were some husbands and single fathers who sought help and advice but the numbers were a great deal smaller. Those seeking advice weren't confined to Crumlin residents. They extended to the leafier and wealthier suburban areas of Kimmage, Terenure and Templeogue.

As a young law student I was stunned by the nature and extent of the family difficulties exposed in consultations with FLAC clients and, in particular, by the desperate need of so many wives for help and the total inadequacy of the law and social services to provide the help they required. The nuns and social workers operating the social service centre during the daytime in St Agnes's provided what help they could for some of FLAC's clients but the majority required legal intervention and I rapidly learnt that our family law was grossly inadequate.

Just starting my second-year legal studies in Trinity College, I knew nothing about family law and I fairly quickly discovered that it was foreign territory for many of the well-meaning solicitors who were voluntarily assisting us in the Crumlin Centre. They, like me, when first volunteering, wrongly anticipated that most of the legal problems requiring help at the centres would relate to consumer issues, accidents, housing problems, medical negligence and wills. As a result, the legal back-up required to ensure clients were properly advised was not always available even when the solicitor on our rota was present. As was inevitable, there were some Friday evenings when the expected solicitor failed to appear.

Working in the Crumlin Centre I learned as much as I could from the more experienced students and the solicitors I met. In my first week I discovered no textbook on Irish family law existed and few articles had appeared in legal journals about the subject. I was surprised to discover that a dependent unsupported wife with children could only take her husband to court to obtain a maintenance or financial support order if she was also deserted by him. Many of the wives I met were living in virtual penury at home with working husbands who kept most of their earnings to themselves or were simply drinking most of it away. Even more shocking was the violence. Battered wives, many who had been their husbands punchbags for years, sought help. Some had at some stage after serious injury reported their husbands to the gardaí but had been told that, as it was "a domestic", the gardaí could or would not intervene. Some who did so, for their troubles, by way of retaliation suffered a second beating. And then there were those who were too afraid to tell anyone and had covered up domestic violence perpetrated by husbands and hoped FLAC could help them. And not only wives but also children were being battered. On occasion, a grandparent sought help because both parents were battering their children. No family law remedy existed to protect a spouse or child from a violent spouse or parent. The assailant could be criminally prosecuted but by and large the gardaí did not want to know. Child care proceedings could in those days be taken by the ISPCC (Irish Society for the Protection of Children) and later by a Health Board but that could result in a child being taken away from home and placed in care and the existing residential homes were appalling. By then, the inadequacy of the child-care system was already to some extent known as a result of publication in 1970 of the Kennedy Report but no government action had been taken. It would be decades later before the extent of child abuse in our residential institutions would be fully revealed. Early on in my work in FLAC, I also learnt that child-care proceedings provided no practical assistance for the circumstances with which I was confronted every Friday evening in Crumlin.

The plight of unmarried mothers and children born outside marriage was also dreadful. Under family, societal and religious pressures to place their children for adoption, few unmarried mothers who retained their children received any child support from their children's fathers, few of the unmarried fathers had any interest in their children's care or welfare, our grossly inadequate laws stigmatised the children as "illegitimate" and they were still commonly referred to as "bastards". Children born outside marriage were also denied the same succession or inheritance rights to their deceased parents' property that applied to the children of a married couple.

I was astonished to discover that our maintenance support laws were based on legislation enacted in 1886 and our child-care laws on legislation enacted in 1908, in each case by the British Parliament in London. Even more extraordinary were our Judicial Separation laws. They had remained unchanged for hundreds of years and were based on law administered by the Ecclesiastical Courts of the Church of Ireland prior to 1870. A few months after volunteering to work in FLAC I discovered in Trinity's library a book written on this topic in the 1880s. It was the only one and nothing had changed since its publication.

Before becoming a law student, like many others my age, I was already familiar with the antiquated lunacy of Irish law in criminalising the sale of condoms, but I had paid little attention to Articles 41 and 42 in the Constitution, dealing with what were described as the "family provisions". Both articles had been covered in our first-year Constitutional Law course in Legal Science but it was only after working in FLAC that I fully realised that these articles were not merely constitutional rhetoric and decoration reflecting the 1930s perspective of the Roman Catholic Church but also pernicious and cruel. The prohibition on divorce contained in Article 41.3 was imprisoning abused and unsupported spouses in failed marriages, while the "inalienable" and "absolute" rights conferred on married parents by Article 42 were imprisoning abused children in failed families. Meanwhile, our child-care system utterly failed to provide children with crucial care and protection.

I started helping out in FLAC because I believed it was

the right thing to do. After about three months I became an angry idealist determined to do what was required to effect constitutional and legal reform.

Throughout the rest of my time as a Trinity law student and during the following academic year, as I completed my solicitors' exams, much of my spare time was devoted to FLAC. About five months after commencing working in St Agnes's Social Service Centre I became director of the Crumlin Centre. It became my responsibility to ensure enough students were present every Friday evening to meet the demand, that we had a fully functioning solicitor rota system and a sufficient number of practising solicitors and barristers available to represent FLAC clients in District Court maintenance cases and other court proceedings. Because of the huge surge in the numbers of those seeking help, legal representation in court became a problem. The numbers requiring free representation in the District Court grew so rapidly that we suffered a shortfall of volunteer solicitors to meet the need. There was also a problem of solicitors on occasion unexpectedly not showing up for a court hearing.

Whenever one of my FLAC clients was involved in court proceedings I believed it important to accompany her to court. At the time, all maintenance and child-support cases from our area were being heard in camera (in private) by District Court Judge Seán Delap, in a District Court based in the Four Courts. Delap knew I was a student involved in the Crumlin FLAC Centre and, in the beginning, allowed me sit inside at the back of the courtroom when cases involving clients of mine were in hearing in private behind closed doors. On occasion, when a client's solicitor was absent when her case was called, Delap had no difficulty with my asking that he delay hearing the case for an hour or so until the solicitor arrived. After a few months had elapsed, when solicitors failed to appear, he invited me to explain in court what the case was about. He would then hear the case, requesting that I ask the client under oath any questions of relevance and later conduct any necessary cross-examination.

By October 1972, I was a solicitor's apprentice commencing third-year Legal Science in Trinity. I was also regularly appearing before Seán Delap in the Dublin District Court, voluntarily representing unsupported and distraught wives and unmarried mothers and cross-examining husbands and fathers. As a solicitor's apprentice and university law student I should not have been doing so but Delap ignored the rules and convention. Very rapidly, at a young age, I became an experienced and confident advocate. By late autumn of 1972, the solicitors on the FLAC Crumlin court rota were representing clients who consulted our other undergraduate volunteers while I was representing my own.

Judge Delap was a great humanitarian. He regarded the 1886 Maintenance Act as outdated and grossly inadequate and gave it a liberal interpretation. As far as he was concerned any employed husband living at home who failed to support his wife was in constructive desertion and a maintenance order would be made. Prior to a wife benefiting from such order it wasn't necessary that the husband physically desert and leave home. Where a dependent wife left home as a consequence of her husband's bad behaviour, he also regarded the husband as in constructive desertion and made a maintenance order for the wife's support. Whilst some of Delap's District Court colleagues took the same approach in the latter circumstances, few did where both spouses continued to live under the one roof. As a result, many unsupported wives advised by some other FLAC centres whose maintenance cases were heard in other District Courts, were left destitute in their home because they were not regarded by the presiding District Judge to be deserted by their husbands.

As director of the Crumlin FLAC Centre, I was also a member of the FLAC Council which was composed of the directors of all the other centres across Dublin. Chairperson of the Council was a UCD law student, David Maloney. David, who was from Tipperary, would later go on to become a solicitor and to be elected to Dáil Éireann as a Fine Gael TD representing Tipperary North constituency in 1981, the same year as me. David was very bright and did a great job ensuring the student organisation operated efficiently, kept good records and maintained good relations with the legal professional bodies. The Council included a UCD law graduate and recently qualified solicitor, Brian Gallagher, who had been involved in FLAC from its inception and had been its previous chairperson. Brian was a year older than me and early on I recognised that he had great judgement and insight. We quickly became friends but what neither of us anticipated was that by 1977 we would become partners in our own legal firm, Gallagher Shatter, and work harmoniously together for thirty-five years.

The number of FLAC clients was escalating monthly and we had no doubt but that there was a need for a State-funded statutory civil legal aid and advice service. Whilst FLAC would later open some centres outside Dublin, it was initially a Dublin-based organisation. We knew there was a need to provide free legal help for spouses and unmarried mothers throughout the country as there was already a trickle of clients coming to centres from various parts of Ireland but it was beyond the competence of a student organisation to fully meet the need that existed.

The objective of FLAC's founders was not only to provide legal help for those who genuinely lacked the capacity to pay for it, but also to campaign for the creation of a State-funded statutory civil legal aid and advice service. Until the autumn of 1972 the primary focus had been on providing legal help. A decision was made to publish FLAC's first major report, to put pressure on the government to provide the badly needed service and to highlight the need for family law reform. The FLAC Report 1972, making the case, was published shortly before Christmas of that year. The director of each centre had to prepare detailed statistics of the number of clients helped and categorise the relevant areas of law. David Maloney coordinated the production of the Report and, with Brian Gallagher's help, I wrote the section on family law. As there was so little public knowledge of the area, I used the opportunity to detail the then current law and also to prescribe the reforms required. I didn't know when doing so that the reforms, then first advocated and later expanded upon in books written by me on Irish Family law, would lay the foundations for family law reform for the following thirty-five years.

Both the Law Society and the Bar Council had given a grant to FLAC (as they continue to do to this day) and we were able to get the report professionally printed. I was officially FLAC's public-relations spokesperson and it was my job to organise a launch of the Report. We launched it at a press conference held in Jurys Hotel in Ballsbridge. The Report's launch was a great success, generating enormous publicity in the next morning's papers and catapulting me into my first radio and TV interviews. The Report acted as a catalyst for a variety of newspaper articles on the inadequacy of our family law, the vulnerability of battered and dependent wives and the reforms government should implement. It also initiated a new debate on the issue of divorce and, as I learnt from Carol, who by then was a Social Studies undergraduate in Trinity College, was instantly added to the Trinity Social Studies curriculum by one of her lecturers.

Following publication of the Report, the first major FLAC public meeting was organised for early 1973. It took place in Dublin's Wynn's Hotel in the city centre on a midweek evening and received a lot of advance publicity in newspapers and on radio. Its focus was on the reforms advocated in the FLAC Report and invitations to attend were issued to the media. We had no idea how many people would turn up to such a meeting on a winter's night to listen to speeches delivered by law students. We were overwhelmed by the numbers. The room was packed with standing room only and the meeting generated yet more publicity.

For my remaining two and a half years as a law student I regularly broadcasted on FLAC's proposed legal reforms and engaged with journalists interested in writing about family law and other legal issues. There was a very talented and dedicated team of law students managing and working in FLAC's law centres, many of whom have since their FLAC days played various distinguished legal roles, including as members of the judiciary. I was simply part of that team and in 1975 I was privileged to act as overall chairman of FLAC. By then the work of FLAC's student army of volunteers was widely recognised.

In 1975, with the assistance of government and voluntary funding, FLAC opened its first full-time law centre, the Coolock Community Law Centre, and employed its first full-time solicitor, George Gill, who as a student had been a FLAC volunteer. The Coolock Centre, which still exists and is now known as the Community Law and Mediation Centre, was designed as a prototype of the centres we were advocating the State should open nationwide. It was the forerunner of today's government law centres. By the time the Centre opened, work had already commenced by a government-appointed committee, the Pringle Committee, examining the need for a comprehensive state-funded system of civil legal aid and advice and the structure through which it could be provided. The creation of the committee was the government's response to FLAC's campaigning and the support drawn from other groups and organisations. Brian Gallagher, who was nominated as FLAC's representative on the committee, played an important role in successfully advocating the law-centre model recommended in the Pringle Report published in 1977. Ultimately, in 1980 a non-statutory Civil Legal Aid and Advice Scheme was established by the government under the aegis of a Legal Aid Board appointed to manage the scheme and a number of government law centres were opened around the country. Before the scheme was announced and established, the European Court of Human Rights held the State in breach of its international human rights obligations in proceedings successfully taken by a Mrs Josie Airey. She successfully complained that the State's failure to provide her with free legal representation for judicial separation proceedings, for which she could not afford legal representation, violated her right of access to the courts. The Airey judgement validated FLAC's advocacy of a state-funded civil legal aid scheme and forced a reluctant Fianna Fáil government to partially implement the Pringle recommendations, eight years after FLAC first publicly advocated such a scheme. It wasn't until 1995 that it was finally put on a statutory footing.

During my time as Director of the Crumlin Centre and

in dealing with PR as a Council member and then as FLAC's chairperson, doing interviews, whether on radio or television, became second nature as did undertaking my own legal and social research. Journalists regularly contacted me for legal background and comment on social issues which were the subject of articles they were writing. Their reliance on a law student's "expertise" was a little crazy and could have resulted in the publication of articles of questionable accuracy. I was always conscious of this and careful to never make any comment or give any guidance without being absolutely certain of its legal accuracy.

One of the journalists in regular contact with me between 1973 and 1980 was Nuala Fennell. Unknown to both of us at the time, we would ultimately be jointly elected as Fine Gael members of Dáil Éireann in June 1981, together with John Kelly, to represent Dublin South constituency. Nuala was then writing for the Irish Press and in the months following publication of the FLAC Report she wrote a variety of articles about the plight and vulnerability of women in broken marriages. Whenever Nuala wrote an article with a family law content she phoned me to ensure the accuracy of what she was writing. Nuala, together with nine other women, formed AIM Group, whose objective was to campaign initially for reform of the maintenance and property laws to provide better financial protection and security in the family home for wives and dependent children. At that time most family homes were owned by husbands in their sole name. A husband could sell the home behind his wife's back and use it as security to borrow money without her consent. When marriages broke down, this created awful problems and this was one, amongst the many issues, addressed in FLAC's 1972 Report. AIM launched their own report in

1973, calling for legal reform and greater protection for battered wives, and in the background, together with other lawyers, I assisted Nuala in the preparation of the report. At an early stage I also met with some of the members of AIM group to detail for them the experiences of many of the women FLAC was assisting. Those I met included Madeleine Prendergast, who was the wife of Peter Prendergast. Peter was destined to become Fine Gael's Secretary General while Garrett Fitzgerald was leader and later Taoiseach. Deirdre McDevitt was amongst the founders of AIM group and would later join Fine Gael, become a lifelong friend and work in Leinster House for many years. When Nuala was a Minister of State in the Department of Justice1982-87, Deirdre worked as her personal assistant. Both FLAC and AIM campaigned for family law reform in the 1973-75 period and Nuala and I stayed regularly in touch. In 1975, Nuala together with Mary Banotti, who would some years later be elected as Fine Gael's member of the European Parliament for Dublin, Anne Magennis and Nuala Campbell, founded Irish Women's Aid and opened the first Irish hostel for battered wives in Dublin's Harcourt Street. By then I was chairperson of FLAC and, at Nuala's request, I organised the provision through FLAC of free legal advice and aid to the women temporarily resident in the hostel.

A copy of FLAC's 1972 Report was sent to every TD and Senator in Leinster House and in 1973 I got the bright idea of holding a meeting in Leinster House for TDs and Senators, to advocate implementation of the reforms detailed in the Report. Liam Cosgrave was Taoiseach, leading a Fine Gael/Labour coalition government and Ritchie Ryan was Minister for Finance. As a member of the Dublin Jewish Students Union I had met Richie when he was a guest speaker at one of our meetings and we had chatted over a cup of tea when the meeting was over. I contacted Ritchie who booked Room 114 in Leinster House, located near the Dáil Chamber, for a FLAC meeting to take place on a Wednesday afternoon when both Houses of the Oireachtas were sitting. We posted invitations to all Oireachtas members and, to my surprise, when the meeting started the room was almost full. There were between forty to fifty present with standing room only.

So in our early twenties both David Maloney and I made our first speeches in Leinster House. I spoke of the need for family law reform whilst David (as Chairperson of FLAC) spoke of the need for a state-financed civil legal-aid scheme. What was astonishing was the number who came to the meeting and the extent to which a group of law students was taken seriously. Sitting at the back of the meeting was Garrett Fitzgerald, who was the relatively newly appointed Minister for Foreign Affairs in the Cosgrave-led Fine Gael/Labour coalition government. At the end of the meeting he came up to me and handed me a note listing the names of each Oireachtas member present. It had never occurred to us to obtain their names and the list enabled us to write to each of them to thank them for coming.

A year later in November 1974 my dad was a patient in St Vincent's Hospital following his suffering severe chest pains. Entering the lift after visiting him I bumped into Garrett who explained he had been visiting his wife, Joan, who was in the hospital. I did not know nor did he say why she was a patient. Much later I learnt that she suffered from severe arthritis. Both FLAC and AIM had been campaigning for reforms for a further year, nothing had changed and the number of FLAC clients was continuing to increase. Paddy Cooney was Minister for Justice and I wrongly assumed nothing was being done. Giving no thought to the fact that Garrett might have been upset that

Joan was in hospital, I instantly and undiplomatically confronted him over the government's lack of action. It was the wrong time and the wrong place and born of the frustration of an idealistic and frustrated youth. I recall him promising that the government would introduce family law reform shortly and saying he would bring it up again with Paddy Cooney. The lift reached the ground floor and we went our separate ways. Driving home I felt guilty and regretted my abruptness. I think that is primarily why I still remember our unexpected meeting in the lift.

In the years that followed I developed an enormous admiration for Garrett. I regarded him as a brilliant Minister for Foreign Affairs, an impressive reformist and a farsighted leader of Fine Gael in the 1977-81 period. I would not again meet him until I was elected as a Fine Gael member of Dublin County Council in 1979 and when I did he clearly had no memory of our previously meeting. However, I have little doubt that if not for my perception of Garrett I would never have joined the Fine Gael party in 1979 nor have then stood for election to represent the Whitechurch area on the Council. Fine Gael's historical baggage would for me have been an insurmountable obstacle. It was my admiration for Garrett Fitzgerald which resulted in my being the first, and, so far, the only member of the Irish Jewish community to seek electoral office as a Fine Gael candidate.

◄►◄►◄►

Fine Gael was anathema to many members of Ireland's Jewish community when I was growing up. It was the party associated with the Blueshirts (the National Guard), the Irish pseudo-fascist group, led by General Eoin O'Duffy who had been Garda Commissioner in the Irish Free State from September 1922 until February 1933. The emergence of the Blueshirts in July 1933 coincided with the emergence of fascist organisations across the Europe of the 1930s. Their mode of dress, their objectives, their adoption of the straight-armed fascist salute of the supporters of Mussolini and Hitler and their dedication to marching was still remembered by the Irish Jewish community in the 1960s and 1970s. The baggage of the Blueshirts and O'Duffy's brief leadership of Fine Gael as its President (1933/34) was added to by Oliver Flanagan's membership of Fine Gael. He had delivered a notoriously strident anti-Semitic maiden speech in 1943 in Dáil Éireann, at a time when Jews were being starved, shot, gassed and incinerated in the Nazi concentration camps. During the course of what can accurately be described as a rant, Flanagan, referring to Emergency Powers Orders directed at the IRA, had asserted that "there is one thing that Germany did and that was to rout the Jews out of their country. Until we rout the Jews out of this country, it does not matter a hair's breadth what orders you make. Where the bees are, there is the honey – where the Jews are, there is the money". Flanagan, originally elected as an Independent TD for the Laois/Offaly constituency, had joined Fine Gael in 1954. He still represented the constituency in the 1970s and would continue to do so until 1987 when he retired and his son Charlie Flanagan, the current Minister for Justice and Equality, was elected.

The presence of Oliver Flanagan in the Fine Gael parliamentary party was sufficient to ensure in the 1960s and 1970s that at election time most members of the Jewish community voted for the Fianna Fáil or Labour parties. Ben Briscoe, like his father Robert (Bob) before him, from 1965 onwards being the only Jewish member of Dáil Éireann strengthened Fianna Fáil's support within the community.

The extraordinary visit made on the evening of the 2nd May 1945 by the then Taoiseach and Fianna Fáil leader Éamon de Valera to Germany's ambassador in Dublin to express his condolences on the death of Hitler, who had committed suicide two days earlier, was long since forgiven and forgotten. The visit, which at the time had sparked international outrage, was perceived by de Valera as an act of courtesy on behalf of a neutral country and as neither "passing any judgements, good or bad".

De Valera's rigid adherence to diplomatic protocol to express condolences on the death of a fascist political tyrant responsible for the death in war and in Nazi concentration camps of millions of people, knowing of the Nazi's anti-Semitism and barbaric atrocities, and at a time when filmed footage of the liberation of the skeletal survivors of the concentration camps had been in international circulation for months, displayed a despicable lack of insight and moral judgement. Yet during the 1960s and 1970s Flanagan's speech prevailed in memory whilst the Irish Jewish community in 1966 paid tribute to de Valera, who was by then President, by funding the planting of a forest of 15,000 trees in Israel in his name. (The 50th anniversary of the Éamon de Valera Forest in Lower Galilee was commemorated in Israel in November 2016 by the unveiling of a plaque). No judgement was passed by the community on the de Valera-led governments in the 1930s and 1940s turning their backs on the Jewish victims of Nazi persecution and the concentration camp survivors of German genocide and denying them Irish resident visas, nor on his condolence visit to the German embassy in 1945. Perhaps this was because Flanagan was perceived as an anti-Semite whilst de Valera was perceived as merely guilty of political misjudgement. De Valera was also regarded as well disposed to Ireland's small Jewish community, having ensured that its "Jewish congregations" were given express constitutional recognition in the State's constitution for which he had successfully obtained popular approval in 1937 in what was then called a plebiscite (today it would be called a referendum). Such recognition at a time when fascist-fuelled anti-Semitism was contaminating politics across Europe elicited much communal gratitude. I have no doubt that it was the largely communal negative view of Fine Gael which shaped my initial perception of the party.

◄○► ◄○► ◄○►

I had no thought of joining any political party when involved with FLAC. My focus was on how to continuously improve FLAC's service and effect reform. When I was still director of the Crumlin Centre, St Agnes's Social Service Centre became involved in what was then referred to as a pilot community care scheme. It involved, amongst other things, ensuring there were weekly coordinating meetings of all of those providing community services in the Crumlin area to improve and coordinate the assistance given to families with difficulties.

Many of the clients we were assisting in FLAC required other community supports and help and for a year I attended the Wednesday afternoon meetings in the Social Service Centre. Doing so was really valuable in helping to ensure clients in need received either Deserted Wife's or Unmarried Mother's Allowance, or Home Assistance, a social welfare payment which would later be replaced by Supplementary Welfare Allowance. It also enabled me to ensure that, where required, a social worker visited a client who could benefit from social work support. The meetings were a great step forward and a forerunner to the community care scheme later applied nationwide. They were also for me a great eye-opener. Some of the nuns engaged in social work had a great deal more understanding of the realities of life and insight than many assumed. I recall an occasion when one of the nuns had observed a distraught wife she recognised leaving the Centre after a meeting with me. Knowing I would not reveal anything that was confidential, she remarked to me at the end of a Wednesday meeting that she had seen Mrs *** leaving, presumed it was a marital problem, that the main problem was they were married just four years with three children, the husband was staying down in the pub because he couldn't cope after work with the pressures at home and that what Mrs *** should do was to take the Pill to ensure they had no more children. (At that time the sale of condoms in Ireland was a criminal offence but sale of the contraceptive pill, in theory to be used as a menstrual "cycle regulator", was not). So far, she told me, she had been unsuccessful in persuading her to do so. Mrs *** had declined the Pill for religious reasons but the nun pledged to have another go. I don't know whether her second intervention worked and helped resolve the marital difficulties but Mrs *** never returned for further legal help.

◄O► ◄O► ◄O►

By 1976 the world had changed. As a result of the work of FLAC, AIM group and Women's Aid campaigning for reform and also a report published by the Commission on the Status of Women, new family legislation was enacted, modernising our maintenance and child support laws, enabling the courts to bar a violent spouse from the family home, requiring the consent of a non-owning spouse for a valid home sale and also for the lawful use of a home as security to obtain a mortgage or otherwise borrow money. It was the first major reform of Irish family law in almost a hundred years and Paddy Cooney, the then Minister for Justice, has never received the recognition he deserves for steering the legislation through both Houses of the Oireachtas. However, a great deal more which remained to be done was comprehensively described in a book on Irish family law written by me which was first published in 1977.

◄○► ◄○► ◄○►

Looking back to that period of my life and the amount of time I devoted to FLAC, I recognise today that it was something of a minor miracle that I successfully graduated as a law student and this is coming from someone who doesn't believe in miracles!

But during my time as a Trinity undergraduate I wasn't exclusively engaged in FLAC and the issues of legal aid and family law reform. I was a hyperactive political activist with a personal agenda. Unlike many of my Trinity contemporaries, I had no interest in student politics or debating societies. My focus was firmly outside the university campus on the world beyond.

Chapter 11

Von Tourist, Von Cup of Coffee

In the early 1970s there was public discussion and debate about the relevance and impact of Article 44 of the Irish Constitution on the island of Ireland. The article gave express recognition to the "special position" of the Catholic Church as "the guardian of the Faith professed by the great majority of the citizens". It also expressly recognised the other religious denominations existing in Ireland at the date of the coming into operation of the constitution in 1937, including, as previously mentioned, the "Jewish congregations". In addition and most importantly, as it still does today, it constitutionally guaranteed freedom of conscience and worship and prohibited any discrimination by the State based on religious profession, belief or status.

The constitutional reference to the " special position" of the Catholic Church was perceived by many as out of date, offensive to Protestants, a barrier to reconciliation between the North of Ireland and the Republic and out of step with post-Vatican Two thinking on the relationship between Church and State. It was proposed that the express reference to the Catholic Church's special position and to the other religious denominations be removed and the government sought submissions on the proposal.

We debated the issue at the Dublin Jewish Students Union (DJSU) and discovered that there were no plans for the Jewish Representative Council of Ireland (an internal Jewish community body with representatives on it from all the synagogues and communal organisations) to make any submission to government. There was a longstanding reluctance within the Jewish community to become involved in national political issues, particularly those perceived to be religiously delicate. Centuries of European anti-Semitic persecution understandably resulted in people just wanting to get on with their lives and not get embroiled in unnecessary controversy – but that was not the perspective of some of us in the DJSU. We were young, idealistic and self-confident and wanted to look beyond the community and play a meaningful role in the country's modernisation and development. As the Irish "Jewish congregations" were expressly referenced in Article 44, I believed there was an obligation to contribute to the debate. A student sub-committee was formed and I drafted its report. The report recommended the deletion of express constitutional reference to both the Catholic Church's "special position" and to other religious faiths and also addressed other issues that we believed discriminatory, including the ban on divorce and the sale of contraceptives. The report was adopted at a DJSU meeting and forwarded to the Jewish Representative Council, asking that it be adopted and furnished to the government. I believed there was virtually no chance of that happening so, to contribute to the public debate taking place, early one evening I drove into town and delivered copies of the report to the offices of the *Irish Times*, the *Irish Independent* and the *Irish Press*. The next day the report generated enormous headlines, substantial media coverage and a crisis.

The report was treated by the media as a major contribution by the Jewish community to an important national debate. Although referenced as the views of the DJSU, somewhere in the coverage the perspective that it was just the view of a group of students got lost. Publication of the report greatly angered Dr Isaac Cohen, who was still Chief Rabbi of Ireland. The first he knew of its contents derived from reading his morning *Irish Times*. I learnt later that day that it was only as a result of the intervention of Maurice (Mossy) Abrahamson, the widely respected chairman of the Jewish Representative Council, that he was dissuaded from issuing a public statement disowning us all.

A few days later, on behalf of the DJSU, I attended an emergency meeting of the Council specially called to discuss our report. Despite Mossy's best efforts the Council could not be persuaded to officially adopt it. Most of the discussion at that night's meeting comprised expressions of outrage at publication of the report and criticism of the chutzpah of the students involved. However, the controversy quickly died down, as the DJSU Report was generally welcomed in public commentary and reflected views expressed by many others outside the Jewish community. About seven months later, on the 5th December 1972, the Fifth Amendment to the Constitution was approved by a considerable majority in a referendum. As a consequence, reference to the "special position" of the Catholic Church and express reference to other named religions, including "the Jewish congregations", were deleted from the Irish Constitution.

The DJSU sub-committee formed to prepare the constitutional submission was composed of me and Carol, Alan Eppel and Trish Tolkin, who later became husband and wife and emigrated to Canada, and Alan Benson who subsequently became the first member of the Jewish community to join Fine Gael (I was the second) and who during my time in politics gave me great political support. Alan Eppel was destined to become Professor of Psychiatry and Behavioural Neuroscience in McMaster University in Hamilton, Ontario. Trish became a lead strategic planner and fundraiser for a major Jewish organisation in Toronto and obtained a doctorate in medical science, specialising in neurolinguistics. And Alan Benson successfully ran with his brother Gerry a travel agency, Easy Travel, based in Dublin, and became President of Junior Chamber Ireland. We were all close friends and Trinity College students. (All three Alans were also former pupils of High School and Alan Eppel was one of those who used to join in the late-night runs.) In the 1970 to 1973 period we founded, wrote, printed and distributed an occasional Jewish communal newsletter called *Ruach*, meaning spirit, which contained both communal news and criticism of communal institutions. In 1971, together with Edie Segal, we formed the Irish Soviet Jewry Committee to publicise the plight of Soviet Jews which other, mostly young, members of the community joined.

◄◦► ◄◦► ◄◦►

There were an estimated three million Jews living in the repressive Soviet Union. The communist Soviet state required that "Jewish" be registered as their nationality on their official identification papers, and anti-Semitism permeated various aspects of everyday life and Soviet society. During the Stalinist era synagogues had been closed, Yiddish writers and actors executed, and many Jews rounded up and imprisoned as "cosmopolitan" enemies of the state. There was no Jewish educational system permitted, Jewish cultural activities were discouraged and no Jewish communal life existed. Jewish nationals were unable to express their identity and were trapped in a country that didn't allow its citizens to emigrate, in violation of the 1948 UN Declaration of Human Rights, which asserted in Article 13 the right of any individual to leave any country, including his own.

In the years following Stalin's death in 1953 there was a stirring of Jewish consciousness and small numbers of Jews started exploring Jewish culture, tradition, religion and history and commemorating the lives of those massacred by the Germans during World War Two. Israel's victory in the Six Day War in 1967 ignited a sense of self-confidence amongst Soviet Jewry and across the Soviet Union an increasing number of Jews became determined to address their plight. Long silenced by censorship, fear of anti-Semitism and reprisals and also separated from world Jewry, they emerged from isolation to voice public support for Israel, to learn Hebrew, explore their Jewish heritage and also to seek permission to make "aliyah" – that is, to move to Israel. A small and growing number became Orthodox and religiously observant. Eventually the demand for aliyah was extended by some to a demand to emigrate to a state of their choosing. During the 1960s and early 1970s each year a small number were allowed to leave but many were refused and others feared the consequences of applying for an exit visa. By the early 1970s many of those perceived as prominent in the making of such demands were the subject of arrest, trials and imprisonment for engaging in anti-Soviet activities.

A number of leading figures were sentenced to long terms of imprisonment, others labelled as insane and put into psychiatric hospitals and a number deported and exiled to Siberia. The location of some of those arrested was unknown and their families experienced enormous difficulty in establishing their whereabouts. Those not arrested or deported were fired from their jobs and many who held prestigious positions, such as doctors, scientists, engineers and university professors, were compelled to undertake menial labouring jobs. Those the Soviet authorities refused a permit to leave became known internationally as "refuseniks".

Having learnt the lesson of the Holocaust, starting from around 1969/70, members of many Jewish communities rallied to their cause and Jewish support organisations emerged in a variety of countries. Their plight became a focal point for global Jewish activism under the campaign slogan "Let My People Go".

We formed the Irish Soviet Jewry Committee as no Jewish support organisation yet existed in Ireland. We demonstrated on their behalf, met with the Soviet ambassador and lobbied TDs about their plight. Those in conflict with the Soviet authorities believed it to be of great importance that they were aware that there was international knowledge of their individual circumstances. This was perceived as affording some insurance that if a family member was arrested there was an international focus on any trial that might follow and that he or she could not be "disappeared", as their disappearance could result in an international outcry. Phone numbers of refuseniks were circulated amongst the various campaigning groups with requests that families be phoned. As a result, in the early 1970s regular phone calls were made from my home in Crannagh Park to courageous and stressed Jewish families residing in Moscow and Leningrad (now St Petersburg) whose applications to leave the Soviet Union and move to Israel had been refused. It was assumed that many of the Soviet phones were being tapped by Soviet security and intelligence bodies, such as the KGB, so the conversations were kept simple, asking about the health and well-being of family members. This ensured that nothing said could cause additional trouble for those we phoned while relaying a message that their existence and plight was known.

One of the difficulties was language. While a surprising number of those phoned could communicate in English, many could not. At an early stage, at a demonstration that we held, a man introduced himself to me as a retired Irish army officer who spoke fluent Russian, and offered to help. He was recruited to assist with the phone calls and in the following months conducted a number of conversations in Russian with Jewish refuseniks in the Soviet Union from our home in Rathfarnham. I have long wondered whether the Special Branch or army intelligence developed any concerns about the extraordinary number of phone calls being made to the Soviet Union from Crannagh Park and whether the officer concerned was dispatched to engage with us to ascertain whether we were a group of subversives and to discover exactly what we were doing. I think that unlikely but, if he was, any concerns that might have existed would have been rapidly dispelled.

The United States played a major role, together with various European countries, in the creation and signing with the Soviet Union in 1975 of the Helsinki Final Act containing accords on security and cooperation in Europe. The Helsinki Accords included provisions requiring signatory countries to recognise and respect religious freedom and to deal in a positive and humanitarian way with applications to emigrate of persons wishing to reunite with their families. Later provisions were also agreed to address any violations. The Accords laid the foundations for increased Jewish emigration from the Soviet Union in the second half of the 1970s and in 1979 the highest number, 51,000, were allowed to leave. However, in the early 1980s there was a new crackdown on Jewish dissidents and those engaging in Jewish cultural and religious activities. The numbers permitted to emigrate were dramatically reduced, being no more than 2,688 in 1982, reducing to 896 in 1984. There were by then many thousands of refuseniks who had for years been denied their right to leave and whose lives were blighted as a result of being fired from their work and Soviet persecution. It wasn't until late in the second half of the 1980s that the attitude of the Soviet government changed, liberalisation occurred and many prominent refuseniks were given exit visas. Then, following the collapse of the Berlin Wall on the 9th November 1989, the dam finally burst. By the end of the 1990s over a million and a half Jews had left the Soviet Union, one million of whom settled in Israel.

In England a Jewish women's group called "The 35s" (so named because it had 35 original members, aged 35 or thereabouts) was created in the early 1970s to protest and campaign on behalf of Soviet Jewry. Subsequently, a group using the same name was founded by members of the Dublin Jewish community. Members of the group visited the Soviet Union to meet refuseniks, fundraised to provide financial assistance to refusenik families and monitored the Soviet governments implementation of the Helsinki Accords. The 35s took over and expanded the work of our Irish Soviet Jewry Committee at a time when we could no longer sustain our involvement. However, I maintained my interest in what was happening in the Soviet Union and in the plight of Soviet Jewry.

In the early 1980s when I became a TD, Soviet Jews were still experiencing enormous difficulties. On the 6th December 1984, to mark International Human Rights Day, I proposed a Dáil motion for which I had secured all-party agreement and which was adopted without dissent. The motion expressed the Dáil's concern over the continued "harassment, arrest and imprisonment" of Soviet Jews, calling for the release of those imprisoned or exiled because of their desire to leave or to exercise their right to freedom of religion or cultural expression, and calling on the Soviet Union to comply with its Helsinki obligations.

The following year, 1985, shortly after Mikhail Gorbachev became Secretary General of the Communist Party of the Soviet Union, I flew to Moscow, together with Fine Gael's erudite and brilliant political strategist, Senator Seán O'Leary, to visit some of the Jewish refuseniks under pressure and in trouble with the Soviet authorities. As a morale booster, for distribution within the refusenik community, we included in our luggage ten copies of the official report of the Dáil debate. The visit was all very cloak and dagger!

We booked through the Soviet travel agency, Intourist, in London as two lawyers intending to participate in a fully organised package holiday in Moscow and obtained the required holiday visas. Our objective was to meet a number of Jewish refuseniks and upon returning home publish a report on their circumstances. To facilitate doing so, we had a list of names and phone numbers and in advance I had liaised with some others who had made a similar trip and who had substantial expertise in the area, and with contacts in the Israeli embassy in London. (At that time the Israeli ambassador to the UK, based in London, was also Israel's non-resident ambassador accredited to Ireland. It wasn't until 1995 that the Irish government agreed to Israel establishing an embassy in Dublin. In January 1996 Zvi Gabay became Israel's first resident ambassador to Ireland.) We were staying at an Intourist hotel in Moscow and we were warned that it was likely that the hotel phones were bugged by the KGB and that some of the families we were going to contact would be under surveillance.

Yosef Begun, a long-term refusenik whose family we intended to visit, had been sentenced to a term of seven years imprisonment for anti-Soviet activities. The Soviet authorities regarded his teaching Hebrew and Jewish culture as his real "crime" but his doing so did not violate Soviet law. His wife Inna and his nineteen-year-old son Boris were denied their right to visit him and they were concerned about his health. Protesting his father's imprisonment, ill treatment and the denial of visitation rights, Boris was on hunger strike in the family's apartment. He had been on hunger strike for almost a month and there was a concern that he would die or permanently damage his health. Alternatively, as had happened in similar cases, there was a fear that he would be arrested, held indefinitely in a mental hospital and force-fed. Before our departure we were informed that the family had been visited a week earlier by three members of the Canadian Parliament who were assaulted in the street when departing. The Soviet authorities referred to the assailants as "hooligans" but an Israeli official believed they were members of the Soviet security service.

On day one of our visit we participated in that morning's organised Intourist bus tour and at lunchtime excused ourselves from the afternoon arrangements. In case of trouble we believed it important that the Irish ambassador and his officials knew we were in Moscow. We made phone contact with our embassy and arranged to meet up with the First Secretary. Believing the embassy to be bugged, we chose an outdoor meeting in Gorky Park. The location seemed particularly appropriate to add to the sense of drama as both Seán and I had read the famous crime novel Gorky Park written by Martin Cruz Smith. Published about four years earlier, it had by then been made into a movie. When asked by the First Secretary what we were doing in Moscow we responded, "Just visiting as tourists!". He didn't believe us and guessed we were up to something but respected our wish to be discreet. We told him we just wanted him to know we were visiting.

In the days that followed, Seán and I became experts on the Moscow underground, meeting various refuseniks in different underground stations, away from homes and phones under surveillance. Each morning we participated in Intourist excursions, sightseeing and museum visits and each lunchtime excused ourselves from the afternoon excursions. On day three our assigned Intourist guide asked what we did each afternoon. Seán just shrugged his shoulders, responding "Oh, we are Irish!" and then winked at her. I have no idea what she made of that explanation but she didn't ask any more questions.

When dealing with Russian officialdom we had been advised that being assertive and authoritative achieved better results than being docile and compliant. The hotel was organised with military precision. Breakfast, we were informed, was from eight till nine and on day one we were each assigned our seat at a breakfast table and requested to furnish our week's breakfast order. Mine was two poached eggs on toast and a cup of coffee. On day two, arriving for breakfast at about eight twenty-five I discovered awaiting my arrival two cold poached eggs sitting on top of a cold soggy limp piece of white toast, accompanied by a cold cup of coffee. We learnt that day that at exactly eight your breakfast order was placed at your designated place on your assigned table and remained there until you turned up! Sitting opposite me all week was an elderly retired grey-haired Englishman with glasses who sat at the table with a small green backpack on his back. He told us that he was a longstanding member of the British Communist Party and was fulfilling his lifelong dream of visiting Russia. Seán labelled him as The Man from the *Morning Star*, then a well-known British communist publication.

We managed to get to breakfast by eight on days three and four, but failed miserably on day five. We had been out late the night before and didn't arrive for breakfast till after eight-thirty. I badly needed a decent cup of coffee and called over the somewhat intimidating tall female attendant whose job it was to service our table. I very nicely asked if she could bring me a fresh cup of coffee. She irritably stood over me, digesting my request, and then shaking her head and wagging one finger in front of my face thundered witheringly: "Von tourist, von cup of coffee!" To which I loudly responded, standing up and banging my fist on the table, "I don't believe the entire Soviet Union will collapse if I am given a second cup of coffee!" The effect was instantaneous. *Morning Star* Man, who had been quietly reading, jumped up startled from his seat, his glasses falling to the ground, Seán looked at me as if I had lost my marbles and the attendant ran towards the coffee percolator across the room. Rapidly returning to our table, somewhat flustered, she poured me a cup of hot coffee. She did the same for Seán and then proceeded to pour coffee into the cold remains of tea sitting at the bottom of *Morning Star* Man's cup. As she returned the coffee pot to its original resting place, our English companion loudly asserted that he would not drink what he described as a "bourgeois American substance"! As far as he was concerned coffee was contaminating the purity of Soviet Communism.

Despite the egalitarian perception of the Soviet Union held by the small number of Irish communist supporters back home we discovered aspects of Soviet society to be seriously less than equal. Adjacent to our hotel was a luxury restaurant serving meals only to diners who were foreign tourists, diplomatic staff or senior Soviet communist officials and other members of the nomenklatura. Specialty stores, known as Beriozkas, also existed which sold goods that were either unavailable in regular shops or simply scarce for hard currency (e.g. dollars or sterling). Access to these shops was similarly restricted and extended only to those Soviet citizens who received income, allowances or gifts in hard currency. On occasion, when travelling in Moscow, we observed queues rapidly form outside regular stores and discovered that such queues were commonplace when it became known some scarce goods were about to go on sale. Included within the category of scarce goods were Levi jeans. On one taxi ride back to our hotel I was offered a ridiculously large sum of money by the taxi driver for the jeans I was wearing, proposing that he would wait outside the hotel while I changed into other trousers in my hotel bedroom. I declined his offer.

Carol was understandably concerned about my safety on the trip and it was agreed I would phone her each evening to let her know that I was okay. Because of likely phone-bugging, she knew that I would not discuss who we were meeting in Moscow, just tourist sites we had visited, meals eaten and other harmless details of our trip. Before my departure we had also agreed on a code should I want to inform her that we were concerned about our security. It involved my using a particular phrase to describe the weather. It was only after we returned home that I learnt that, when referring to Moscow's weather on calling her the third evening, I had unthinkingly partially used the coded phrase we had agreed. Until I cheerfully and obliviously phoned her the following evening she had been worried that our arrest was imminent!

When we first arrived at the Intourist hotel we had each been required to hand our passports for record purposes into a hotel office and we were informed that they would be returned that evening. We doubted this, as we already knew it was likely our passports would be retained until our departure. On the afternoon of day four in Moscow we were to visit Boris Begun who was on hunger strike, and his mother Inna. We decided, if the security services were going to beat us up and possibly arrest us, it would be a good idea to retrieve and have our passports in our possession. While they would provide no protection from assault, they might ensure the Soviet police would contact the Irish embassy should we end up in hospital or arrested. The question was how to retrieve them? A simple request for their return seemed a good idea, so I accompanied Seán to the hotel passport office where he knocked on its closed window.

A woman slid the window open and aggressively, in good English, asked what we wanted.

Giving our names and room numbers, Seán simply responded, "Our passports, please."

To which she responded, "Vy do you vant them?"

"Oh, because they are ours," he replied in his best, most charming Cork lilt with a friendly smile.

And with that, to our amazement, Soviet bureaucracy crumbled and our passports were returned.

Upon our arrival outside the apartment block in which the Beguns lived, we saw a large closed vehicle with a large protruding device on its roof which we believed had the capacity to monitor ordinary conversation inside their apartment. Upon entering their apartment and introducing ourselves to Inna we found Boris on a bed looking gaunt, tired and pale. Both of them were competent English speakers. Our verbal exchanges were a series of irrelevant pleasantries, our real conversation being conducted through exchanging notes. We learnt of the pressure they were under from the Soviet authorities and of failed attempts to visit Yosef Begun. Boris was adamant he would remain on hunger strike unless his father was released and we explained that we did not believe his action would secure his release. I had been informed that Boris had become religiously observant and I referenced rabbinical authorities asserting suicide to be contrary to Jewish law and values. What Seán O'Leary didn't know was that I already had an intimate understanding of how little impact Jewish law may have on a person intent on taking his or her own life. The Israeli ambassador to Ireland, based in London, had asked us to communicate a request from Israel's Ashkanazi and Sephardi Chief Rabbis that Boris should resume eating and I did so. In response, he insisted he would continue his hunger strike protest.

After about an hour we departed, unsure of what might happen next. We walked past the surveillance vehicle and down the street. Much to our relief no assailants intervened and we successfully hailed a passing taxi.

The hunger strike continued. Shortly after our return to Dublin I read a newspaper report that Boris had ended his hunger strike following his receipt of a phone call from one of Israel's Chief Rabbis.

The visit brought home in a very stark way to Seán and me what it was like to live in a totalitarian state and the extraordinary courage of the Jewish refuseniks who were demanding their rights to religious freedom and to emigrate.

We understood that once we had met with the Beguns the Soviet authorities, if they did not already know, would learn why we were in Moscow. So, the evening after visiting their home, we met again with the Irish Embassy's First Secretary, fully briefed him on our exploits and asked could he arrange for us to meet an official in the Soviet Foreign Ministry to express concern about the Soviet treatment of Jewish refuseniks. To our surprise, our requested meeting was rapidly arranged and took place the next day. Knowing we were both members of the Houses of the Oireachtas, the Soviet official initially courteously listened. We each concluded that thereafter when refuting our concerns he exhibited little conviction and enthusiasm for his own narrative.

Not all the families were under surveillance and one evening we enjoyed a very traditional Jewish meal in a small high-rise Soviet apartment. Three refusenik families were present and very excited to learn of our Dáil motion and debate. They were also delighted to receive the Dáil Reports containing the speeches delivered during the debate for distribution to members of the refusenik community. We carefully explained the very limited impact of Dáil Éireann on world affairs and that the Dáil motion was mainly of symbolic value in conjunction with similar motions passed in parliaments of other European democracies. No mention was made by either of us of the *Skibbereen Eagle*!*

---

*On the 5th September 1898, the *Skibbereen Eagle,* a provincial Irish newspaper published in a small town in West Cork, achieved international prominence by famously warning Nicholas the Second, the despotic Czar of Russia, that it was keeping its eye on him. Its editor, Frederick Potter, asserted that the *Eagle* "will still keep its eye on the Emperor of Russia and all such despotic enemies – whether at home or abroad – of human progression and man's natural rights which undoubtedly include a nation's rights to self-government. 'Truth', 'Liberty', 'Justice' and 'The Land for the People' are the solid foundations on which the *Eagle*'s policy is based." The idea that a small local paper in the South West of Ireland could scrutinise and call to account the Russian Czar struck a chord and was a cause not only of international curiosity but also of some bemusement.

One of the refuseniks whose predicament I had mentioned in the Dáil debate in 1984 was Yuli Edelstein who had been arrested on fabricated charges of drug possession and whose trial was then pending. By the time we visited the Soviet Union he had been sentenced to three years imprisonment and was in a labour camp in Siberia near the Mongolian border. Yuli and his family, like all the families we visited, ultimately secured their freedom and left the Soviet Union. Having emigrated to Israel, he became a distinguished and respected member of the Knesset, the Israeli Parliament. Almost thirty years after our visit to Moscow, Yuli visited Dublin as the Speaker of the Knesset on a reciprocal visit following the visit to Israel of Seán Barrett TD, as Ceann Comhairle (i.e. Speaker of Dáil Éireann). Yuli was surprised to learn that, when under arrest and in prison in 1984, his plight had been described by me in the Dáil Chamber in a debate on the persecution of Soviet Jewry. I gave him a copy of the Dáil motion and transcript of the debate as recorded in the official Dáil reports. We could never have predicted that, thirty years after the Dáil debate, he and I would meet in Leinster House as parliamentarians representing Ireland and Israel. Yuli could also not have anticipated that he would in June 2017, as Speaker of the Knesset, become the first Israeli to address a chamber of the Russian Parliament in both Hebrew and Russian, having thirty-three years earlier been framed, prosecuted and convicted by Soviet Authorities for the "crime" of teaching Hebrew and Jewish history.

I have, of course, yet again, got way ahead of myself. It is now time to return to 1973 and a major event that if omitted will result in my being in terrible trouble from which you, dear reader, will be unable to rescue me!

Chapter 12

A Wedding and Two Funerals

End-of-year Legal Science exams took place in September of each year and in September 1973 I was scheduled to take my third-year exams. The last exam concluded at five o'clock on Friday 21st September and by seven-thirty I was to be in Carol's parents' home in Greenlea Road in Terenure for a pre-wedding family dinner. Carol and I were scheduled to marry in Adelaide Road Synagogue two days later, on Sunday 23rd September.

Our engagement was something of a surprise to my dad. I had proposed to Carol four months earlier in May and we decided we should marry before the start of the next academic year. Without first asking Dad, I assumed Carol would live with me in Crannagh Park. His instant reaction, upon being informed of our engagement, was to ask where we would live when we were married and to remind me we were both still Trinity students with no independent income. When I said I had presumed we would live together in Crannagh Park with him, he smiled broadly, visibly relaxed and congratulated us both. I think he momentarily feared he would shortly be left to live alone.

Betty and Friam Danker, Carol's parents, were delighted at the news and, within days of our engagement, wedding plans were being hatched. I wanted a small wedding but Carol's mum had a different notion. Carol, her first and oldest daughter (she had two more and a son) was to marry before her twentieth birthday and there had to be a big celebration. At an early stage I surrendered, focused on my exam studies and let Betty, Friam and Carol get on with it in consultation with my dad. Betty and Friam were particularly good and decent people, they and my dad got on extremely well and since Carol and I had become an item I had spent a great deal of time in their home and Dad had regularly visited. Both of us had over the previous three years regularly joined them for Friday night Shabbat dinners and by the time of the engagement we were family in everything but name. The small wedding I had envisaged with about thirty-five guests evolved into a large wedding with about two hundred guests!

As the wedding arrangements were being implemented, Dad organised the installation of central heating in Crannagh Park, had a new kitchen installed with the benefit of Betty and Carol's advice and the house painted. He was determined to have it modernised before Carol moved in. The engagement and pending wedding seemed to ignite in him a new sense of optimism and hope for the future.

In the lead-in to our marriage everybody around me was in an increasing state of excitement while I remained quietly focused on my pending exams. As the examinations had only just ended I was practically braindead at the pre-wedding celebratory Friday-night dinner in Carol's parents' home. It was only on the next day, Saturday, it dawned on me I would have to make a speech at the post-wedding ceremony dinner. As a youngster, I had attended a few weddings but like most children and teenagers I had taken absolutely no notice of anything said in wedding speeches. Delivering a wedding speech was unfamiliar virgin territory. On the Saturday afternoon I disappeared into my bedroom, made a few notes and assumed when the time came everything would work out fine.

Sunday arrived, the sun shone all day and we celebrated our marriage in Adelaide Road Synagogue without a hitch. The Shelbourne Hotel was the venue for the dinner and St Stephen's Green the appropriate location for the wedding photos. The two hundred guests arrived, there was a drinks reception and then everyone sat at their designated table. Up until that moment everything had been going very well. As far as we knew, sitting at the top table and being served our food, everything continued to go well. It was only when the meal ended that we discovered a significant number of guests had been served their desserts before their main course. To be different, Carol's mum had hit on the idea of a variety of small dishes being served instead of a large main course and, as both courses included different sorts of pastries, as a result of a kitchen mix-up some guests received the sweet dessert pastries before those containing meat, fish or vegetables. This was only a minor issue compared to my speech which remains a source of embarrassment to this day.

The wedding guests were subjected to a narration on the need for law reform, the plight of Soviet Jewry and quotes from Alexander Solzhenitsyn, one of my favourite authors. Towards the end of my speech I managed to mention our mutual parents and concluded thanking those present for their generous wedding gifts. Relieved the speech was over I then sat down. Five minutes later, to my horror, I realised

I hadn't once mentioned Carol. But by then things had gone from bad to worse!

The next speaker was Rabbi Zalmon Alony, a brilliant Jewish scholar and author, who I knew well and greatly liked. He had been a rabbi in Dublin for many years and I had been invited to his home for Friday evening dinners on a number of occasions during my pre-FLAC days. Rabbi Alony was engaged in a futile but well-intended quest to convince me to be a more religiously observant member of the Jewish community and we had spent hours together on Friday nights past discussing and debating Judaism. I believe he recognised that he was unlikely to succeed but enjoyed our discussions. So by the time of our wedding he knew me very well. This, however, wasn't apparent to the wedding guests. Rabbi Alony was born in Russia and despite his many years in Dublin his English was poor. He opened his speech by wishing mazel tov to both "Anne and Carol" on their marriage and, clearly linguistically confused, continued to call me "Anne" throughout his speech, much to everyone's amusement. The suppressed giggles resulting from each reference to me as Anne turned into explosive laughter when, referring to Carol's popularity, he proclaimed with a smile that "She is well known to many men throughout the community". This generated such a sustained mix of laughter and applause that he joyously repeated it.

Sitting at the top table you are totally exposed and on view. With each reference to Anne, to avoid laughing I resorted to my well-practised technique of counting to one hundred as a distraction and managed to remain looking serene. But when there was a repeat reference to Carol being known to many men, she and I made the fatal mistake of glancing at each other, my defences disintegrated and we both started laughing. I laughed so much the tears rolled down my cheeks. Fortuitously, Rabbi Alony was so engaged in addressing our guests that he didn't notice and continued talking. For weeks afterwards, whenever Carol answered our home phone to friends looking for me, they asked to speak to Anne but no one dared ask her to identify the "many men" by whom she was well known!

The final disaster was my honeymoon arrangements. Instead of organising our honeymoon together I had convinced Carol to allow me to do it as a surprise. I wanted to do something out of the ordinary and for some reason I thought going to Tunisia would be exotic and different. About ten days before our wedding there was some health scare connected with Tunisia and I changed the booking to a week in Sweden followed by a week in Denmark. I have no idea now why I chose Sweden and Denmark. Due to exam pressures, I had done no research and didn't realise how cold the weather can be in each of those countries at the end of September and early October. In short, we took off with summer clothes, froze every time we ventured outside, consumed large amounts of coffee and alcohol to stay warm, ran out of money because I didn't realise how expensive Sweden and Denmark were compared to Dublin, changed our flights and flew home two days early.

Flying home early from honeymoon was not a good omen for a successful marriage in the eyes of relations and friends. However, we survived the trauma. It also had the advantage that Carol took over organising and booking all our future holiday travel and hotel arrangements. She does so still.

Following our honeymoon, we lived with my dad in Crannagh Park and resumed our studies in Trinity College and all our other activities. Dad was delighted to have both of us around and the next twelve months passed very quickly. I completed my final exams in Legal Science in

September 1974 as Carol entered her final year in Social Studies. Obtaining an academic law degree in Trinity did not entitle me to practise as a solicitor, which was my objective. In order to be able to do so I then set out to complete Law Society solicitors' exams by the end of the 1974/75 academic year. As no book existed on Irish family law, I also continued the research I had been engaged in throughout my time in FLAC and commenced writing an academic text on Irish family law.

◄○► ◄○► ◄○►

Suddenly, in early November 1974, Dad took ill and was admitted as a patient in St Vincent's Hospital. He was diagnosed as having had what were described as heart murmurs and detained in hospital for about two and a half weeks. Having been monitored and been given some minor treatment, he was discharged and I drove him home on the afternoon of Wednesday the 27th November. He was in great form and delighted to be out of hospital. At around three o'clock the next morning Carol and I awoke to a terrible gurgling sound coming from his bedroom. I rushed in and found him convulsing and unable to speak. He was clearly in the midst of a massive heart attack. By the time an ambulance arrived he was dead. He was 58 years old.

My dad's death was totally unexpected. His consultant in St Vincent's had downplayed his cardiac difficulties and there was no suggestion of any immediate fatal risk. Rushing into his bedroom I had witnessed the devastating cruelty and violence of his catastrophic cardiac failure. Like the image of my mother lying immobile on our kitchen floor, it is an image as stark today as the night it happened. As I rushed to phone 999 I had no belief in his survival. By the end of my emergency call there was nothing but silence and I knew he had gone. It was the second time within ten years that I experienced an ambulance calling to 14 Crannagh Park and transporting the lifeless body of a deceased parent to a hospital morgue.

Jewish funerals take place without delay. Dad's funeral took place on the afternoon of Thursday 28th November 1974 in the Jewish cemetery in Dolphin's Barn. It was a very large funeral. Nearly all of our wedding guests were there and many others. Unknown to me, Dad had reserved a plot beside my mum's grave and he was laid to rest beside her.

Early in the morning before the funeral the likeable and dynamic young Chief Rabbi, David Rosen, visited my home. I informed him that, in defiance of tradition and as my dad had asked following my mother's death, I would not be sitting shiva. It was unprecedented and he expressed concern that my actions would be viewed by others as showing a lack of respect for my father. I explained that my actions, in fact, reflected my respect for my dad's view of the world, which I shared, and were in compliance with his wishes. I also explained to him how personally traumatic I found sitting shiva for my mum at the age of fourteen. It had aggravated not ameliorated the trauma.

Both Carol and I were distraught at my dad's death and had no wish to share our distress with strangers. We were determined to spend our time with each other and with good and close friends as we came to terms with it all. I know that my decision not to sit shiva caused much consternation within the Jewish community at that time but, looking back on it now, I have no regrets. It was the right decision for us and one that I know my deceased dad would have favoured.

Despite the passing of time, there are many regrets that remain. Like my mum, Dad died far too young. At least, unlike my mum he died from natural causes, leaving aside legitimate questioning of the level of medical expertise involved in his diagnoses and treatment. I would have liked to have learnt more from him about our family history over the preceding hundred years, the relationship between him and my mum, and also the illness which led to her suicide to better understand why she so deliberately ended her own life and did not even leave a note. I would also have liked to discover why Dad's mother, my grandmother Leah, was such a difficult and embittered person. Twenty-three-year-olds, no matter how smart they are or think they are, don't often ask many of those sorts of questions and I never asked enough of them. I also regret that he missed out on so much that he would have enjoyed, such as becoming a grandfather, living with Carol and me for a longer time and some of my various exploits as a lawyer and politician. A further regret is that he didn't live long enough to benefit from the enormous advances in ophthalmology which might have restored his eyesight and enabled him to again enjoy reading. He was a kind, good and principled man who never had any opportunity to fulfil his true potential and who never overcame the loss of my mum and his brother Jack.

By the time Dad died my grandmother was in a coma, unconscious in the Jewish Home. She was being sustained on a drip and by medication. She had been wishing Dad dead for many years but never awoke to learn her wish had finally been granted. Had she momentarily come round it is unlikely she would have understood as for some time before sinking into a coma the Alzheimer's had completely taken over and there were no more periods of lucidity. Just three weeks after Dad's death, on the 24th December, she died and yet again we visited the Dolphin's Barn cemetery. There were neither tears nor sadness. Just an enormous sense of relief that she had ceased to be part of my life.

In just fifteen months our lives had been utterly transformed and I had become an orphan. Carol's parents were enormously supportive as were our close friends, and somewhere in the background there remained my Aunt Gertie. We knew our only option was to look to the future and make the most of it.

Chapter 13

Life Goes On

The twelve months following my dad's death were frenetic. By the end of June 1975 I had sat all the exams required to qualify as a solicitor and Carol had successfully completed her Social Studies course and obtained her degree. She was more successful than me. Whilst I had no difficulty with the legal subjects, I failed the solicitor's compulsory Irish exam. I had neither spoken nor read any Irish since my Leaving Certificate five years earlier, had not taken the Irish exam seriously and done no more than a few hours' advance study. I had been overconfident and too distracted by my main project, writing my family law book, and also my work as chairperson of FLAC.

From early morning till late in the evening throughout the first eight months of 1975, when not involved with FLAC, I spent most of my time either writing and researching at home or in Trinity's main library. My intention was to have a major portion of the first draft of the book complete by the end of August and then to return to it at the beginning of the following June and I managed to achieve that objective.

I was very single-minded and determined. The book, *Family Law in the Republic of Ireland* was intended to not only comprehensively document the state of the law but to also put it in its historical context and prescribe the reforms urgently required to address the diverse realities and difficulties of modern Irish family life. At no stage was I inhibited by the reality that I was only twenty-three going on twenty-four years of age, had only just graduated from Trinity and had not yet qualified as a solicitor. My confidence in my capacity to complete the project derived from my almost four years of voluntary work in FLAC, the many speeches on the subject I had delivered, unofficial tutorials I had conducted to assist Social Science students in Trinity and the research I had personally conducted to learn as much as possible about Irish family law. I passionately believed that the law should protect the vulnerable and individual personal rights and, where it could do so, help to resolve and not exacerbate family difficulties, and be child-centred. I regarded the rule of law as central to a properly functioning democracy. Antiquated laws, out of touch with the daily reality of individuals' personal problems, that discriminated against women and failed, in practice, to protect the welfare of vulnerable children, in my view brought the law into disrepute. I also had no tolerance for the hypocrisy of pretending that our law and the constitutional prohibition on divorce in some magical way prevented marriage breakdown and protected the best interests of children. I had, looking back on it now, some very big insights for an early-twenties, recently graduated law student. Nevertheless, they are insights that have endured and motivated me throughout my life.

From September 1975 until May 1976 work on my family law book was parked as Carol and I resided in Amsterdam. Instead of undertaking a post-graduate law course in a major American or English university I had opted for the Europa Institute of the University of Amsterdam. The Institute offered a one-year diploma course on European law, politics and economics. Ireland had only joined what was then the European Economic Community (the EEC) in 1972 and few lawyers knew anything about European law. I saw it as a great opportunity to explore that area while moving away from pure law and studying economics and politics. Having visited Amsterdam with the Trinity athletics team over four years earlier, I also relished the prospect of living in and exploring a city I had fallen in love with. Also, Carol liked the fact that Amsterdam was closer to home than Harvard or Yale in the United States which were the alternative options I was seriously considering.

On the 31st August 1975 I ended my time as FLAC chairperson and early in September Carol and I packed all our luggage into the Mini-Minor Gertie had given me when I was seventeen and travelled by ferry to England and on to Holland.

The trip was uneventful until we drove into the Amsterdam suburbs. About fifteen minutes' away from the apartment we had rented with the assistance of the university, we got a puncture. Having hauled out all the luggage packed in the boot, accessed the spare wheel and replaced the punctured one, reinstated the luggage and driven a couple of miles, we ground to a halt with a second puncture. An hour later, we finally arrived at the apartment after a local garage had replaced the second punctured wheel. It was an inauspicious start.

Our apartment, located near the famous Rijksmuseum on Roelof Hartplein, was wonderfully spacious, with a picturesque large open fireplace in an antique-furnished sitting room. In the centre of a large bathroom, on four legs stood an impressively ornate nineteenth-century bath which we discovered comfortably accommodated both of us.

We spent nine happy months in Amsterdam. Carol worked in a part-time job in the university and we met a multi-national group of students from across the globe who had been attracted to the course, which was conducted in English. I chilled out and stopped working at a frenetic pace. I was fascinated by European law and hugely enjoyed the lectures and reading material on politics and economics. Many comfortable and cosy evenings during the cold of the Dutch winter were spent sitting and reading by a blazing log fire.

We drove all over Holland and loved its proximity to other countries. We drove to Belgium, Luxembourg and France and spent a wonderful weekend in Paris. Despite the opportunity to do so, we did not visit Germany. I don't believe when in Amsterdam we ever considered driving there. At that time I simply regarded Germany as the country responsible for the greatest catastrophe ever suffered by the Jewish people and there was nothing about Germany that I then wished to see. It wasn't until the early 1990s, accompanied by Carol, that I first visited Germany on a Fine Gael political trip together with John Bruton and the late Jim Mitchell. The Germany of today is, of course, an entirely changed country. It is the state in the European Union which most humanely responded to the current refugee crises resulting from global conflicts, terror and famine. Its government has also in recent decades, as a member of the European Union, been amongst those

European States which have displayed the greatest understanding of the complexity of the problems which Israel has to address to ensure its continued existence and future security. Despite some views to the contrary, I believe it has also been a good friend to Ireland in assisting our addressing our relatively recent catastrophic financial difficulties and bank failures.

Anne Frank's house and the attic in which she hid from Holland's Nazi German occupiers during the Second World War was one of the first places we visited in Amsterdam and subsequently revisited on at least three further occasions with friends who came to stay with us. Of course, all our visitors also wanted to see the famous Red Light district. There was something both intriguing and enormously sad about the many attractive women on show in the succession of brightly lit windows, seductively selling transient sexual intimacy, some gesturing to passersby to attract their attention.

One of our favourite places in Amsterdam was the Albert Cuyp market with its marvellous fruit, vegetables, cheeses, spices, olives, fish and flowers. On a sunny day it was and still is a delightful place to visit with its wonderful produce, colour and aromas. Close your eyes and stand strategically in certain locations and you are transported to the centuries-old aroma of Jerusalem's Arab souk. Perhaps that is why I liked it so much.

Amsterdam was also a great place for restaurants. For the first time we experienced the wonders of an Indonesian Rijsttafel in one of Amsterdam's many Indonesian restaurants. A Rijsttafel [rice table] comprises twenty to thirty small dishes of fish, meat, eggs, vegetables, rice and condiments and it can vary to exclude meat or fish or to be solely vegetarian. It became our favourite restaurant food during our time in Amsterdam and one Rijsttafel shared was more than enough accompanied by rice crackers. Carol and I still, every couple of years, make a weekend trip to Amsterdam and an evening Rijsttafel meal is always on our itinerary.

Our time in Amsterdam passed very quickly. The seasons changed and children skating on frozen canals were replaced by cruise boats full of sightseeing tourists. I finished the thesis I had selected for completing my Europa Institute course, which was on the European Community's Equal Pay Directive and Irish Law. In it, I concluded that our statutory provisions then violated Ireland's obligations under the Directive to ensure women received pay equal to that received by men for equal work.

About six weeks before the course ended I returned to Dublin and successfully repeated the solicitors' Irish exam. While in Dublin I met Brian Gallagher for lunch to ask whether upon my return to Dublin, once my family law book was complete, his dad, Richard, in whose law firm he worked, would be agreeable to my working for free in their office for a few months to gain additional experience. Unknown to me, Brian had come to lunch intending to ask whether upon my return to Dublin I would come and work with him and his dad. It was agreed that I would but, sadly, before I commenced work in the Hume Street offices of what was then Richard F Gallagher & Son, Brian's dad was diagnosed with terminal cancer. I would never have the privilege of working with him.

Back in Dublin in early June I revisited the original chapters contained in my family law book and substantially revised and updated them. As I had expected, my break from writing resulted in my being able to critically reconsider everything previously written and the resulting new and additional insights were invaluable. The Family Law (Maintenance of Spouses and Children) Act had only become law in early April 1976 and a chapter had to be composed detailing its provisions which transformed our maintenance support laws. In response to campaigning by Women's Aid, AIM Group and FLAC for greater protection for battered wives, the Act also for the first time conferred express power on the courts to bar a violent spouse from a family home. This meant an explanation of the new legal provisions facilitating a court application for a Barring Order also had to be written. It wasn't until July 1976 that the Family Home Protection Act completed its passage through both Houses of the Oireachtas. By the end of the third week in August I had completed the chapter on its provisions which ensured a spouse could not sell the family home or use it as security to obtain a mortgage without the consent of the other spouse. It also contained provisions to encourage husbands and wives to own homes in their joint names.

The enactment of both Acts was hugely encouraging as they each contained many of the badly needed reforms that had been at the forefront of FLAC's campaign and about which I had repetitively spoken. For me it confirmed my perspective that a coherent and comprehensive evidence-based account of the additional reforms required could act as a catalyst not only for legislative but also for constitutional change. It was my intention that my book should act as that catalyst and, over the years, its various editions have done so. However, I did not anticipate that some of the reforms I then advocated would take over thirty-five years to become a reality and that a major one of enormous importance, the creation of a specialist unified family court to adjudicate on family law disputes, would not by now have been achieved. For me that is a very major and personal disappointment.

Somewhere in the middle of the summer of 1976 I buried myself for some days in the State archives, which were then in Dublin Castle, to read papers recently released on the preparatory work undertaken on the drafting of the personal rights and family provisions contained in the Irish Constitution, to identify material of value to include in the book. By accident one day I came upon old Department of Justice archived files containing correspondence received in the 1930s from Jewish families desperately trying to escape Nazi Germany, pleading for visas to live in Ireland. The files also contained the racist vitriolic anti-Semitic advice to reject all such pleas given to the Department by the notorious Irish ambassador in Berlin, Charles Bewley, warning of Jewish contamination of Catholic Ireland. Sadly, the Justice Department acted on that advice. With great difficulty I determined to finish my book and refocused on files and papers relevant to the drafting of the 1937 Constitution, promising myself that I would one day revisit Bewley's rabid bigotry. Thirty-five years later, upon my becoming Minister for Justice and Defence, my knowledge of the content of the Justice Department's archived files partly motivated my prioritising the action required to change the departmental mindset and end the gridlock creating up to a four-year delay in the processing of citizenship applications. I also devised and inaugurated the holding of citizenship ceremonies to formally acknowledge and celebrate the acquisition of Irish citizenship by foreign residents in Ireland. Unfortunately, I did not have the time required to fulfil my second objective of comprehensively reforming our outdated and fragmented immigration and asylum laws, and addressing the circumstances of both those in direct provision and the large number of undocumented migrants who have been resident in the Irish state for many years.

◄o► ◄o► ◄o►

By early October 1976 my family law book was finished. I gave Brian Gallagher a copy and his feedback was invaluable, resulting in my making further revisions. When visiting Dublin in the spring of that year, I had met with the Institute of Public Administration in the hope that the IPA would publish it and had given them a copy of the existing draft. Just after we returned to Dublin in June 1976, I was informed that the Institute had arranged for the book to be read by a retired civil servant who was a qualified but non-practising lawyer. They had been advised that the substantive description of the law and its historical background merited the IPA publishing the book on condition that the third segment of each chapter, criticising the current law and proposing reforms, be deleted. The advice they were abiding by was that it was quite irregular that such content appear in a legal textbook. The book, I was told, should solely focus on current law and not contain personal views on its inadequacies and how they should be addressed.

I was totally gobsmacked. As far as I was concerned the case for reform was a central part of the book. In no circumstances could I agree to what was proposed. Having made enquiries about possible publishers, I met Seamus Cashman who had established Wolfhound Press just two years earlier in 1974, as a literary and cultural publishing house. Today, Seamus is widely recognised as an accomplished poet. Seamus had never published a legal textbook and had no means of knowing whether the book would sell or sink or whether the twenty-five-year-old he was talking to was a little bonkers. I knew nothing about publishing, was convinced the book would have an audience and needed his help. A deal was done. I would pay for the printing and binding and Wolfhound Press would publish and distribute the book. In return, I would receive a greater portion of the book's hoped-for profits than authors were then usually paid. We also agreed that I would be actively involved in the book's promotion.

What Seamus didn't know was that I did not have the funds to pay for the printing. I was counting on there being sufficient advance sales to pay the print bill. Talks with the Law Society resulted in it agreeing to insert a flyer and an order form in its monthly *Gazette* sent to solicitors and to sponsor the book's launch in the Society's headquarters in Blackhall Place. It all worked out. Before publication day the number of pre-paid advance orders received more than covered the cost of the print run.

Family Law in the Republic of Ireland, a 350-page treatise on Irish family law, was published in the spring of 1977, flew out of the bookshops and within a short time became the first legal textbook to appear in the top ten of the bestsellers list. It became the bible on family law relied on by the judiciary, the legal profession and various groups and organisations advocating for law reform and, within a short time, extracts from the book were being cited in High and Supreme Court judgements. By September, when it appeared on the book lists of various university courses for the start of the 1977/78 academic year, a second print run was required.

Publication of *Family Law in the Republic of Ireland* coincided with Brian Gallagher and I becoming partners in what became the solicitors firm, Gallagher Shatter. I had been working with Brian since the late autumn of 1976 and we enjoyed working together. On the 6th April 1977 Gallagher Shatter was launched on the world.

Brian had already been successful in a major case of constitutional significance entitled the State (Healy &

Foran) v The Minister for Justice and Others. In it, the Supreme Court delivered a landmark decision determining the State to have violated the constitutional rights of two alleged young offenders by failing to provide criminal legal aid to ensure their proper legal representation. In the years that followed, the firm would be involved in many seminal and groundbreaking cases, both at home and in Europe. From time to time, we would encounter difficulties and obstacles as we attempted to break the mould and challenged the antiquated practices of the legal profession but when commencing work as partners we knew nothing of that. Neither did we know that we would work together as great friends for thirty-five years without a cross word ever being exchanged between us.

And neither of us anticipated that within a few weeks of our forming our partnership, Carol and I, when visiting France, would believe we were about to die!

Chapter 14

*Cliffhanging, Reflections on Life
and Dead Sea Shenanigans*

It was early May 1977. Carol had accompanied me to Paris where I was attending an international conference on family law on behalf of the Law Society. When the conference finished we were heading to the South of France for a week's vacation. Our intention was to hire a small car, a Fiat 127, drive to Cannes, stay there for a few days, then leave the car at Nice airport and fly home. Calling to collect the hire car in Paris we were offered and accepted at no extra expense the bigger, longer and more comfortable Renault 16. The company needed it returned to their Nice agent and we were happy to oblige.

We planned a two to three-day drive along the 900-kilometre route, stopping in various cities, towns and villages along the way and doing some sightseeing. The drive was enjoyable and uneventful, despite poor showery weather, until just after darkness had fallen on the evening of the second day out of Paris.

I was driving cautiously at about 40 kilometres an hour

on a wet, unlit, dark, winding, narrow road located on the Massif Central. As we approached a sharp bend, two glaring headlights suddenly appeared travelling at speed on the wrong side of the road heading directly at us. I instantly swerved to the right and braked, the car skidded on a narrow grassy verge, the right side of the car dipped and we then descended into black nothingness. As so frequently portrayed on TV and in movies, although it all happened in milliseconds, it momentarily felt as if we were descending in slow motion. I had time to say, "We're going over a cliff," – Carol responded, "I know," – and the stricken car's fall gathered speed. We both believed we were about to die. Suddenly with a jarring thump the descent stopped. The car was on its side but fortunately the Renault was fitted with seat belts which held us in place. Other than our headlights there was total darkness. Neither of us knew what had stopped the car's descent or whether it would break through whatever had done so. Due to the amount of cloud cover neither the moon nor any stars were visible and neither of us could determine, looking down through Carol's passenger-seat window how much further we might fall should the car resume its downward plunge.

Considering the unexpected circumstances, we both remained inexplicably calm.

Carol asked quietly, "What should we do?"

I replied, "Let's get the hell out of here!"

Bizarrely, at that moment, unknown to him, Michael Crawford intervened!

Just a short time earlier we had both enjoyed watching together an episode of the excellent BBC comedy series *Some Mothers Do 'Ave 'Em* in which Crawford played the mercurial, accident-prone Frank Spencer. The episode had portrayed Frank sitting in the driving seat of a Morris Minor, the back of which delicately hung over the side of a cliff, with Frank and his wife Betty fearing being propelled over the cliff should they attempt to exit the car.

Carol asked, "What if we dislodge the car by moving and it continues to fall?" at the same time as the same thought struck me.

Hanging out on the side of a cliff, shrouded in darkness, we both thought of Frank Spencer and started laughing. It was probably more hysteria than amusement. In the sit-com Frank and Betty were ultimately okay but that wasn't mentioned by either of us. Agreeing we had no choice, I carefully opened my door, unclipped my seat belt and stuck a leg out. Feeling around with my foot, I was hugely relieved to make contact with terra firma – the sloping side of the cliff. I grabbed Carol's hand and exited the car, pulling her out after me as she unclipped her seat belt. We carefully and slowly crawled on hands and knees towards the road above us until we were near the clifftop and could progress no further. At that point the slope ended and the remaining stretch, although not very far, was straight up and a sheer climb.

As we'd edged up the cliff I'd heard someone call out "*Qui est mort?*" [Who is dead?[. The unexpected response was my ghostly voice from below asking, "*Pouvez vous nous aider, s'il vous plaît?*" [Can you help us, please?].

My request generated a lot of excitement. There was a hubbub of conversation and people hanging over the side, holding out hands. We grabbed on to their hands and we were pulled up by a number of people onto the wet grass verge. It was an enormous relief to reach safety.

We discovered that a small crowd had gathered. No one identified themselves as the driver of the car that had headed straight for us and I assumed that he or she had simply driven on. We learnt that the driver of a car travelling some way behind us had seen us going over the cliff and the others gathered were drivers and passengers of other cars that had stopped. Miraculously, neither of us was hurt. Within a short time the gendarmerie from the local village arrived with two large trucks, mounted with big searchlights and hydraulic hooked pulleys. When the searchlights shone on the car we discovered that about thirty feet down there were two trees growing at right angles out of the side of the cliff and that the front right side of the car had lodged on one and the back right side on the other. There were no other trees close by. Had I been driving any faster the car would have shot over one or both trees. Had I been driving a Fiat 127 instead of the Renault 16, the smaller car would not have been long enough to be caught by the two tree trunks and would most likely have bounced off one and continued its descent. By asking us to drive the Renault 16 to Nice, the car rental company had enabled two randomly growing trees, probably many years earlier seeded by passing birds or the wind, to save our lives.

Within thirty minutes of the trucks arriving, the car had been hauled back onto the road. It was undamaged save for two dents where it had crashed into the tree trunks. Having established that I was able to drive, the gendarme in charge drove slowly ahead of us, lights flashing, down the mountainous road to the nearby town. He took us straight to a small local inn, booked us in for the night and offered to pay for the room if we didn't have enough money to do so. Then he promised to arrange for a local mechanic to check out the car overnight to ensure it was safe to continue our drive. We assured him we could pay for our room and thanked him for his help. He was enormously kind and went much further than duty demanded to ensure we were okay. We were lucky to be alive. There was no barrier at the location where we had slid over the cliff. The gendarme told us that the drop was hundreds of feet down and that about two months earlier a couple had died when their car went over the cliff at the same location.

Carol and I both still recall our night at the inn. Having showered and changed we were served a wonderful meal of a variety of fish, fries and salad and drank an awful lot of wine. Neither of us can truthfully recall how many bottles of wine we drank but we do remember going to bed very drunk. We repetitively toasted our good luck in surviving the ordeal with the Jewish toast "L'chaim!" ("To life!") The innkeeper joined in the celebration of our survival unharmed and refused to accept payment for the wine or the meal.

We both that night reflected on how an unexpected random event can have a catastrophic impact and end or destroy a life. For some months afterwards, it felt as if we were living on borrowed time.

The following day, the Renault was returned and we were assured it was safe to drive. On returning to Ireland we sent the gendarme a letter of thanks and a gift of Waterford Crystal glasses.

We continued on our journey to Cannes. Neither of us had previously visited the South of France and we had four enjoyable days exploring its shops and restaurants. Unfortunately, the weather remained poor and there was little opportunity for sitting out in the sun by our hotel pool. We didn't care. We were just happy to be alive.

A less traumatic memory of that holiday is a visit to the home of an elderly distant French relation, whose name I no longer recall. He lived in a beautiful apartment overlooking the Cannes sea front. I had first learnt of his existence when I was sixteen years old. Grandmother Leah, with no forewarning, disappeared, leaving a note behind announcing she had gone to France to marry a distant cousin. Two days later when she phoned, Dad discovered that she had turned up uninvited at the man's apartment in Cannes and announced she was staying. Two weeks later she returned dejected to Crannagh Park, declared the whole thing a mistake and never elaborated further.

We had the relation's name and address, so we dropped a note into his apartment saying we would love to meet him and left our hotel phone and room number. The next morning we received an invitation to lunch.

His apartment was stunning, full of beautiful antique furniture with the ambience of a residence from the previous century. He was in his eighties, physically frail but with all his faculties intact, and had a great sense of humour. He spoke little English but we managed to converse reasonably in French, Carol being a great deal more fluent than me. He recalled my grandmother's unexpected visit. The word I remember he used to describe her visit was "fou" (crazy) and he smiled. We learnt that not only had he never proposed to her but that also there had been no contact between them for many years before her uninvited arrival.

We spent nearly three hours with him. He was being cared for by a live-in housekeeper who was an extraordinarily talented cook. The modest lunch we had expected turned out to be a five-course meal. Having finished the soup and what Carol and I presumed to be the main course, the actual main course arrived. As we struggled our way through it, he offered a second helping of everything we had eaten, insisting we were still growing young people, repetitively urging us to "mange, mange!" (eat, eat!). Dessert eaten, coffee and petit fours finished, conversation exhausted, he grew tired and we gave our thanks, said our goodbyes and staggered out of the apartment. Neither of us today remember any other meal we ate during that visit to Cannes but we each vividly remember the wonderful afternoon spent in his company and the laughter. We had told him of our dramatic cliff fall and that memorable afternoon luncheon evolved into a celebration of the fact that all three of us were alive. "L'chaim" was the toast repeated again and again after each glass of wine was poured.

Carol and I agreed after our cliffside adventure on the importance of making the most of life because none of us can know with certainty what tomorrow might bring. Between the two of us I am the one most remiss in that department as I have not, over our many years together, taken sufficient time out to simply enjoy life and I have devoted far too much time to law and politics. A former and great Secretary General in the Department of Defence, Michael Howard, trying to get me to slow down in 2012, in a reflective moment advised me that few people sitting in a rocking chair at the age of seventy-five, looking back on their lives, regret that they did not spend more time at work. But, he said, many regret they did not take more leisure time and also spend more time with family, friends and with those who they would have liked to have got to know better. It is an important insight. Life for all of us is a transient and, ultimately, a terminal experience and Carol and I are very fortunate that our lives did not simultaneously and prematurely end just four years into our marriage at the bottom of a cliff in France.

In pursuit of our philosophy to make the most of life, we took off to Israel for a three-week vacation in the summer of 1978. Carol had never visited Israel and it afforded an opportunity to meet up with an Israeli couple we had become friendly with in Amsterdam and to explore Israel together. The plan was to stay with our friends for five days and then go travelling.

We flew to Heathrow and then took an El Al flight to Tel Aviv. Everything was going well until we arrived in Tel Aviv airport and our luggage failed to appear, never to be seen again. We arrived in our friends' home with nothing other than the clothes we were wearing. The next day we each bought three pairs of shorts, three light tops, swimwear, a small knapsack and jogging shoes which proved to be all we required for the entire stay. We realised that most of the contents of the full case we had each packed were totally unnecessary. It was a useful lesson in the benefits of travelling light that has stayed with us down the years.

We travelled throughout Israel and visited places I had visited before and parts I had not previously seen. The Old City of Jerusalem was calm, safe and busy. Without fear of a bomb explosion, of being shot, a knife attack or of being run over by a vehicle driven by a terrorist, we could stroll through the hustle and bustle of the souk and other parts of the Old City and the more modern West Jerusalem. We could also safely hang out in a street café or bar, people-watching, while drinking coffee, orange juice or beer and eating delicious falafel and hummus with pitta bread and olives.

While in Jerusalem we visited Yad Vashem, the World Holocaust Remembrance Centre. The Centre comprehensively details the history of the Jewish people in the period leading into the Holocaust, narrates its unimaginable horror in words, pictures, works of art and film and remembers the six million Jewish victims. It contains many personal items found in the concentration camps and Jewish ghettos, including an exhibit of shoes of children who were murdered in the Nazi gas chambers, their bodies then incinerated and turned to ash. It is a chilling and emotionally stressful place to visit. It starkly depicts the barbarity and inhumanity of Hitler's Nazi Germany and the active complicity of the many thousands of collaborators of other nationalities who enthusiastically assisted the Nazis to implement their genocidal objective of creating a Judenfrei Europe (a Europe free of Jews).

It was in Yad Vashem that my assumption was confirmed that Ireland's neutrality during World War Two would not have saved the small Irish Jewish community from being slaughtered as part of Hitler's "Final Solution" had Germany successfully invaded Great Britain. A map on display in Yad Vashem contained Adolph Eichmann's wartime estimate of the number of Jews to be targeted for extermination across Europe. Amongst those designated on the map were 4,000 Jews living in Ireland. Clearly, in Hitler's world after Great Britain, Ireland was next.

I have over the years attended many Holocaust memorial events, at some of which I have delivered orations. In remembering all of those who perished during the Holocaust I believe it is also important that Irish people know and understand that had Hitler succeeded in his objectives, our State would have become a site for mass murder. The unanswerable question is who and how many in the Ireland of that time would have collaborated with German occupiers to eliminate Ireland's small Jewish community?

One day into week three of our visit to Israel we were splashing our feet in the salty water of the Dead Sea when we saw a bus arrive. It stopped some distance away and a group of middle-aged, very pale-faced men and women descended from the bus, together with two priests. It was August and very hot, well into the 30s Centigrade. All the men were dressed in suits and ties and the women also looked seriously overdressed for the heat of the Israeli mid-afternoon summer sun. The priests were dressed exactly as you would expect to see a priest dressed in Dublin on a cold autumn day. We were wearing light tops and shorts and were, by then, very suntanned.

The group walked in our direction. As they came towards us, we overheard some conversation and our suspicions were confirmed. They were all Irish. Neither of us could understand how they could cope with the heat in the clothes they were wearing. One of the priests was clearly leading the group and was engaged in a biblical discourse on the Dead Sea and the general area.

Being bad people, we decided to have some fun and engage in some shenanigans. Carol, whose Irish is superior to mine, cheerfully greeted them "as Gaelige" [in Irish] not mentioning that we were from Dublin. "Conas atá tu?" ["How are you?"] she asked. She then engaged one of the priests in an animated conversation. They all looked astonished as they assumed we were Israelis. The conversation over, the priest completed his dissertation, no one removed any clothes to dip into the salty seawater and, obviously sweating profusely, they headed slowly back to their bus.

I had just nodded and smiled and said nothing, so on their departure I threw in a "Slán!" ["Goodbye!"]. As they walked off we could hear them excitedly discuss how extraordinary it was that we spoke fluent Irish. I wonder how many people upon their return home heard the astonishing story of the two "Gaeilgeoir" [Irish-speaking] Israelis they met during their visit to the Holy Land!

Chapter 15

Family Planning Irish Style

On the 16th June 1977 a general election took place. The Fine Gael/Labour coalition government, led by Liam Cosgrave as Taoiseach, was replaced by a Fianna Fáil government, led by Jack Lynch as Taoiseach, with a large Dáil majority. It seemed to me that it was highly unlikely that the new government would take any worthwhile initiatives on the many outstanding legal and social reforms FLAC and many women's organisations had been advocating. I was by then chairperson of CARE: The Campaign for Deprived Children, an organisation founded by Seamus Ó Cinnéide advocating major change in our children's law and services. The law was completely inadequate and the services grossly dysfunctional but there was little interest within any of the political parties in effecting change. If CARE had been listened to and the reforms we were advocating in the 1970s been implemented, one of the more recent scandals and failures exposed might have been avoided.

After the general election I decided to try and get inside the political process instead of lobbying from the outside. To do so, I had the bright idea of standing for election to the Seanad [Senate] on the Trinity College panel of Seanad candidates. I had never closely followed the Seanad elections which occurred after each general election and knew nothing about the dynamic of Trinity Seanad election campaigns. As a candidate I was totally clueless. Having secured a small list of prominent former graduates willing to be named as my supporters, and devised and printed a leaflet which was delivered by post to all Trinity graduates registered to vote, I sat back and waited to be elected. I assumed the publicity around publication of my family law book and past media coverage of my promoting FLAC and CARE-related campaigns for legal and social reform would result in a successful outcome. I was wrong. When the first count was announced I wasn't even in the running for a seat, having secured only a miserable 186 first-preference votes. I was rapidly eliminated, my vote distributed to other candidates and ultimately the three candidates to represent Trinity in the Seanad were announced. They were Trevor West, a longstanding Trinity Senator, Conor Cruise O'Brien who had lost his Dáil seat having been a controversial Labour minister in the outgoing government, and Mary Robinson, a Senator since 1969 who had received substantial public prominence campaigning for lawful access to contraceptives and for legislation she had unsuccessfully attempted to have enacted on the issue.

I understood it had been unrealistic of me to expect to beat any of those elected but I regarded the vote I had secured as pretty abysmal and embarrassing. I determined that should I ever again be an election candidate I would be a lot more professional. I realised that I had a great deal to learn.

Some months after Garrett Fitzgerald assumed the leadership of Fine Gael from Liam Cosgrave, I decided to try and influence Fine Gael policy in the hope that the party would put some pressure on Fianna Fáil to implement badly needed reforms. John Boland TD was the Fine Gael Health spokesperson and Michael Keating TD the Law Reform spokesperson. Having contacted each of them, they were happy for me to voluntarily undertake some behind-the-scenes work and draft some Dáil questions which they tabled. I found Keating pleasant and genuinely interested in a variety of issues. Boland was gruff and uncommunicative. I was never sure what his real views were on any issue. While I provided some help to Keating in the 1977-79 period, my engagement (I wouldn't call it a relationship) with Boland ceased in 1978. It ended on the day I informed him that Carol was running a family planning and advice clinic in a shop on Harcourt Road, near Dublin's Kelly's Corner. I believed Boland should know as it was likely the clinic would generate some publicity and I did not want him to think I had concealed her involvement from him. After that conversation he ceased contacting me or returning my phone calls. At the time I suspected that he feared I was some anti-clerical left-wing sex-mad radical. It is more likely that he simply concluded it was politically expedient that he did not accidentally get entangled in any controversy that might involve the clinic as a result of any association with me.

For Fine Gael, family planning and contraceptives hit a political erogenous zone and were political hot potatoes. Since 1935 the importation of contraceptives into Ireland for sale and their sale in the State was a criminal offence, although their importation for personal use or their actual use did not violate the law. In practice, however, the law presented no barrier to the sale on prescription by pharmacies of the contraceptive pill. This was because the pretence was employed that it was sold as a menstrual-cycle regulator and not primarily for contraceptive purposes. The difficulty was that not all women could take the contraceptive pill and not all occasions of intimacy involved advanced planning!

When still in Trinity I was delighted when the constitutionality of the law was successfully challenged by a Mrs Mary (known to her family as May) McGee, with the Supreme Court in 1973 acknowledging that the law wrongly denied married couples reasonable access to contraceptives. In doing so, the Court determined it interfered with their right to plan their families and violated their right to marital privacy.

In response to the Supreme Court decision, in 1974, the Fine Gael Minister for Justice, Paddy Cooney, on behalf of the Fine Gael/Labour government brought before the Dáil controversial legislation to regulate the importation, manufacture and sale of contraceptives. Although the legislation was conservative and restrictive, making the purchase of contraceptives by "an unmarried person" a criminal offence, it was perceived as a liberal reform because it facilitated their purchase by "married" persons. (It said nothing about the use of contraceptives by the unmarried!) Its provisions were vehemently opposed by some Fine Gael and Labour TDs and also by the Fianna Fáil party, who disagreed with the Supreme Court and believed the law should continue to reflect Roman Catholic Church teaching. Fine Gael was compelled to allow a free vote to accommodate the party's internal divisions and as a result the Bill had been defeated. Sensationally, without any forewarning, the Fine Gael Taoiseach, Liam Cosgrave, together with his Fine Gael colleague Richard Burke, the Minister for Education, had taken the unprecedented step of voting against their own government's Bill. At the time I regarded the defeated Bill and a lot of the debate relating to it as more relevant to the Ireland of the 1930s than the realities of the 1970s.

Throughout the 1970s the growing Irish women's movement had protested against Ireland's outdated and restrictive laws on contraception and campaigned for reform. There was little real enthusiasm for effecting meaningful reform within Fianna Fáil and Fine Gael, and some divisions on the issue continued to exist within the smaller Labour Party. As a result organisations sprang up to get around the legal restrictions. The Family Planning Association, Family Planning Services and the Well Women Centre opened and not only provided family-planning counselling and advice but also made contraceptives freely available to those who sought them in return for a donation. The "donation" formula was perceived as providing protection against the possibility of being prosecuted for their sale or for importing them for sale. Fortunately, the Customs and gardaí turned a blind eye to the importation into the State of large volumes of condoms and other contraceptive devices and never questioned the "donation" not "sale" formula.

Much of the work undertaken in the three services was voluntary. They were all based in Dublin, couldn't fully meet the needs in the city and no services existed in the rest of the country. However, the provision of non-directive expert advice and counselling on family planning and crisis pregnancies was a crucial and vital service that the country sadly lacked, which each service provided.

From the time Brian Gallagher and I commenced working together, we provided legal advice to Family Planning Services (FPS) and, in 1978, on behalf of FPS we initiated High Court Judicial Review proceedings to overturn a ban imposed by the Censorship Board on a family-planning leaflet FPS had been publishing for some time. A judgement later delivered in similar proceedings successfully taken by the Family Planning Association, against a ban imposed on a similar leaflet it published, ensured the success of the FPS action. The bans generated the inevitable controversy. Carol, who was a qualified social worker, was particularly incensed by the Censorship Board's bans and believed additional family-planning services, including counselling were required. In 1978, together with two friends, she opened the Harcourt Family Planning Service on Harcourt Road. It was located in one of the premises my dad had originally jointly owned with my Uncle Jack, which I had inherited from Dad following his death. Operating rent free, their expenses were minimal. For about a year and a half Carol and her two friends provided free family planning counselling and advice, undertook pregnancy testing (for which they could lawfully charge) and provided condoms in return for donations. The service closed down shortly before the end of 1979 because all three were pregnant and shortly due to give birth!

Of course, the Harcourt Road Three hadn't planned simultaneous pregnancies. Early in 1979 Carol and I decided the time had come to start a family as had, unknown to us, one of Carol's friends working with her in Harcourt Road. However, the announcement of the third pregnancy was both unexpected and particularly welcome as for some considerable time the couple concerned had experienced difficulty in conceiving and specialist reproductive assistance had been unsuccessful. There was clearly something in the air in Harcourt Road! Visitors to the Family Planning Service in November 1979 may have had serious doubts about the reliability of the family-planning advice provided and the various brands of condoms on display as all of those working there were in an advanced stage of pregnancy.

Unsuccessful in finding reliable replacements for the first quarter of 1980 when all of the babies were due, just before Christmas 1979 the service closed its doors. But that was not the only Shatter involvement in reproductive politics.

Shortly prior to Christmas 1978 the Health (Family Planning) Bill was published on behalf of the Fianna Fáil government by Charlie Haughey, the Minister for Health, who a year later would take over from Jack Lynch as Taoiseach. Requested by the *Irish Times* to write a serious article analysing the Bill and its implications, I found the task virtually impossible.

The objective of the legislation was to regulate family planning services, to confine the sale of contraceptives to pharmacies and only permit their sale where medically prescribed. Ireland was to become the first country in the world in which a doctor's prescription was required for the lawful sale of a packet of condoms. Moreover, a doctor was only allowed to provide the required prescription to a person who in the doctor's opinion sought "contraceptives for the purpose, bona fide, of family planning or for adequate medical reasons and in appropriate circumstances".

The importation of contraceptives for sale on prescription in pharmacies was permitted but the Bill rendered it unlawful to import contraceptives to give away in return for donations. While the Bill permitted travellers to import contraceptives as part of their "personal luggage" when entering the State, it only did so where their "quantity is not such as to indicate they are not solely" for the travellers' "personal use". Whilst condoms in luggage were okay, it seemed bringing a condom into the State in a jacket pocket was to become a criminal offence. It was also to be an offence to import them as a gift for a friend.

The Bill, although on a serious issue, was a gift to comedy and raised more questions than it answered. How was a doctor to determine whether contraceptives were sought for purposes other than family planning and what did that mean? Did prescribing condoms to simply enjoy safe sexual intimacy and to avoid contracting a sexually transmitted infection fall foul of the law? When writing a prescription was the doctor to specify the "sensitivity" factor of the permitted condom and its colour? As the courts had confined "family rights" under the Constitution to married couples, was it unlawful to furnish a single person with a prescription for contraceptives? If so, should doctors before prescribing contraceptives and pharmacists before selling them require the production of a marriage certificate?

Chaim Factor (1979)

And there was a requirement that they be used in "appropriate circumstances".

Did this mean a patient had to designate the location or room in which anticipated sexual intercourse would take

Chaim Factor (1979)

place for a doctor's approval? In assessing whether a patient seeking condoms was acting bona fide, was the doctor required to ensure the patient would only engage in sexual intimacy with their spouse and did this "good faith" condition require a verification home visit? While prescriptions for the pill could be relatively straightforward, directing that a patient take one a day, what about condoms? Before issuing a prescription was a doctor to look into the whites of the eyes of each male patient to determine whether he was a five, ten, fifteen or twenty condoms a month man? And these were only some of the questions raised by the Bill!

For the customs authorities the Bill had a unique set of difficulties. Whilst travellers were allowed to import condoms in their "luggage" for their "personal use", no guidance was given on how to determine the maximum number of condoms any individual traveller could be expected to use nor did the Bill specify a "use by" time frame! There was also no way in which anyone could establish whether a particular condom had been used by the traveller who imported it after it had been disposed of by the user! Of course, if such a law was enacted today and it required for verification purposes the collection by a government agency of all used condoms, DNA testing could check whether a condom's contents matched the DNA of the traveller claiming to have imported it for his "personal use". An entire new industry together with thousands of new jobs could result from such a brilliant political initiative! Whether this is something worth considering is for you to judge.

Chaim Factor (1979)

The Bill was legal nonsense but was regarded by some political commentators as politically astute or "cute". Instead of the article requested by the *Irish Times*, over the 1978 Christmas break I rapidly wrote a short satirical book on the Bill entitled *Family Planning Irish Style* which was brilliantly illustrated by cartoons drawn by Chaim Factor, a good friend and accomplished artist and sculptor. By early March 1979 the book was printed, published and launched by then Senator Mary Robinson who many years later, in November 1990, would be elected President of Ireland.

The launch took place in the Old Dublin Restaurant in Dublin's Francis Street, owned by Maurice and Bertha Cohen, who were close friends. To mark the occasion Chaim's original illustrations were framed and exhibited on the restaurant's walls. It was the second occasion Francis Street had played a big role in my life.

It was the *Irish Time*'s original request for an article which triggered the idea for the book. Someone in the paper was obviously delighted with it as it gave the launch great coverage and reproduced one of Chaim's very funny cartoons. To our delight, within a short time of publication it appeared in the bestsellers list and within four weeks it sold out and a second print run was required.

A week prior to the book's publication Charles Haughey described his Bill as "an Irish solution to an Irish problem". I don't know whether he ever read our parody of his legislative initiative but we did delight in extracts from *Family Planning Irish Style* being quoted during the parliamentary debates on his Bill. Its bizarre provisions were enacted by the 23rd July 1979.

The legislation was totally out of touch with social reality on an issue of huge importance to many people. Whilst a ministerial order was made bringing it into force on the 1st November 1980 and it remained on the statute books unchanged until 1985, it was never fully enforced and did not have the effect intended. Family Planning Clinics continued to supply contraceptives and no one was ever arrested and prosecuted for importing more condoms in their luggage than they were physically capable of personally using. What I didn't know or anticipate in 1979 was that six years later, as a TD, I would participate in the Dáil debate on the legislative amendments made to Haughey's Act which resulted in the enactment of the liberalising Health (Family Planning)(Amendment) Act 1985. While it repealed some of the restrictive provisions contained in the 1979 Act and enabled the sale of condoms without prescription, as a legislative measure to reflect and address social reality it still had a common-sense deficit. In a State with significant numbers of children conceived as a result of intimacy between teenage boys and girls, it confined the lawful sale of condoms without prescription to over-18s. There was little likelihood of sexually active or promiscuous fifteen or sixteen-year-olds calling in to their family doctor for a prescription for condoms. It wasn't until 1993 that this age restriction was totally removed.

For me, Haughey's legislation and the publication of *Family Planning Irish Style* had unanticipated consequences. During the first six months of 1979, Haughey's Bill generated substantial public controversy, with the Catholic Church resolutely opposed to the measure despite its restrictive legislative idiosyncrasies. Iconic broadcaster and *Late Late Show* host, Gay Byrne, found the topic irresistible and in late April or early May 1979, together with Anne Connolly of the Well Woman Centre, I was a guest on the show. Displayed on a table in studio was a variety of different brands and types of packaged condoms supplied by the Well Woman Centre which were discussed and explained by Anne Connolly in response to questions from Gay Byrne. When finished with the table and its display, Gay then turned to me and I responded to questions about the content and peculiarities of the Haughey Bill. The show went well but added fuel to an already-running controversy. It was the first time condoms in their varied colours and designs had been prominently displayed on RTÉ television and there was a public outcry and howls of outrage from those who vehemently on theological grounds opposed any type of what was called "artificial contraception". Criticism was voiced that the show threatened Catholic moral values (such criticism was not uncommon down the years) whilst those campaigning for reform who disliked Haughey's Bill were delighted with Gay Byrne's courage. In the annals of the *Late Late* that particular show joined many others which today are regarded as having broken down barriers, positively contributing to a more tolerant Ireland, freed from the suffocating influence of the Catholic Church.

Life is full of coincidences. Just a few days before the *Late Late* was broadcast, Peter Prendergast, who was Fine Gael's general secretary, phoned me to enquire whether I was interested in being a Fine Gael candidate for the Whitechurch area, which included Rathfarnham, Knocklyon, Ballyboden and all of Ballinteer, in the forthcoming June local elections. As a result of my experience assisting Michael Keating, out of admiration for Garrett Fitzgerald and motivated by my dislike of Haughey and Fianna Fáil's approach to politics, just two months earlier I had joined the Terenure branch of Fine Gael. I joined Terenure because it was Ritchie Ryan's branch, its members met near to our home and I knew no one in my local Rathfarnham branch. Running as a local election candidate seeking membership of Dublin County Council had never occurred to me and I knew nothing about local government. Intrigued by the proposition, having discussed it with Carol, twenty-four hours later I confirmed my interest. Prendergast informed me that a week later (three days after the *Late Late Show*), a convention would be held for the local Fine Gael members to select their two candidates and he would arrange for me to be proposed as a candidate. As I knew none of the voting members and had never been at a political convention, I explained that I believed it unlikely I would succeed in being selected. "Well, if you are not," he responded, "Garrett will put you on the ticket but please don't tell anyone that." Somewhat naively I believed Garrett Fitzgerald knew of and valued my various involvements. I would later discover he knew nothing about me, understandably had no memory of our previously meeting and that in matters of candidates and organisation he relied entirely on Peter Prendergast's skill, insight and political intuition.

Prendergast made it clear to me that to avoid upset it was preferable I was selected at the Convention rather than be imposed on the ticket by Fine Gael headquarters and arranged that I meet up with Anne O'Connell, who he explained was secretary of the Emmet Branch (named after Robert Emmet, the Irish Republican and rebel leader, executed for treason in 1803 at the age of twenty-five) in Rathfarnham. Anne was an experienced political operative and she was assigned to tune me in, introduce me to the voting convention delegates and mind me.

We hit it off the moment we met. She was voluble, extrovert and unconventional. I learned that a large number of the Emmet Branch members were also members of the Ballyroan Ladies Bridge club in Rathfarnham. Anne played bridge there regularly and the Emmet Branch had a substantial number of voting delegates. In the days that followed she drove me around to the homes of every one of them to canvass their support. There was not enough time to meet all the delegates from other branches but we managed to visit some and left letters in the homes of those we missed.

Everything seemed to be going unexpectedly well till the Saturday morning after my *Late Late Show* appearance. Early that morning, Alan Benson, who had for some years been a member of the Mount Merrion branch of Fine Gael, phoned. He was unusually agitated. Alan had history in Fine Gael, being among a number of Mount Merrion members who kicked up an enormous row when in 1974 Dick Burke, who represented the constituency in the Dáil, had voted against Paddy Cooney's Family Planning Bill. I had told Alan my name was to be proposed as a candidate for election to Dublin County Council. Although he believed our family planning and contraception laws required radical change, he was concerned my political career would be finished before it got started as a result of the previous night's TV show.

"Why in the name of God did you go on that show just three nights before the Convention? Do you not realise how conservative some of the Fine Gael branch members are?" he asked.

"My views on our contraceptive laws aren't exactly a State secret!" I replied, and then to cheer him up I continued, "Well, look on the bright side – at least I didn't model one and put it on display in all its glory!"

His good-humoured response to that is unprintable. All I will record here is that the phone call ended with a lot of laughter.

My lobbying of the Fine Gael members continued throughout that weekend and I discovered they weren't all as conservative as Alan feared. A number were delighted with my *Late Late* appearance and thought it would prove of great electoral benefit. Others were less enthusiastic. By the Sunday evening I discovered that a small number of members were spreading the rumour that I was a rampant abortionist!

The convention took place in a packed meeting room upstairs in the Yellow House pub in Rathfarnham. Candidates proposed and speeches delivered, the voting took place. Anne O'Connell was convinced from the feedback that a nomination was in the bag. I had my doubts, despite my lack of political experience. When the result was announced, I had failed to get the nomination by two votes. The selected candidates were a sitting councillor, Myles Tierney, and George McHugh, a member of the Ballinteer Branch. Anne O'Connell was devastated. I was just relieved that I had come close and not made a fool of myself. Two days later I was added to the ticket.

There were four councillors to be elected to represent the Whitechurch area and Fine Gael had no hope of winning more than two seats. Usually Fine Gael headquarters adding a candidate generated local controversy but despite my addition making it more difficult for both Myles and George to win a seat there was no hassle. As a sitting councillor Myles had great insight and expertise on all the local major and minor council issues and very generously took time out to give me a very helpful detailed briefing. Throughout the campaign both Myles and George were totally decent and honourable and we each worked as hard as possible to generate support.

Looking back on it now, I had a very benign introduction to the rough and tumble of electoral contests under the proportional-representation system in a multi-seat constituency. I would later learn that the contest for votes can generate destructive hostility, mistrust, and poisonous rivalry between candidates nominally running together as colleagues within the one party.

Anne O'Connell minded me throughout the 1979 local election campaign. I absented myself from Gallagher Shatter for most of the three weeks preceding polling day and under Anne's tutelage canvassed morning, noon and night. Carol was working in Harcourt Road and most mornings just Anne and I tramped the housing estates of Knocklyon, Rathfarnham, Ballyboden and Ballinteer. In the afternoons and evenings we were accompanied by the bridge club members of Emmet Branch and some other branch members. Most evenings and every weekend Carol joined us. Anne ran the operation with military precision. In addition to door-to-door canvassing, leaflets were printed and dropped, I held coffee mornings together with Carol, shopping centres were repetitively visited and church Masses attended. Over three weekends I was a continuing presence outside shopping centres greeting customers and outside churches engaging with parishioners after Mass.

The churches and shopping centres also figured in our weekday schedule, the day starting with my meeting those exiting early morning Mass. Over the three weeks I met many of the same voters seven or eight times. By week three I was on first-name terms with hundreds of people I hadn't ever met before our campaign started.

The campaign was extraordinarily intense and to add to the excitement at the start of its first week, having carried out her own pregnancy test, Carol announced to my delight that she was pregnant. Our first child was due in just over seven months.

Whilst I treated the campaign seriously there was a legion of funny incidents. Standing outside Rathfarnham Church's gates one very windy weekday morning as the first parishioners exited the church doors after ten o'clock Mass a huge gust of wind blew Anne's very wide and long skirt up in the air around her waist as she loudly proclaimed "Feck, I forgot to put my knickers on!" I instantly had a vision of our being arrested for Anne flashing outside the church gates and I convulsed in laughter. As she scrambled to push the elevated skirt back down I was relieved that the approaching elderly parishioners were sufficient distance away to have not fully appreciated the carry-on. I cheerfully greeted them as they passed by, looking as if butter wouldn't melt in my mouth.

Standing at the front door of a house in Rathfarnham, emphasising my dedication, Anne informed the woman she was talking to that upon my election I would be opening a weekly clinic in Rathfarnham but failed to explain what type of clinic. "Grand then, I'll be down to Dr Shatter for the false teeth so," she happily exclaimed.

The *Late Late* regularly came up at doors as a positive. "And what flavour do those condoms come in?" was an enquiry from a woman in her mid-50s with a wink and a mischievous twinkle in her eye.

But it wasn't all plain sailing. "You're the Jewish abortionist" was the accusation at one door and some negative comment and hostility over the contraceptive issue emerged during week two of the campaign. It was, however, a good deal less than I anticipated and by the end of the campaign I believed my *Late Late Show* appearance to have been a positive.

Of course, I was a candidate in one of the most liberal constituencies in Ireland. I also discovered that I had substantial support from members of the local Church of Ireland community because of the High School and Trinity College connections. Not only did I meet many of the parents of former High School mates but many parents whose children were then High School pupils. My greatest disappointment was when one of my former teachers, who I particularly liked, upon our meeting outside his house on the Lower Dodder Road announced to my surprise that he wouldn't even give me a preference vote because Fianna Fáil was his party.

◄○► ◄○► ◄○►

Polling day arrived and much of it was spent standing outside Ballyroan polling station in Rathfarnham shaking hands and urging voters to give me their No 1 vote. I was accompanied by Carol and an army of Emmett Branch members and supporters covered in *Vote Shatter No 1* stickers.

In the late afternoon I was verbally accosted by an angry middle-aged man who announced he was a Knocklyon resident and a potential Fine Gael supporter. He was not going to vote for me or any Fine Gael candidate because no one from the party ever had the courtesy to call to his house to seek his vote. Upon my asking, he detailed the exact location of his home which was a detached property in Knocklyon at the end of a long driveway. Knowing the area had been comprehensively canvassed, I immediately knew the answer.

"Do you have a very large Alsatian dog?" I asked.

"I do," he answered, looking puzzled.

"Well, five nights ago my wife, Carol, who is pregnant, had to run down your driveway and slam your gate shut to escape from your barking Alsatian when it viciously charged at her. If not for the dog you would have been canvassed," I quietly explained. The wind taken out of his sails, I then called Carol over, saying, "This is the guy whose dog chased you."

The aggression disappeared. Looking embarrassed, he apologised and promised me his No 1 vote. Exiting from the polling station, he gave me a friendly pat on the back, saying "I did that" and walked to his car.

Carol had five nights earlier been lucky to avoid getting bitten (as would happen to me some years later when canvassing in a by-election) but was delighted she had secured a first-preference vote. She regarded it as a small victory on the political battlefield!

The election over, the count followed. Much to my surprise I topped the poll with 2,497 first-preference votes. Closest to me and also elected to the Council was Fianna Fáil's Tom Kitt with 1,552. Tom in 1987 would go on to be elected as a TD and some years later become government chief whip. Myles Tierney who secured 1,142 votes was also elected once the transferred votes were counted, including 600 votes secured by George McHugh. Many of those who had canvassed throughout the three-week campaign were at the election count to celebrate the result, including Alan Benson. Having previously worried over my *Late Late* appearance he now laughingly explained my victory as the South Dublin pro-condom vote.

I attributed the successful outcome to my enthusiastic army of canvassers and their general: the Ballyroan Ladies Bridge club members and Anne O'Connell. After the debacle of my Seanad election candidacy, I had, thanks to them, at the age of twenty-eight successfully taken the first step on the political road leading to Leinster House.

Chapter 16

Horsehair, Two Goldfish and a Newt!

During 1977 to 1981 I spent a large amount of my time working as a lawyer. Becoming a member of Dublin County Council added to my work burden but I am an early riser, and on days when afternoons were taken up with Council meetings, I frequently made up for my absence from our law firm by starting work sometime between 5 am. and 6 a.m. on files I took home. A second edition of my family law book was scheduled to be published in 1981. Commencing January 1980, when not under office pressures, I found early morning an ideal time to write uninterrupted by phone calls. By April 1981 the second edition was completed and its publication was launched by the then President of the High Court, Mr Justice Thomas Finlay, at a reception held in the Law Society in July 1981.

◄o► ◄o► ◄o►

From the moment Brian and I were open for business as Gallagher Shatter we were inundated with a broad range of challenging and interesting legal work. My particular focus was on constitutional and family law. Publicity from publication of my family law book resulted in an upsurge in the already large number of family law clients advised by the firm before my arrival. They presented with a wide variety of family difficulties. Each of us having been deeply involved in FLAC for many years, we willingly voluntarily advised and represented before the District Courts a substantial number of women who could not afford to pay legal fees. By 1980 we realised that we were representing so many non-fee-paying clients that the annual salary paid to our secretarial and back-up staff exceeded the modest sum each of us was earning as partners! As the increase in client numbers had required that we move premises from Hume Street to Ely Place, based on the firm's expenses we realised it was not sustainable to operate on that basis. Fortunately, the government-sponsored law centres opened in 1980 and that enabled us to take a more commercial approach and to confine pro bono cases to those which fell outside the state civil legal-aid scheme, such as constitutional actions, or unique actions of difficulty and merit to which we believed we could bring particular expertise.

In the first year of our working together, other than in District Court proceedings where litigation was involved, like all other solicitors I instructed barristers to both draft court papers and undertake court advocacy on behalf of clients I was advising. The barristers I instructed that year had all previously been instructed to represent clients by either or both Brian and his father, were very accomplished, and the vast majority were destined for judicial appointment to the High Court and a number onwards to the Supreme Court. As they negotiated the settlement of family law disputes or acted as advocates in court, I realised that the differences between what I had been doing in the District Court and what they were doing in the High Court were primarily the stage setting, the greater range of issues that could be addressed and the greater time afforded to the High Court to consider the complexities of a family dispute. I also discovered in some cases that I had a greater familiarity with relevant aspects of family law than the barristers instructed who arrived in court with a copy of my book amongst their papers.

Although legislation pioneered in 1971 by Des O'Malley, when Minister for Justice, for the first time enabled solicitors conduct advocacy in all our higher courts, such advocacy in reality had continued to be the exclusive preserve of barristers who were members of the Bar Library based in the Four Courts. I determined to take the plunge and from early 1978 gave clients the option of either my acting as their advocate in High and Supreme Court cases or going the traditional route of instructing one or more barristers (counsel) to do so. Most of those who consulted with me and who had to resort to court proceedings took the first option.

My undertaking High Court advocacy work resulted in significant savings to clients in legal fees. Whilst additional solicitor's fees were charged for the additional work involved, they were substantially less than the additional fees clients would have incurred if, as was traditional, both senior and junior counsel represented them in court.

As a twenty-seven-year-old recently qualified solicitor, my appearing in the High Court representing clients without counsel upset and annoyed some members of the Bar Library, whilst others took it in their stride. The former regarded it as an impertinent disruption and threat to the comfortable status quo. It also annoyed some solicitors. I believe that on occasion they found it difficult to explain to their clients why they were paying for three or four lawyers to represent them in court when their spouse required only one!

In the early years of my acting as an advocate in the High Court there were occasions when I found myself opposed in court by a virtual army of experienced lawyers comprising two senior and one junior counsel accompanied by one or two solicitors. I was usually accompanied only by one of our firm's apprentices or assistant solicitors whose role was to take notes when I was on my feet in court, hand relevant papers to the judge when required and marshall witnesses in and out of the courtroom.

Prior to a court hearing family proceedings, it was usual on the day of the hearing to engage in discussions to attempt an amicable resolution of a family dispute, even where such resolution had not earlier proved possible. In marital-breakdown cases this involved agreements being negotiated and reached on behalf of estranged spouses to enable their permanent separation and to resolve a variety of issues in dispute, including those relating to maintenance support, finance, property, child custody and contact/access, ownership of and residence in the family home and succession (inheritance) rights. The option of divorce did not exist because of the constitutional ban and did not become available until after the divorce referendum held in 1995.

In the first few months of my solely representing clients in the High Court, some Senior Counsel declined to directly talk to or engage with me as they considered doing so contrary to Bar Library etiquette or beneath their dignity. Their solicitors were dispatched to negotiate attempted settlements and with some amusement I observed from a distance heated discussions within my opposing legal teams about the dilemma posed by my not being accompanied by one or more of their Bar Library colleagues. Inevitably, where positive progress was made in my initial engagement with an opposing solicitor and complex issues were involved, the barristers got over themselves and eventually engaged directly with me. After the first nine months or so most barristers who experienced initial difficulty with my approach, whilst not entirely happy, became reconciled to my representing clients without counsel. A small number for some years did not and clearly deeply resented having to negotiate with a mere solicitor.

In the early days the prevailing court etiquette highlighted for me the extent to which the Irish legal profession was captured in an eighteenth-century English colonial-era time warp. As a solicitor I could competently present a case in the High Court wearing my business suit but the barristers opposite me were required to wear a uniform including gowns and wigs made of horsehair that would not have been out of place two centuries earlier in the English royal court of George the Third. I believed family disputes sufficiently traumatic for those involved without such unnecessary antiquated regalia intimidating and upsetting estranged spouses and adding to the trauma of family litigation. I rapidly concluded that less not more formality would be beneficial and, just over ten years after I commenced undertaking High Court advocacy, I succeeded as a TD in having enacted, from the opposition Dáil benches, my Judicial Separation and Family Law Reform Act 1989 which radically reformed our separation laws. In doing so, it provided more comprehensive financial and property protections for dependent spouses, encouraged the resolution of family disputes by mediation and controversially, with much Bar Library resistance, ended the wearing of wigs and gowns in family law cases by both judges and barristers. The Act of 1989 also laid the crucial legal foundation for the successful referendum held in 1995 which ended the constitutional ban on divorce and facilitated the enactment of divorce legislation.

Court seating was another area of confusion, absurdity and complexity. Traditionally, Senior Counsel sat at a large front-row table in the High Court with Junior Counsel sitting behind them on what is called the "junior bench" with totally inadequate space for court papers and legal textbooks. Solicitors traditionally sat below the judge's dais on the far side of the table looking at the barristers engaged in the court hearing. As a solicitor advocate I was entitled to share the seating used by Senior Counsel to present my client's case and question witnesses. On two occasions different Senior Counsel, upon walking into court before the judge's arrival, as I arranged my papers for an imminent court hearing, ordered me to move off to the other side of the table. On the first occasion I simply and quietly refused. On the second occasion I again refused, this time responding with good humour and a smile, saying that an application requiring me to do so could be made to the judge, who that day happened to be the President of the High Court, Mr Justice Thomas Finlay. A few minutes later Judge Finlay's crier placed some papers and a copy of my family law book on the judge's table, the judge came into court, those present stood up and bowed and they sat down only after he had done so. The court registrar started calling over the names of the family cases to be mentioned or heard that day and the court progressed its business. No application was made for a judicial order to have me evicted to the other side of the table!

There were occasions both in the early and in the following years when family cases commenced hearing in the High Court in the Four Courts and a Senior Counsel representing the other side did not appear, resulting in the instructed Junior Counsel alone undertaking the court advocacy. When that occurred I regarded it as totally bizarre that Bar Library and court etiquette required Junior Counsel, who were frequently older and more experienced than me, to sit behind me and struggle with balancing important papers on an obviously inadequate space. I thought it nonsensical that in such circumstances my opponent could not use the vacant part of the large front table that was available for use by a Senior Counsel. Fortunately, during the early years not all High Court family cases were heard in the main Four Courts building. Many were heard in Ormond House which was located on Ormond Quay, just a few minutes' walk from the Four Courts building. In that High Court room there was one long table at which both senior and junior counsel could sit together side by side. It was when representing clients in Ormond House that a number of unexpected and funny incidents occurred.

In those days a regular occurrence was spouses petitioning the court for what was known as a Divorce a Mensa et Thoro. In fact it wasn't a divorce at all but merely a court separation decree. ("Mensa et Thoro" was the Latin terminology for "bed and board". Some thought a better translation would be "bed and bull"!) The client I was representing was alleging her husband guilty of cruelty and unnatural practices. A separation sought on the ground of unnatural practices was a rarity and it was the first time I had pleaded such a case. Walking into court I was carrying a number of heavy old law reports containing judgements delivered by the Ecclesiastical Courts of the Church of Ireland over one hundred years earlier which illustrated conduct that constituted an unnatural practice. Most of the examples given concerned odd and intimate behaviour with farm animals. Bending over the legal practitioners' table to place the books of reports on it, I heard a ripping sound. Reaching behind me I discovered, to my horror, that the entire seam of my suit trousers had split and the material was hanging limply down on both sides. I rapidly sat down to await the judge's arrival. Fortunately, my client and her estranged husband were sitting along a side wall and were totally oblivious to my personal dilemma and remained so when ten minutes later I stood up, leant back and opened the case to the court, hoping my suit jacket was providing my exposed area with some cover. During the course of my court opening I had to describe for the judge past examples of various lurid incidents detailed in the law reports as unnatural practices knowing that my semi-naked bottom, covered only by a brief pair of underpants, was partially on display through the courtroom window. Luckily, we were three floors up and no one was sitting behind me as the court hearing was held in camera, that is in private. Only the estranged couple and their lawyers were allowed in court. When the court adjourned for lunch I had just enough time to drive home, change my suit and return to the courtroom before the case continued.

Family law and marital breakdown disputes are always both sad and very traumatic for those involved. It is crucial that this is always understood by their lawyers but there are occasions when something unexpected happens and restraining laughter borders on the impossible.

In one of my earlier cases, amongst the many serious complaints made by a wife was an allegation that prior to marriage her husband had persuaded her that on random occasions he suffered from unexpected temporary blindness and that the only cure for his blindness was immediate intercourse, with him having a successful climax. It was the climax which he claimed restored his lost sight. I could see the judge's incredulous reaction to this part of her evidence and then committed the cardinal sin all lawyers should avoid. I asked a question to which I did not already know the answer.

"And did the cure always work?" I enquired as an afterthought.

"Ah, Mr. Shatter," she exclaimed, "most times it did but sometimes we had to have a second run at it!"

Luckily, with that her evidence concluded.

I sat down having heard the unexpected response and waited for the husband's barrister to commence cross-examination but there was nothing but silence. I looked up at the bench and all I could see was the judge's head dipped down as low as possible and his shoulders shaking. Looking at my opponent, he was waiting for the judge's silent laughter to stop with an enormous grin on his face. I couldn't then restrain myself from laughing. The poor client sat looking bewildered in the witness box until everyone resumed a serious demeanour, service resumed and the case proceeded. As the outcome was successful she never questioned me about my laughter in court.

Another time in the Four Courts I was representing an estranged wife separating from a parsimonious husband and the main dispute was over maintenance support. He was clearly a difficult client and must have insisted that his barrister, when cross-examining my client, ask questions that no sane barrister would ever want to ask. As it happened, he was represented by a very good member of the bar with considerable expertise in family law. He had also in its early days been involved in FLAC and would later in his career be a distinguished member of the judiciary. His riding instructions clearly were to establish my client was profligate with money.

Towards the end of his questioning her on her maintenance claim and household expenditure he asserted, "And you have two dogs," and then asked, "How much do they cost to feed each week?" After she had responded the next question was "And there is a cat. How much each week does the cat cost?" Upon her answering, he stridently continued, as no doubt required by his client, "And there are two goldfish and a newt. How much each week do they cost?" As my client spluttered and the judge looked askance, I turned around and gave the barrister a you-can't-be-serious look. He responded with a wink and sat down, having completed his cross-examination. Sitting at the front of the court I had to ram a handkerchief into my mouth to restrain my laughter. I have little doubt that it was the last question asked which resulted in my client benefiting from a particularly generous maintenance-support court order. Unfortunately, the question wasn't answered by my client, so I never got to know the weekly cost of feeding two goldfish and a pet newt!

There was, of course, little room for laughter when dealing with broken marriages, child kidnappings, child custody fights and adoption disputes, but helping resolve very real personal problems and finding constructive, beneficial, just and fair solutions to family conflict without the need for a court contest was always the most satisfying outcome. Resolving a family conflict in this way avoided the uncertainties of a judicial decision and enabled estranged spouses and parents, with legal assistance, to construct their own solution. Estranged parents doing so also enhanced the possibility of them fully co-operating with each other in implementing sensible arrangements which facilitated each of them maintaining a meaningful relationship with their children. Understandably, in domestic child kidnappings and adoption disputes this was rarely possible. In High Court nullity proceedings, in which a court order was sought that a marriage was null and void, a judicial determination was essential as no couple could by agreement nullify their marriage.

A readily identifiable difficulty with family court proceedings is that while some members of the judiciary hear and determine family cases with great insight and expertise, others utterly lack the capacity to do so. When commencing legal practice with Brian Gallagher I presumed this was just a District Court problem but I rapidly learnt it extended into the High Court. When some years later the Circuit Court acquired a major role in family cases, it was also clearly evident in that court. This difficulty persisted throughout my thirty-five years of legal practice which ended in 2011. It is the reason why for decades I advocated the creation of specialist family courts with specially skilled and trained judges assisted by fully trained supportive back-up personnel and a state-wide in-court mediation service. It was my announced objective when Minister for Justice to establish such courts and have them up and running by October 2015 but this never happened because of my unexpected premature departure from government in May 2014.

At a very early stage when I first represented clients in the High Court the unsuitability of some members of the High Court judiciary to hear family cases became clear. Unfortunately, as family cases were heard in private to protect the anonymity of family members, this was concealed from public view. For many years I believed it was in the public interest that contentious family court cases have greater transparency and as Minister for Justice I finally had an opportunity to facilitate this. The Courts Act 2013, which I steered through the Dáil, now grants media access to report family law court hearings on condition that the anonymity of family law litigants continues to be preserved. Unfortunately, very limited use has been made to date of the access given to do so.

I was genuinely shocked by two examples of outrageous and inappropriate judicial behaviour which occurred in my early years of High Court advocacy in the late 1970s.

A young couple had married and, due to the husband's psychological difficulties, after the passage of six years their marriage remained unconsummated. There was no identifiable physical barrier to sexual intercourse, medical evidence confirmed the wife remained a virgin and counselling and psychiatric assistance had not solved the problem. The husband's consultant physician confirmed that he had referred the husband to a consultant psychiatrist because there was no physiological reason for the difficulties he was experiencing. Whilst they remained on good terms the couple concluded, having received legal advice, that the High Court should be asked to declare their marriage null and void on the ground of impotence. The case was heard by the High Court and I represented the wife. The judge was well known for his gruff manner but I expected he would bring some humanity to a court hearing which was obviously enormously difficult for the couple and which involved two clearly distressed, articulate and educated young people.

I initially explained the background to the case and the content of the medical and psychiatric reports. My client was then called to give evidence. Unusually, the judge insisted she remain standing in the witness box throughout her evidence and not sit down. It was necessary for the court to hear evidence of the unfortunate couples attempts at intercourse and of their inability to fully engage but the level of detail the judge required of their intimacy was way beyond what I believed was necessary or appropriate. The greater the detail, the greater her distress until she dissolved into tears. The judge insisted she continue to stand, despite my request that she be permitted to sit down, because he wanted "to have a full look at her to judge her veracity".

My client was an attractive woman who had dressed smartly for court. During her evidence I became increasingly disturbed by the judge's manner of staring at her and looking her up and down but had to remain respectful towards him. Upon her evidence concluding, the husband's barrister had no questions. The required medical evidence given was unchallenged and the husband confirmed the truth of what the court had already been told. Noteworthy for a family law case, the couple were not at war or in conflict with each other. They each in their evidence informed the court they remained friends and regretted that they had no choice but to go their separate ways. Their evidence was given more in sorrow than in anger. There could be no reason to doubt their veracity or to conclude that they had fabricated a false story to legally end their marriage and be free to remarry.

At the end of the evidence, having detailed the relevant law, I expected the annulment decree sought would be granted. Instead the judge announced he would deliver judgement another day. Some weeks later, delivering a written judgement, he threw out the case stating that he was not satisfied with the evidence he had heard nor believed that their marriage had not been consummated. He had little doubt the couple had agreed to end their marriage and essentially concluded they had collusively given perjured evidence. There was nothing said in court on which the decision delivered could be properly based. I was outraged by the judgement delivered and the treatment of my client. To this day I believe that my client's attractive physical appearance alone resulted in the judge disbelieving the evidence given by her and her husband of his sexual difficulty. In his head no man could fail to perform with such an attractive woman. The denial of the nullity decree and the judge's pejorative comments caused my client enormous distress which I'm sure was shared by her husband.

The indefensible decision of the High Court judge resulted a year later in 1979 in my first Supreme Court appeal. Having read the court papers, the transcript of evidence and heard legal submissions, the Supreme Court granted the nullity decree concluding that "a decree of nullity was the only verdict open to the court on the evidence given", and severely criticised the High Court judgement. Delivering the Supreme Court's judgement, Judge Seamus Henchy's criticism of the High Court judge was withering. "It is not in accordance with the proper administration of justice to cast aside the corroborated and unquestioned evidence of witnesses, still less to impute collusion or perjury to them, when they were not given any opportunity of rebutting such an accusation," he firmly stated. He then added: "To do so in this case was, in effect, to condemn them unheard which is contrary to natural justice."

Whilst I was delighted with the Supreme Court outcome, I knew that if a different judge had first been allocated to hear the couple's case, the appeal to the Supreme Court would have been unnecessary. It was a stark illustration at an early stage in my career as a young lawyer of the uncertainties surrounding the outcome of court proceedings, no matter how straightforward a case may appear. What I didn't know was that thirty-six years later I would re-learn that lesson in a very personal way when losing High Court proceedings I felt compelled to initiate to defend my good name and reputation. I also did not know that, having been the Minister responsible for the creation of a Court of Appeal, established to improve the efficiency of our court system, and having successfully appealed to that court, I would then become embroiled in a Supreme

Court appeal that awaits hearing. Central to it all, coincidentally, is the principle that "to condemn" someone "unheard" is "contrary to natural justice". Oddly, I would travel a full circle since my very first appearance as an advocate before the Supreme Court. Life truly is a funny and unpredictable business but the inside story of all of that is for another day.

An example of inappropriate judicial behaviour in a family court action with less serious consequences occurred in a child kidnapping case heard in the High Court in which my opponent was a young junior counsel, Adrian Hardiman, who would many years later be appointed as a judge to the Supreme Court. In 1978 a two-year-old child was kidnapped from his mother in Belfast by the child's father. At the request of the RUC, members of the gardaí stopped the father in the Republic on the main Belfast to Dublin road and the child was temporarily placed in care with the Eastern Health Board. I was instructed by the North's child-care authority to seek an emergency court order for the child's return home to Belfast. Court papers prepared, they were served on the father, who was being held in Garda custody. The mother travelled by train to Dublin for the court hearing and the father was escorted to court in handcuffs by two Garda members. I understood there was no legitimate explanation for the father's conduct – the parents and child had always lived in the North – and that, if they had a disagreement over the child's care, it should have been resolved by the courts in Northern Ireland.

After the judge had first read the court papers, I detailed the applicable law and asked that a court order be made placing the child in his mother's custody and that she be allowed take him home to Belfast. Adrian Hardiman had barely started his replying court submission when the court adjourned for lunch.

The child had been brought to the Ormond Hotel on Dublin's Ormond Quay, which was close to the Four Courts, by an Eastern Health Board social worker and during lunchtime I accompanied the mother to the hotel as she wished to spend some time with her child. I asked the social worker to remain in the hotel with the child to enable mother and child rapidly return to the North if the court orders sought by me were granted.

The court was to resume at two o'clock but the judge failed to appear until about twenty past two and when he did he was intoxicated. Adrian Hardiman attempted to argue that the father was entitled to bring his child to Dublin, explained that he wanted custody of his child because the parents had broken up and proposed that the Dublin courts should hear a full-blown custody case and not the Northern Ireland courts. Worse for wear after a liquid lunch, the judge had no interest in Hardiman's argument. He constantly interrupted his submissions shouting, "You've got no case, you've got no case!" and "I'm sending the child up North!". Each time he uttered "You've got no case!" the judge leant forward and then falling back into his chair with his right leg kicked the back of the wooden divide which separated the judge from the court registrar's seat. Each kick produced a load thud, drowning out Hardiman's voice and resulted initially in the startled registrar jumping up from his seat. Hardiman continued to struggle to be heard but was getting nowhere. At the ninth or tenth thud as the judge fell back into his chair, Hardiman simply gave up despairingly and sat down.

"Right then!" the judge exclaimed. "Child to be released by Health Board to the mother, custody to mother, child to be immediately returned to the North, Registrar can inform the Health Board." Having granted all the court orders I sought, he then stood up and tottered out of the court through the judge's door.

Having furnished the court registrar with the phone number of the social worker's supervisor, I then rushed back with the mother to the Ormond Hotel. After the social worker had checked she could release the child, I put mother and child in a taxi to be driven back to Belfast. I anticipated that because of the manner in which he had been treated in the High Court, Hardiman might attempt to seek emergency intervention by the Supreme Court to temporarily stop the mother's departure. I knew the judge's conduct had been totally improper but I believed the correct outcome had been achieved. From my knowledge of the background, I believed the father's court response had no merit but I had some sympathy for Adrian Hardiman's plight. He was entitled to expect the judge would at least listen to his submissions before reaching any final conclusions.

Later that afternoon I learnt that Hardiman had been unsuccessful in seeking the Supreme Court's intervention. Had he been successful, it would have made little difference. By the time the court would have sat it was likely mother and child would have been within a few miles of crossing the border or would have already done so. As mobile phones did not then exist the mother would not have been contactable nor would there have been sufficient time for the gardaí to intervene.

There were, of course, many good High Court judges at that time hearing family law cases. Among the best were the President of the High Court, Judge Thomas Finlay, who was soon to be appointed Chief Justice, Judge Donal Barrington initially appointed to the High and then to the Supreme Court, Liam Hamilton later President of the High Court and then Chief Justice, and Judges Herbert McWilliam and Mella Carroll. They and some others applied a great deal of insight and common sense as well as legal expertise to the hearing and resolution of family conflicts and disputes.

The biggest and most far-reaching case in which I was involved in the late 1970s was what became known as the Murphy Tax Case. Knowing our willingness to litigate interesting constitutional cases on a "no foal, no fee" basis, Yvonne Scannel, a Trinity law lecturer involved in an organisation entitled The Married Persons Tax Reform Association, referred to me a married couple, Mary and Francis Murphy, both of whom were schoolteachers, to act as plaintiffs to challenge the constitutionality of our income-tax laws.

The challenge was based on the fact that had they not married and instead cohabited they would together incur a lower income-tax bill than the sum they were obliged to pay as a married couple. The contention was that our income-tax laws discriminated against married couples and the extra tax burden imposed on them violated the pledge contained in Article 41 of the constitution "to guard with special care the institution of marriage and protect it against attack". The case had enormous implications for our tax system and I knew its outcome would impact on many married couples throughout the State. I had no doubt that it would be resolutely and vigorously opposed by the State with Bar Library big guns instructed to defend the status quo. This was not a case for me to litigate on my own.

Rory O'Hanlon, a Senior Counsel who had been frequently instructed to represent clients by Brian's dad and Brian, was recruited to the cause and Mary Robinson, who was then a Junior Counsel. Rory some years later was appointed a High Court judge and there is no need for me to again reference Mary's future career path. Gallagher Shatter and counsel all agreed to charge no fees if the case was unsuccessful.

In the nine months' lead-up to the Murphy court hearing, an enormous amount of work was undertaken to identify comparative cases and judgements of relevance from across the globe, and a number were unearthed. Some I obtained from family law lawyers with whom I had been engaged in international family law work and some others from lawyers I had met at law conferences abroad. I can still recall wading through the English translation of a labyrinthine judgement of over 150 pages of the Greek courts that I received from a well-meaning Greek colleague, attempting to identify something relevant to our case contained in it. I was practically braindead by the time I had finished reading it and concluded that it said nothing that mattered that could assist in winning the Murphys' case.

The Murphys' constitutional claims were successful. The High Court judgement of Liam Hamilton in their favour, delivered in October 1979, was appealed to the Supreme Court and upheld by it on appeal in January 1980. In addition, the State was ordered to pay the Murphys' legal costs. For the Supreme Court appeal, Dermot Gleeson, a future Attorney General, replaced Rory O'Hanlon who was unavailable, and our legal team was boosted by the addition of the well-known Senior Counsel, Kevin Liston. By the time of the Supreme Court hearing, the State was represented by three senior and one junior counsel as well as the chief state solicitor's office, and the Murphys by two senior counsel and one junior in addition to Gallagher Shatter.

It was a huge victory which ensured that the State could never again require a married couple pay greater income tax than the tax payable by a cohabiting unmarried couple with an identical income. The Murphys, who were a modest quiet couple, were thrilled with their victory. So was I and the rest of our legal team. Our delight was justified as not only had we positively contributed to the State's constitutional jurisprudence and eased the tax burden of many thousands of married couples across the country, we were also going to get paid for doing so! We had been happy to represent Mary and Francis Murphy for free as we believed the taxation laws unfairly discriminated against married couples. However, getting paid for the work done was an additional welcome bonus.

Chapter 17

Psychopaths, Ducks and a General Election

Politically 1979 to 1981 was for me a learning experience. By the time I was elected to Dublin County Council the gloss had gone off the Taoiseach Jack Lynch's stunning general-election victory for Fianna Fáil in 1977 which had restored that party to government with an overall Dáil majority. The Fianna Fáil victory had resulted from a giveaway election manifesto promising the abolition of rates and car tax, reduced income tax and increased government expenditure. The State's finances were in a vulnerable position and had rapidly deteriorated as public expenditure and borrowings increased and revenue resources decreased. A second oil crisis and increases in petrol prices contributed to the mix, together with internal Fianna Fáil unrest following the local elections. By December 1979 Lynch was gone and Charlie Haughey had taken over as Taoiseach and leader of Fianna Fáil. Up until the general election of June 1981, despite a famous television address by Haughey, telling the nation of our need to tighten our belts, the State's finances continued to deteriorate.

Haughey attracted strong emotions. Those interested in politics either hated or loved him. Few were politically neutral. For me Haughey was the guy who had at the start of the troubles in Northern Ireland got too close to the IRA, whose evidence I disbelieved in the Arms Trial, and who was a political charlatan and hypocrite prepared to manipulate any issue, no matter how sensitive and no matter what its impact on people's lives, to gain personal political advantage. I believed his Family Planning Bill epitomised the type of cynical politics that should be consigned to the dustbin of Irish history.

I saw Haughey as a politician obsessed with power for power's sake, whilst I regarded Garrett Fitzgerald as genuinely committed to economic and fiscal sanity and also constitutional and social reform. I had been an accidental local election candidate with Fine Gael leanings who at Peter Prendergast's instigation had secured a county council seat for Fine Gael. By the time of the June 1981 general election I had become a true believer. Haughey securing the leadership of Fianna Fáil, the manner in which he treated some Fianna Fáil TDs I then personally respected, such as George Colley whose daughter Anne I had worked with when she was a FLAC law student volunteer, and the outright thuggery of some of Haughey's supporters, substantially contributed to my political education. They epitomised everything I despised in politics. As a result of Haughey becoming Taoiseach I became determined to stand as a Fine Gael candidate in the general election that would take place to elect members of the 22nd Dáil.

◄०► ◄०► ◄०►

My first two years on Dublin County Council were informative and hectic. There were far more Council meetings to attend than I expected, at which a broad range of local issues were addressed. A substantial number of new housing estates had either been recently constructed or were under construction and there were continuing problems caused by developers failing to properly finish estates. These included roads left in poor condition, pathways not constructed or properly finished, open spaces not properly landscaped, trees and shrubs not planted, signage not put in place, builders' waste left dangerously abandoned, street lighting not properly working, amongst other things. This generated understandable concern from local constituents and resident associations and I was shocked to discover the casual approach taken by the Council to having these problems addressed. While it was usual that developers received enforcement notices from the Council demanding that planning conditions be complied with and outstanding works properly completed, I believed the Council to be far too slow, as the planning enforcement authority, in taking developers to court. As a consequence, they felt under no real pressure to rapidly resolve the very real difficulties they created for those who purchased homes from them. I quickly learnt that by tabling motions at Council meetings to require the initiation of court proceedings, I could speed the process along and ensure developers were put under pressure to comply with their obligations. My doing so was regularly welcomed at the many resident association meetings held throughout the Whitechurch electoral area.

I discovered that being a councillor required my attendance not only at afternoon and evening council meetings but three to four nights a week at local Fine Gael branch or constituency meetings and also meetings of local, community, sporting, school and resident organisations and bodies. Some nights could involve both Council meetings and two or more local meetings, some of which were more interesting than others.

It worked out that from Mondays to Thursdays Carol put up with me not finally returning home till around eleven most nights. As often as possible, unless stuck in the city centre for an evening council meeting, I came home for tea around quarter to seven to again hit the road by eight.

Our greatest excitement was the birth of our son Dylan in January 1980. He was a healthy contented baby and his arrival brought a whole new dimension to our lives. My coming home for a quick tea before night-time meetings meant that I could spend an hour or so with him before he settled down to sleep. I was anxious to avoid becoming just a weekend parent but at times it was difficult because of work pressures. It was all very hectic and Carol was amazingly tolerant of my absences and supportive of my work. I tried on Fridays to ensure I finished work and arrived home or at Carol's parents' home for the Friday evening Shabbat dinner between five and six, and I avoided attending any meetings on Friday nights.

This pattern of work continued throughout my time as a councillor and continued following my becoming a TD in 1981, the only difference being that frequently it was midweek late-night Dáil sittings that delayed my returning home at a reasonable hour.

Being a County Councillor was a great eye-opener. I was surprised to discover more could be achieved as an active member of the Council than I anticipated. Prior to my election I would have had little respect for the role of the councillor in Irish life. I learnt that if I prioritised an issue and was persistent and constructive, real results could be achieved, although on occasion progress was painfully slow. Ballyroan library is a good example.

In the years preceding my election, the Rathfarnham

community had substantially grown. For years a plot of land had been reserved beside the local Ballyroan church to construct a library. The library was badly needed and repetitively promised at election times. I discovered when elected that plans for the library existed but had not been finalised and no funds had been secured for its construction. During my early years on the Council I prioritised getting the library project underway and securing the required funding. Ultimately I was successful and construction commenced in 1984 and the library finally opened two years later in 1986. As an avid reader I was utterly astonished that such a large community with so many local schools lacked the basic facility of a library. Once building commenced I greatly enjoyed checking out its progress each time I drove past the construction site to visit close friends who lived nearby.

Over the years when I was a member of Dublin County Council, there were occasions when Council meetings were enormously entertaining. An unforgettable moment occurred during a heated discussion on the quality of water in County Dublin. A Fianna Fáil Councillor for dramatic effect during his critical speech held up for all to see a small bottle containing a murky substance to complain about the amount of "orgasm" in his local water! Of course, he intended to highlight the "organisms" not the "orgasm" in the water. Like a shot, Fine Gael's Nora Owen, who, like me, was first elected to the Council in 1979 and who later became Minister for Justice in the coalition government formed in 1995, remarked "We don't have those interesting things in the water in my area!" About fifty per cent of the councillors and Council officials present collapsed laughing whilst the speaker together with the rest present just remained silent and looked puzzled. It was their silence and puzzlement that I found the most entertaining.

There were other similar unforgettable contributions to Council discussions. During a serious discussion about the vulnerability and safety of elderly people living alone, a genuinely concerned Fine Gael Councillor urged the installation by the council of emergency alarms adjacent to the beds of the elderly to enable them to ring for help "if sick or dead"! How the Council could revive the dead was never explained.

The issue that took up most time during my first term on Dublin County Council was the County Dublin Development Plan. The Council as the Planning Authority for County Dublin was legally obliged every five years to conduct a review of its Development Plan. The function of the Development Plan was to prescribe "the development objectives" for the Council's area. A central issue was land zoning and future land use – that is, whether land should be solely or primarily used for residential, commercial, industrial, agricultural or other purposes. The preservation, improvement and extension of parks and other amenities, the location and designation of motorways and roads, the extension and provision of water supplies and sewage services were also major issues. Development-plan decisions made by the Council not only had a major impact on local communities and prescribed a roadmap for residential and economic development across County Dublin but could overnight turn landowners into multi-millionaires and enormously benefit construction companies.

The review had been initiated in 1977, some two years before I was elected to the Council and was well under way when I became a member in June 1979. Between January 1979 and May 1980 twenty special meetings of the Council were held to discuss variations to the development plan initially proposed by Council officials. From July to October 1980 the proposed plan went on public display.

During that period 447 written representations were received by the Council. These resulted in 173 oral hearings between January and April 1981. Councillors received reports on both the representations received and the oral hearings that took place. Between July 1981 and September 1982, thirty-six Special Council meetings were held to consider further amendments to be made to the plan originally put on display. A second public display of the new draft amendments followed in November/December 1982. This produced a further 4,570 representations resulting in a further fifteen Council meetings. The process finally concluded on the 31st March 1983 when at a Council meeting the new development plan was adopted.

Various controversies occurred during the development-plan process over proposed land rezonings but the difficulties experienced were not as dramatic as those which arose with regard to the planning process subsequent to the County Council elections of June 1985 and during the undertaking of the next development-plan review, which commenced in 1987. Unknown to me in the early 1980s, it would result in allegations of corruption being made against a number of County Council and Oireachtas members and also the County Manager George Redmond, the creation of a Tribunal of Inquiry which commenced its work in November 1997 and did not deliver its final Report until March 2012, findings that a significant number of councillors were the recipients of corrupt, improper or inappropriate payments, and also criminal prosecutions. In addition, there would be multiple court proceedings initiated, challenging both the Tribunal's procedures and final conclusions, some of which would be successful. The Tribunal's hearings and conclusions reached into the heart of government and caused a political cataclysm, involving a Fianna Fáil Minister for Foreign

Affairs, Ray Burke, who resigned from office and later served a prison sentence and also engulfed and ended the political career of a Fianna Fáil Taoiseach, Bertie Ahern.

I always perceived my role as a councillor and as a TD as engaging in public service but as the years passed it became clear that a minority of politicians perceived attaining public office as creating an opportunity for self-service. Those who were the recipients of corrupt payments during my time as a member of Dublin County Council displayed outrageous contempt for the trust vested in them by their electorate, their honest Council colleagues and the general public.

<hr/>

As I had promised, following my election to Dublin County Council I opened a weekly advice clinic in Rathfarnham. It was located in the office of a friendly solicitor close to Rathfarnham Garda station. Most of those I met there had genuine problems to be resolved, many of them resulting from dysfunctional responses to issues by the Council or government departments. Often, when followed up, the problems were solved but on occasion bureaucrats simply went into denial and dug in their heels. When that occurred, an inventive response was required to resolve the problem.

For many years a Rathfarnham couple who enjoyed maintaining a nicely planted colourful back garden had happily lived in Marian Crescent, Rathfarnham. Suddenly one day after a downpour their garden was flooded but they didn't know why. In the weeks that followed it was again flooded each time there was heavy rain. Not only did the flooding destroy their garden it crept up to their kitchen door. They discovered Council workers had been laying new pipes and were convinced that the Council's works were responsible. Council officials denied this, insisted there must be some leak in their domestic water pipes and, despite my best efforts, refused to take any action. The couple's plumber could identify no cause for the flooding on their property. Following one particularly heavy downpour they had a virtual lake over two-foot deep, occupied by ducks who flew into their garden and made it their new home. Upon the wife phoning me to tell me about the ducks, I immediately contacted the *Southside People*, the local free paper, and accompanied by a photographer and reporter drove to their home. The ducks featured in a large front-page picture illustrating the couple's plight, accompanied by an exclusive story in the paper's next edition. Having failed to resolve the problem for over four months, within a week council engineers discovered pipes newly laid by Council workers adjacent to the couple's home to run off water into the public drainage system were wrongly located and directing all the accumulated water underneath their back garden wall. Resolution of the problem became locally known as "The Battle of the Ducks". A little publicity can occasionally be very effective in getting things done!

Humour was not confined to Council meetings. Over the years some of it resulted from my weekly meetings with constituents in my advice clinic. On one dark and miserable November Thursday evening, having met and dealt with a queue of constituents, I was informed that a suspicious and intimidating guy accompanied by a vicious-looking Alsatian dog was the last person waiting. It was agreed that should it sound as if I was in difficulty a phone call would be made to the adjacent Garda station by my Fine Gael helper. The man was then sent in to me. Usually I tried to keep meetings informal by sitting beside the constituent,

---

chatting and taking notes. This time I sat behind the solicitor's desk and watched warily as a very tall sombre man wearing a long dark raincoat approached my desk and sat down with his Alsatian beside him. The dog looked particularly alert and menacing as it stared at me over the desk. I was concerned it might be ordered to pounce.

After the man introduced himself to me, he very quietly said, "We need more psychopaths and I'm told you're the man."

I thought I had misheard and, apologising, asked him to repeat what he had said.

"Psychopaths," he said. "We need more of them."

"Ah, more psychopaths," I responded, nodding knowingly, and slowly wrote down the words "psychopaths needed" on my notepad below where his name and address had been recorded.

"I'm told you're the man who gets things done," he explained expectantly.

Going into my best caricature politician mode, I assured him I would do my best about the psychopaths.

Satisfied, he stood up and, followed by the dog, walked back towards the door, turned around to face me and slowly reached into both raincoat pockets. Without saying another word, he carefully pulled out two bicycle clips, bent down, clipped up his trouser legs, turned right and exited the room.

Through the window I watched him unlock his bicycle which was attached to outside railings and cycle away up the road with his dog running proudly beside him. It was only as he fitted on the bicycle clips that I had realised, relieved, that it was more "cycle paths" not "psychopaths" that he was seeking! Up to that point I had always called them "cycle lanes". Since that Thursday night many years ago, for me, forever more they remained "psychopaths"!

248

◄o► ◄o► ◄o►

It was only during the Council election campaign that I discovered the enormous delays being experienced by people in having landline phones installed. Mobile phones did not exist and landline phones were provided through the totally inefficient Department of Posts and Telegraphs. People in need of a phone could wait months and, in some cases, years for a phone to be installed in their home. I also discovered a vibrant political industry resulting in people who had a phone believing its installation to be a special favour due to the representations of a local Fianna Fáil TD or as a result of some special ministerial intervention. On a number of occasions, following my election as a Councillor, I attempted to have phones provided by directly contacting the government department and sometimes but not always this proved successful. It was all totally mad.

The situation in South Dublin seemed particularly bad so I created STAG (the Southside Telephone Action Group) as a vehicle to campaign for reform of the creaking antiquated telephone service. The other nominal members of STAG were Carol, Anne O'Connell, Alan Benson and also Nick Cummins, a Fine Gael Emmet Branch member who became a good friend. The truth is STAG was just a front organisation to generate a media platform for me to campaign as its chairperson for a modern telephone service and secure media attention for the difficulties of South Dublin residents. It worked unexpectedly well and the campaign generated both valuable local and national publicity, including newspaper editorials deploring the state of the phone service. I also found that when contacting the department about phone applicants' difficulties as chairman of STAG, I received a far better response from its civil servants than the response received wearing my hat as a Fine Gael County Councillor. The temptation when making such calls to describe myself as the leader of the Stag Party was enormous but I managed, with some difficulty, to keep that thought to myself!

◄o► ◄o► ◄o►

Some months subsequent to my *Late Late* appearance I was contacted by the producer of Gay Byrne's morning radio show. I was asked as an experiment to participate in a show with Gay, as a "legal eagle" answering legal questions live on air and told if my doing so went well it might be made a regular feature. I readily agreed because it sounded like fun. I did my first show, it all went very well and I enjoyed the experience. The show was inundated with letters seeking legal guidance on a variety of questions and for over a year I participated in one show each month, excluding the summer break period, answering questions asked in letters and also live on air in response to listeners who phoned in. Gay was by then very well established as our most famous and best-known RTÉ broadcaster but I discovered he had no airs and graces and I really enjoyed my experience of broadcasting with him. Most times after a radio programme he took me off to the RTÉ canteen for a cup of coffee and a chat about either the issues of the day or the previous week's *Late Late Show*.

In late April or early May 1981, the Fine Gael convention to select candidates for the Dublin South constituency to run in the general election took place. I successfully came through the convention to run on a ticket that had a total of five Fine Gael candidates. Within a few days of my selection being publicised, Fianna Fáil wrote to RTÉ demanding that as I had been selected as a general election candidate, my involvement in Gay's radio show should end. Although the election had not yet been officially called and was some weeks away, the station capitulated to Fianna Fáil's demands and, with some minor controversy, my role as the *Gay Byrne Show*'s legal eagle ended. During the election campaign I discovered that many constituents who rarely listened to Gay in the mornings because they were at work had read about the controversy in the newspapers, believed I had been wrongfully targeted by Fianna Fáil and for that reason intended to vote for me. I concluded that Fianna Fáil's protest had contributed positively to my chances of election to Dáil Eireann. They would have been better off staying shtum as, once the election was called, longstanding broadcasting election rules would have automatically excluded me from the show.

◄o► ◄o► ◄o►

Selected with me were the sitting TD and well-known legal academic and UCD law professor John Kelly, Nuala Fennell, Tom Hand who was a member of Dublin County Council representing Dundrum, and Alexis Fitzgerald who was a member of Dublin Corporation. It was unusual to select five candidates to contest five Dáil seats. Fine Gael were relatively certain to win two seats and securing the third was a stretch. Today's conventional political wisdom would confine the party candidates to three, for fear the party vote would be overstretched and that not enough votes of a candidate eliminated under our multi-seat proportional representation system would transfer to the surviving party candidates. Peter Prendergast was convinced that running five would maximise the Fine Gael vote which would benefit from John Kelly's political profile and the public profile attached to both me and Nuala from our campaigning and media engagements.

Our main electoral competitors were Fianna Fáil's Síle de Valera, Niall Andrews and Seamus Brennan and the Labour Party's John Horgan. De Valera and Andrews were both sitting TDs as was Horgan, and Brennan was Fianna Fáil's former general secretary. It was a high-profile constituency, the competition was fierce and it was a target for substantial media attention. The enthusiasm generated by Fitzgerald and hostility to Haughey resulted in our having a huge army of canvassers, some rigidly attached to individual Fine Gael candidates, others floating between each of us. Daily door-to-door canvassing, greeting people after Mass and at shopping centres, meeting parents outside schools, coffee mornings, leaflet drops and newsletters together with hundreds of political posters were our campaign's bread and butter and reflected the approach of all parties nationally across the different constituencies. But the Fine Gael Dublin South campaign was more intense than many as a result of our having five candidates. Unfortunately, I discovered that the internal tensions derived from the competition to get elected generated suspicion and paranoia that damaged relationships. I don't believe the damage to the friendship between me and Nuala, for which we were both at fault, was ever fully repaired after the 1981 campaign.

Some of the tensions resulted from campaigning initiatives Prendergast would suggest to an individual candidate to fuel the competition, which he would offset with a different suggestion to another candidate. For Prendergast maximising the numbers elected rather than a bias towards any individual candidate was the game plan but this was not always understood and certainly not appreciated by a candidate who believed he or she was being unfairly disadvantaged.

As with everything else in life, the campaign threw up its funny moments. John Kelly hated canvassing and had to be literally cajoled around the constituency. Politically John was the best-known and most controversial candidate on our local Fine Gael ticket. It was a huge electoral advantage being a sitting TD and he was regarded as a sure bet for re-election. On occasions when we canvassed together he regularly disappeared into a voter's house for a cup of tea or coffee or a whiskey when offered and on a couple of evenings we lost him and had to double back and knock on the doors of houses already visited to discover his whereabouts. He also seemed to relish lengthy doorstep discussion with dyed-in-the-wool unconvertible Fianna Fáil voters which, to the annoyance of some, delayed the canvass.

Our objective was to ensure every house in the constituency was visited at least twice by a candidate and if possible three or four times to secure the vote. To avoid candidates bumping into each other, canvas schedules were exchanged. They worked fine till halfway through week two of the campaign when one candidate seemed to repetitively ensure that their leaflets were dropped into people's letter boxes a couple of hours before my arrival in an estate. I viewed that with a mix of annoyance and amusement as by then there were so many campaign leaflets from all the candidates doing the rounds I doubted that any totally sane person was reading any of them.

The weather was fine for much of the campaign and an enormous amount of door-to-door canvassing was undertaken. One of the oddest moments occurred during the second week of the campaign. It was a bright sunny morning and I was canvassing with a Fine Gael pal I had known for some time. I do not remember how or why we got on to the topic but as we were chatting away between

houses engaging in some banter he announced he had been
circumcised twice! On that basis he contended that
although born Catholic he could be regarded as more
Jewish than me. He went on to explain that at the age of
twenty-nine his medical specialist had diagnosed
circumcision as the cure for a physiological problem. Some
weeks after his unexpected surgery he was informed
insufficient skin had been removed and new skin had
grown back. Unfortunately for him a second circumcision
was required. Happily (perhaps " happily" is something of
an exaggeration) the second surgery was more competently
undertaken. It was both a painful and unfunny event in his
life but his telling of the story was hilarious. Canvassing
had to be suspended for about ten minutes as each time we
attempted to walk up someone's driveway, before either of
us pressed a doorbell, one of us collapsed laughing. We
remain friends to this day and thirty-eight years later he
remains the only person I know to have been snipped twice!

As a personal campaign initiative before the election,
Peter Prendergast encouraged me to replicate an election
ploy successfully used by the German Christian Democrats
in a relatively recent German election. He suggested I
distribute balls with my name on them. I purchased 10,000
coloured bouncy rubber balls the size of tennis balls which
were sourced by a good friend, Bryan Wolfson, who was a
partner in a toy-import business and I had the slogan
"Shatter is on the Ball" printed on them. We gave them
away outside supermarkets, schools and late night in pubs
over the last ten days of the campaign and they went down
a treat. Within a couple of days they were widely laughingly
referred to by the most respectable of Southsiders as
"Shatter's balls" and were sought by children and adults
alike wherever I canvassed. Unlike election literature the
balls endured and I still regularly meet people who recall

receiving a ball from me during their childhood. They were so successful that I repeated my ball giveaway in many of the general election campaigns that I subsequently fought, including the 2016 general election. Unfortunately, Nuala didn't appreciate my balls and complained bitterly about them, unaware that the idea that I distribute them originated from Peter Prendergast. Of course, Peter was not responsible for the slogan on the balls. That was my idea.

The General Election vote was scheduled for the 11th June 1981. One of the funniest incidents during the election campaign occurred the night before voting took place. Tom Hand was expected to secure a strong first preference vote in his local Dundrum Council area and if he was eliminated from the count while I still remained in the race it was important that I secured some of his transfers. To do so, at Peter Prendergast's suggestion, on the night before polling day the last of my balls were handed out at front doors to Dundrum residents by some of my supporters. That evening's canvass and the campaign over, I dropped by our local campaign headquarters in Dundrum to thank anyone there for their work. As I walked into the hallway I spotted, through an open door, our director of elections propped up by the fireplace, obviously having had a few drinks too many and clearly not sober, trying to focus as Tom Hand bitterly complained from somewhere behind the door that "Shatter's fucking balls are all over my estate!" Concluding discretion to be the better part of valour, I rapidly retreated to my car and departed before either of them spotted my presence!

The election over and the count completed, John, Nuala and I were elected for Fine Gael and Seamus Brennan and Niall Andrews for Fianna Fáil. As far as the media was concerned the big shock was Fianna Fail's Síle de Valera's failure to get elected. Less attention was given to Labour's

John Horgan, a decent man I liked, losing his Dáil seat.

As far as the Fine Gael members of Dublin South were concerned, we had pulled off a great political victory which we hoped would help propel Fine Gael into government in coalition with the Labour Party. However, when the seats won in all the constituencies were counted, the two parties together fell short of an overall Dáil majority. I assumed that the support required to make up the numbers would be obtained from other TDs who had opposed Fianna Fáil's return to government. In the immediate aftermath of the election the formation of the new government was not my immediate concern as that was an issue to be addressed by Garret Fitzgerald.

Carol and I, together with our group of canvassers and supporters, celebrated the fact that just two years after my first being elected to Dublin County Council I was now a Dáil deputy at the age of thirty with an opportunity to influence government decisions and pursue an agenda of legal and social reform to which I was personally committed. I had no realistic insight into how difficult it is for a young idealistic outspoken deputy, who is a backbench member of a large political party in government and who has no relationship with their party leader, to achieve anything worthwhile and to play a role other than make noise and act as lobby fodder, voting with the government on every issue. I still had a lot to learn.

Chapter 18

Being Seen but Not Heard

It has been both challenging and strange revisiting the first thirty years of my life, leading into my being first elected to Dáil Éireann. Much of it was either forgotten or parked somewhere in the deep recesses of my mind, waiting to be rediscovered. The journey I have travelled writing this book has given a new immediacy to events of long ago and awakened a curiosity I had never previously experienced about my family background, its influence on how I see the world and how I cope with or react to adversity. It has also been a beneficial escape from events of the past three years, the many false accusations made and the media frenzy which unexpectedly turned my life upside down. There are moments in life when there is a value in reconnecting with your roots and with what has helped frame the person you are. It is also important to overcome and adjust to the trials and tribulations of life and live in the present with your eyes firmly on the future. I have relearnt that lesson writing this book and also enjoyed again laughing at events I had half forgotten.

Upon my election to Dáil Éireann in June 1981 as an enthusiastic still-wet-behind-the-ears TD, I had no idea what the future would bring. I remember little about my first few months as a Dáil Deputy other than my readjusting to a new life as a full-time politician whilst retaining a full-time involvement in my legal practice. Fortunately, shortly before the election I had completed writing the second edition of my family law book so it no longer took up any of my time. As usual, my weekday work started between 5 and 6a.m. and ended between 10 and 11 p.m. I continued, as far as was possible, to keep politics and law out of Friday nights and my weekends so that Carol and I had some real quality time together. By the time of my election to the Dáil, our son, Dylan, was one and a half years old and a busy inquisitive little boy interested in everything around him and quite rightly demanding attention. It wasn't until March 1983 that our daughter, Kelly, would be born.

The Fine Gael/Labour coalition government formed on the 30th June 1981, when the 22nd Dáil first convened, had a slim majority and was dependent for its political survival not only on support from all the elected Fine Gael and Labour Party deputies but also on the support of two newly elected Independent TD's, Jim Kemmy who represented Limerick East constituency, and Seán Dublin Bay Rockall Loftus, who represented Dublin North East constituency. (Seán, an environmentalist, had changed his name to draw attention to his campaign issues.) At an early stage it was clear that the government's majority was precarious and in the lead up to Christmas I remained campaign-ready, aware of the possibility of the government falling and an early election. I rapidly learnt that backbenchers on all occasions were simply expected to vote with the government and not to be heard criticising the action of government or individual ministers. Despite the government's dependency on its backbenchers for its survival, little value was attached to their views. I had expected something different from a government led by Garret Fitzgerald as Taoiseach and realised, as a newly elected deputy, it would take time to make any real impact. I was disappointed to discover that no value of any nature was attached to the expertise I had acquired in my voluntary work or to my knowledge of the inadequacy of Irish family law and our child-care system or to the detailed reform agenda contained in the second edition of my book on family law. But it was early days and exciting to be one of the 166 deputies elected to Dáil Eireann.

The 1981 general election resulted in the election of three Jewish members of Dáil Éireann, the largest number since the foundation of the State. Considering the small size of the community, which by that time had shrunk to about 2,130 people, this was seen by many as remarkable. Typically, each of us were members of different political parties. Ben Briscoe was re-elected as a Fianna Fáil TD representing the Dublin South Central constituency having been in the Dáil for many years. Mervyn Taylor, elected as a member of the Labour Party was, like me, a first term Dáil Deputy, and represented the Dublin South West constituency. In the months and years that followed we got on well at a personal level but we discovered we each had different perspectives on a variety of domestic political issues.

One of the stranger events in my early weeks in Leinster House was meeting Oliver Flanagan who had continued to represent the Laoise-Offaly constituency since his egregious anti-Semitic Dáil speech in 1943. I was sitting with four Fine Gael TDs having lunch in the members' restaurant when Flanagan joined the table. Up to that moment we had not been in each other's company other than when attending meetings of the Fine Gael parliamentary party or voting in the Dáil Chamber. Conversation throughout lunch was about the uncertain political situation and the likelihood of another general election. After a couple of colleagues had departed the table, out of the blue, Flanagan initiated a conversation about his once meeting Moshe Dayan, the famous Israeli military leader who as Minister for Defence was credited with achieving Israel's victory in the Six Day War. His description to me of how impressed he was with Dayan resonated as a "some of my best friends are Jews" stereotypical unconvincing disclaimer of bigotry and his mechanism for ingratiating himself with me. I wasn't particularly impressed but saw no purpose in a confrontation over a speech delivered by him almost forty years earlier. If he had at some time met Dayan I did not expect he had reminisced with him over his 1943 call in the Dáil on the Irish government to "rout the Jews out of this country". I quickly moved the conversation into other territory and we never again discussed together anything to do with Israel, Judaism or the Irish Jewish community.

In the years that followed, as political controversy on the issues of family planning, contraception, divorce and abortion swirled around, Oliver Flanagan and I were always on opposite sides of each debate. Flanagan favoured the prescriptive theological rigidity of the Catholic Church and maintaining the status quo whilst I favoured liberal reforms to address the reality of modern Ireland's long-ignored social, medical and family issues. Oliver Flanagan ceased to be a TD in 1987 and his son Charlie was elected in his place. I found Charlie to be entirely different to his father and in the years that followed his election we became good friends. Upon my becoming Minister for Justice and Defence in 2011 and ceasing to be chairperson of the

Ireland/Israel Parliamentary friendship group, which I founded, Charlie took over the chair. We will never know what view his father would have taken of him doing so.

◄o► ◄o► ◄o►

In March 1981 IRA prisoners in Long Kesh prison in Northern Ireland, in what were known as the H-Blocks, had commenced a second hunger strike over their demand that they be recognised as political prisoners and that their treatment be different to that of ordinary criminals – for example, that they be allowed to wear their own civilian clothes and be exempted from prison work. It was a demand to which the British government led by Margaret Thatcher could not readily capitulate. I had no sympathy of any nature for the IRA but believed a more intelligent and nuanced response than was forthcoming from the British government was required to resolve the developing crisis resulting from the death and martyrdom of some of those who had led the hunger strike. The hunger strike was continuing at the time of the election of the Fine Gael/Labour government. By then four hunger strikers had already died and two had successfully been elected to the Dáil. The hunger strike finally ended in October 1981 by which time a total of ten prisoners had died. Whilst there was no formal recognition of the prisoners' political status, in order to end the strike most of the prisoners' demands were ultimately agreed.

Brian Gallagher was a member of the Catholic Church's Irish Commission for Justice and Peace which sought to constructively resolve, in a practical way, the dispute between the hunger strikers and the British government and to end the hunger strike. Together with other members of the Commission, during the summer of 1981, Brian visited some of those on hunger strike and engaged in talks with representatives of the British government to bring about a resolution, but unfortunately the Commission did not succeed in its mission.

As a newly elected TD with no involvement of any nature in issues relating to Northern Ireland there was no constructive role I could play. However, I had concerns that the visceral dislike of the IRA and its murderous campaign of violence, which I and many others shared, was a barrier to intelligently resolving a crisis that could only act as a recruiting agent for the IRA and increase its public support within the nationalist community. Upon my expressing this view I was disappointed to discover that some of my Fine Gael parliamentary party colleagues were not at all happy, some misinterpreting it as my being sympathetically disposed towards the IRA. This was, of course, completely untrue.

One of the things I have learnt in life is how there can be humour in the midst of strife. During that summer I returned to our law firm late one afternoon having attended a meeting with representatives of one of the family-planning clinics to discuss what could be done to ensure the new coalition government enacted legislation to replace Haughey's Family Planning Act of 1979 and didn't capitulate to the opposition of the Catholic Church. Sitting in the reception area, waiting to meet Brian to discuss what further steps the Commission for Justice and Peace could take to resolve the hunger strike, I found the Commission's Chairman, the Auxiliary Bishop of Dublin, Bishop Dermot O'Mahony. We briefly discussed the developing situation in the North and the Bishop's insights into what could be done to prevent the death of more prisoners. I was impressed with the Bishop who was clearly a little despondent that the Commission's intervention had not proved successful. As I climbed the stairs to my office it struck me that we had a very strange legal practice. While one partner was agitating to liberalise the family-planning laws and to ensure contraceptives were readily available for those who required them, the other was an active member of a Catholic Church Commission voluntarily working with members of the hierarchy!

Twenty-eight years after my meeting Bishop Dermot O'Mahony in our office, he was severely criticised for mishandling and covering up complaints of child abuse by a Commission of Investigation in the damning Murphy Report, published in November 2009, which addressed clerical child sexual abuse in the Catholic Archdiocese of Dublin. The Commission's Report asserted that the Commission "established" that by 1995 "he was aware of thirteen priests", within the representative sample it examined, against whom allegations of abuse had been made and which the Bishop had failed to properly address. Coincidentally, amongst the priests named was a Father Ivan Payne for whom he had supplied a reference to the Diocese of Sacramento, even after Payne had admitted to being a child abuser.

Well before publication of the Murphy Report I had learnt all about Ivan Payne but I did not know the full story of Bishop O'Mahony's involvement with him. In 1992 Gallagher Shatter had issued the first ever civil action for child abuse taken against Desmond Connell, the Archbishop of Dublin, as the head of the Dublin Diocese, and also against Payne seeking damages on behalf of one of Payne's victims, the courageous Andrew Madden. Andrew when a young altar boy had been sexually assaulted by Payne when Payne was serving as a priest in the Cabra parish in Dublin. Initially, the Church defended the proceedings and denied all liability but the case was ultimately resolved by an out-of-court settlement. It was the first of its kind. Although the church insisted that Andrew Madden sign a confidentiality clause, out of his concern for other victims of clerical abuse and because the Church remained in public denial of the extent of the scandal, Andrew subsequently publicly told his story.

Shortly after Andrew first consulted Tim O'Sullivan, a partner in our law firm, I was consulted by a client with marital difficulties who had already sought a Catholic Church annulment of her marriage and who wished to initiate High Court family law proceedings. I was astonished to discover that the priest attached to the Church's Dublin Regional Marriage Tribunal in Drumcondra, which adjudicated on church nullity cases and who was appointed to interview her was Father Ivan Payne. I also learnt that he had been given the title Vice Officialis which is conferred on a priest appointed to act as a diocesan Bishop's adjutant judicial vicar. Andrew's allegation against Ivan Payne was not new to church authorities. It had been known for some time. It was difficult to fathom how a priest against whom serious allegations of child abuse had been made could be appointed by church authorities to the Marriage Tribunal to conduct interviews with nullity applicants about the most intimate aspects of their married life. Although Andrew Madden's settlement was concluded in 1993, I later learnt that Payne retained his position in the Marriage Tribunal until 1995, the year when Andrew Madden revealed his identity and told his story. Payne was later prosecuted on a series of sample charges of indecently assaulting nine boys between the ages of eight and eleven years of age over a period of twenty years and also for indecent assaults on Andrew Madden. In January 1998 he pleaded guilty to all charges and was ultimately sentenced to six years imprisonment. When the Report of the Murphy Commission was published in 2009, I was Fine Gael's Front Bench Spokesperson on Children and I had to respond to the Report on behalf of the party. This is just one of the many examples of the unexpected connections that occurred over my thirty years as a member of Dáil Éireann between legal issues which involved Gallagher Shatter and political events. They could not have been predicted when I was first elected to the Dáil in 1981.

Prior to Christmas 1981, as is usual, the Dáil went into recess for the holiday break. Shortly after Christmas, Carol and I, together with Dylan, who was by then nearly two years old, were booked on an Aer Lingus flight for a two-week vacation in Tenerife. I was determined that we would have some family time together away from the demands of politics and law. I also wanted time to reflect on my first six months as a TD and the reality of how politics worked.

My admiration for Garrett Fitzgerald had been the primary motivation for my joining Fine Gael and, contrary to his cuddly public image, I had found Garrett a difficult and distant person with whom to engage. On occasions when I had attempted to engage him in conversation in Leinster House he was always distracted and my perception, be it right or wrong, was that he believed together with other newly elected deputies I had no meaningful role to play in the development of government policy or legislation.

Sitting in the front row of the plane, we waited for boarding to finish. When it looked as though all passengers had boarded two seats to my right still remained vacant. About five minutes later Garrett and his wife Joan boarded and sat in the two empty seats. Garrett was sitting directly across the aisle from me. I gave him a friendly hello to which I received a mumbled response. The plane door was closed, we slowly taxied down the runway and took off. Garrett sat reading a book and engaged in some conversation with Joan for the next two hours. On a second occasion I attempted a conversation. There was a one-sentence response and he then returned to his book. I understood that he was taking time out and wished to relax, as I did, but I was taken aback by his lack of response and his failure to engage in any conversation of reasonable length. I concluded that either I had during my brief period in the Dáil unknowingly said something to offend him or he had no idea who I was. During the third hour of the flight as drinks were served I made some further comment that ensured he knew at least that I was a member of the Fine Gael parliamentary party but to no avail. There was yet another single-sentence reply, he then turned to say something to Joan and I gave up.

Carol thought Garrett was extraordinarily rude and said so to me. After all, he was my great political idol and my election to the Dáil, like that of many other Fine Gael TDs, was instrumental in him becoming Taoiseach. Even if he had no wish to converse, the exchange of a few meaningless pleasantries would have satisfied the circumstances. With less than an hour of the flight left, Dylan, who had been briefly sitting on my lap, climbed down, stood in the aisle and then unexpectedly kicked Garrett's left leg. As I lifted Dylan, put him back on my lap and simultaneously apologised to a slightly flustered Taoiseach, I also silently applauded Dylan's first spontaneous political initiative. As far as Carol was concerned Dylan certainly was his father's son. As far as I was concerned, Dylan's unexpected intervention proved without doubt that life really is a funny business!